GUITAR TAB

budgetbooks

ROCK GUITAR HITS

ISBN 978-1-4234-9282-5

HAL•LEONARD®
CORPORATION
7777 W. BLUEMOUND RD. P.O. BOX 13819 MILWAUKEE, WI 53213

Visit Hal Leonard Online at
www.halleonard.com

CONTENTS

According to You

Words and Music by Andrew Frampton and Steven Diamond

Gtrs. 1-3 & 6-8: Drop D tuning:
(low to high) D-A-D-G-B-E

Gtrs. 4 & 5: Tune down 1 step:
(low to high) D-G-C-F-A-D

*Symbols in parentheses represent chord names respective to detuned guitar.

**Gradually lift P.M.

Chorus
Gtrs. 3 & 4 tacet
B♭5 (C5)
C5 (D5)
D5 (E5)
G5 (A5)
him, I'm beau - ti - ful, in - cred - i - ble. He can't get me out - ta his head. Ac - cord - ing to
Rhy. Fig. 2
Gtr. 2
Rhy. Fig. 2A
Gtr. 5 (elec.)
B♭5 (C5)
B♭(♯4) B♭5
C5 (D5)
D5 (E5)
G5 (A5)
him, I'm fun - ny, ir - re - sist - a - ble, ev - 'ry - thing he ev - er want - ed.
End Rhy. Fig. 2
End Rhy. Fig. 2A

Gtrs. 2 & 5: w/ Rhy. Figs. 2 & 2A (1st 4 meas.)
B♭5 (C5) C5 (D5) D5 (E5) G5 (A5)
Ev-'ry-thing is op-po-site, I don't feel like stop-ping it. So, ba-by, tell me what I got to lose. He's
*Gtr. 6 (elec.)
mf
w/ dist.
*Doubled throughout
B♭5 (C5) C5 (D5) N.C.
in-to me for ev-'ry-thing I'm not, ac-cord-ing to you.
Gtr. 6
Gtr. 2
Gtr. 5

Interlude
Gtr. 6 tacet
N.C. B♭5 (C5) F5 (G5) N.C. B♭5 (C5) F5 (G5)
2. Ac - cord - ing to
Gtr. 4
8va
Gtr. 2
Gtr. 5
Verse
Gtr. 2: w/ Rhy. Fig. 1 (3 times)
Gtrs. 4 & 5 tacet
F5 C5 D5 B♭5
you, I'm bor - ing, I'm mood - y, and you can't take me an - y place. Ac - cord - ing to
Riff C
Gtr. 3
End Riff C
Gtr. 3: w/ Riff C
F5 C5 D5 B♭5
you, I suck at tell - ing jokes 'cause I al - ways give it a - way.
Gtr. 6

Gtr. 3: w/ Riff A
F5 C5 D5 B♭5
I'm a girl with the worst at - ten - tion span. You're the boy who puts up with that, ac-cord-ing to
Gtr. 3: w/ Riff B
Gtr. 6 tacet
F5 C5 (D5) G5 (A5) N.C.
you, ac - cord - ing to you. But ac-cord-ing to
Gtr. 4
Gtr. 2
P.M.
Chorus
Gtrs. 2 & 5: w/ Rhy. Figs. 2 & 2A (1 1/2 times)
Gtr. 4 tacet
B♭5 (C5) C5 (D5) D5 (E5) G5 (A5)
him, I'm beau - ti - ful, in-cred - i - ble. He can't get me out - ta his head. Ac-cord-ing to
Riff D
Gtr. 6

B♭5 B♭(♯4) B♭5 C5 D5 G5
(C5) (D5) (E5) (A5)
him, ___ I'm fun - ny, ir - re - sist - a - ble, ___ ev - 'ry - thing he ev - er want - ed. ___
B♭5 C5 D5 G5
(C5) (D5) (E5) (A5)
Ev - 'ry - thing is op - po - site, I don't feel like stop - ping it. So, ba - by, tell me what I got to ___ lose. He's
End Riff D
B♭5 C5
(C5) (D5)
in - to me for ev - 'ry - thing I'm not, ac - cord - ing to you. ___
Gtr. 6
Rhy. Fig. 3
Gtr. 2
End Rhy. Fig. 3
Rhy. Fig. 3A
Gtr. 5
End Rhy. Fig. 3A

Bridge
Gtrs. 5 & 6 tacet
**D5
B♭maj7(no3rd)
F
Asus4
A
I need to feel ap-pre-ci-at-ed, that I'm not hat-ed, oh, no.
*Gtrs. 2 & 3
*Composite arrangement
**Chord symbols reflect basic harmony.
Gtr. 3 tacet
D5
B♭maj7(no3rd)
B♭5
Why can't you see me through his eyes? It's too bad, you're mak-ing me diz-zy.
Gtr. 4
Gtrs. 2 & 3
Gtr. 2
P.M.
Guitar Solo
Gtrs. 2 & 5: w/ Rhy. Figs. 2 & 2A
B♭5
(C5)
C5
(D5)
8va
Gtr. 4
loco
D5
(E5)
G5
(A5)
P.M.
P.M. P.H.
Pitch: A

B♭5 B♭(♯4) B♭5 C5
(C5) (D5)
8va
D5 G5
(E5) (A5)
3. But ac - cord - ing to
Verse
F C G5 N.C.
(G) (D) (A5)
me, you're stu - pid, you're use - less. You can't do an - y - thing right. But ac - cord - ing to
Gtr. 4
Gtr. 1
Chorus
Gtr. 1 tacet
Gtrs. 2 & 5: w/ Rhy. Figs. 2 & 2A (1 1/2 times)
Gtr. 6 : w/ Riff D
B♭5 C5 D5 G5
(C5) (D5) (E5) (A5)
him, I'm beau - ti - ful, in - cred - i - ble. He can't get me out - ta his head. Ac - cord - ing to
Gtr. 4

B♭5 (C5) B♭(♯4) B♭5 C5 (D5)
him, I'm fun - ny, ir - re - sist - a - ble,
8va
D5 (E5) G5 (A5)
ev - 'ry - thing he ev - er want - ed. Ev -
Gtr. 4 tacet
B♭5 (C5) C5 (D5) D5 (E5) G5 (A5)
- 'ry - thing is op - po - site, I don't feel like stop - ping it. Babe, I'll tell you what you've got to lose. He's
Gtrs. 2 & 5: w/ Rhy. Figs. 3 & 3A
B♭5 (C5) C5 (D5)
in - to me for ev - 'ry - thing I'm not, ac - cord - ing to you.
Gtr. 4
loco
Gtr. 6

B♭5
(C5)
F5
(G5)
B♭5
(C5)
F5
(G5)
You, _ you, ___ ac - cord - ing to you, ___ you, _ you. ___ Ac - cord - ing to ___
Gtr. 4
15ma
w/ bar
steady dive
w/ bar
steady ascent
*Harm.
w/ bar
steady dive
steady ascent
slack
-4 1/2
Pitch: G
-2 1/2
-4
-2 1/2
*Harmonic located approx. four-tenths the distance between the 2nd & 3rd frets.
Gtr. 6
Gtr. 2
Gtr. 5

Outro
Slower ♩ = 115
Gtr. 4 tacet
Fsus2
(Gsus2)
Csus2
B♭sus2
you, I'm stu - pid, I'm use - less, I can't do an - y - thing right.
Gtr. 6
*Gtrs. 7 (acous.)
& 8 (elec.)
mf
let ring throughout
*Gtr. 8: w/ clean tone
Gtr. 2
Gtr. 5

Adam's Song

Words and Music by Tom De Longe and Mark Hoppus

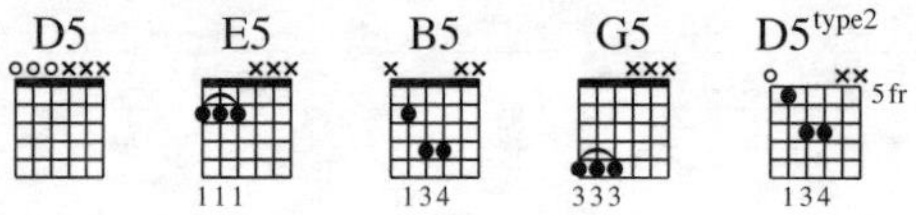

Gtrs. 1, 2, 3 & 5;
Tune Down One Whole Step:
① = D ④ = C
② = A ⑤ = G
③ = F ⑥ = D

Gtr. 4; Drop D Tuning;
Tune Down One Whole Step:
① = D ④ = C
② = A ⑤ = G
③ = F ⑥ = C

G5
B5
G5
to go on. You'll be sor - ry when I'm
in the hall? Please tell Mom this is not her
Interlude
Dsus4
Em
Bm
Gtr. 1: w/ Rhy. Fill 1, 2nd time
D/G
gone.
fault.
Gtr. 1
let ring
Dsus4
Em
Bm
Gtr. 1: w/ Rhy. Fill 1, 2nd time
D/G
let ring
Chorus
Gtrs. 1, 2 & 3: w/ Riffs A, A1 & A2, 2 times, 3rd time
Gtr. 4: w/ Rhy. Fig. 3, 2 times, 3rd time
D5
E5
B5
G5
1., 2. I nev - er con - quered, rare - ly came. Six - teen just held such bet - ter days,
3. I nev - er con - quered, rare - ly came. (But) to - mor - row holds such bet - ter days,
Gtrs. 1 & 2
mf
w/ dist.
simile on repeat
Gtr. 1
Gtr. 2
divisi
* Gtr. 2 to left of slash in TAB.

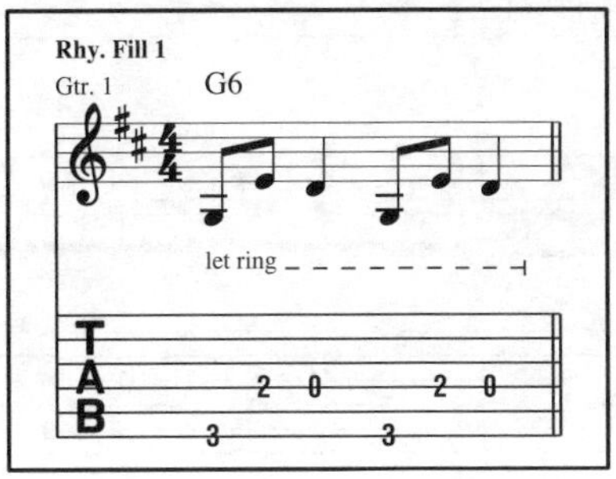
Rhy. Fill 1
Gtr. 1
G6
let ring
T
A
B

D
Em
B5
G5
days when I still felt a - live. We could-n't wait to get out -
days when I can still feel a - live, when I can't wait to get out -
Gtr. 2
Gtr. 1
D5
E5
B5
G5
Rhy. Fig. 3
End Rhy. Fig. 3
Gtr. 4 (elec.)
w/ dist.
side. The world was wide, too late to try. The tour was o - ver, we'd sur - vived.
side. The world is wide, the time goes by. The tour is o - ver, I've sur - vived.
Riff A2
End Riff A2
Gtr. 3 (elec.)
w/ dist.
Riff A1
End Riff A1
Gtr. 2
Gtr. 1
Riff A
End Riff A

To Coda
1.
Gtrs. 1 & 2: w/ Riffs A & A1
Gtr. 4: w/ Rhy. Fig. 3
D5
E5
B5
G5
I could-n't wait till I got home to pass the time in my room a - lone.
I can't wait till I get home to pass the time
Gtr. 3
Interlude
Gtr. 1: w/ Rhy. Fig. 1, 2 times
Gtr. 3 tacet
Bm
D/A
D/G
D/E
D/G
2.
G5
Interlude
Gtr. 3 tacet
D
open
Gtr. 4
Gtr. 4 tacet
* Dadd4/A
in my room a - lone.
Gtr. 5 (acous.)
mp
let ring throughout
Gtr. 1
w/ clean tone
let ring throughout
* Chord symbols reflect overall tonality.
Gtr. 5
Dadd4/G
Dadd4
Dadd4/G
Asus2
A5
Gtr. 1

Gtr. 5 tacet
Dadd4/B
Dadd4/G
Dadd4
Dadd4/G
Asus2
A5
Dadd4/G
Gtr. 1
Dadd4
Dadd4/G
Asus2
A5
Dadd4/B
Dadd5/G
D.S. al Coda
D5
D5/G
play 3 times
D5/A
D5/B
D5/G
Coda
Segue to "All the Small Things"
G5
D5type2
Gtr. 4
in my room a - lone.
Gtr. 3

All Over You

Words and Music by Edward Kowalczyk, Chad Taylor, Patrick Dahlheimer and Chad Gracey

Tune Down 1/2 Step:
① = E♭ ④ = D♭
② = B♭ ⑤ = A♭
③ = G♭ ⑥ = E♭

Intro

Moderate Rock ♩ = 126

G A Dsus2 A
for be - in' strange Our love is no oth - er
End Rhy. Fig. 2
F# G A Dsus2
than me a - lone, for me all day Our love is
Harm.
A F# G A
Gtrs. 1 & 2: w/ Rhy. Fills 1 & 1A, 2nd time
like wa - ter an - gels pinned down and a - bused hey hey
w/ dist.
Rhy. Fill 1
Gtr. 1
G A
Rhy. Fill 1A
Gtr. 2
TAB

Chorus
Gtrs. 1 & 2: w/ Rhy. Fig. 1, 2 times, simile
G F♯ Bm A Dsus2
All o - ver you, All o - ver me the sun, the fields,
the sky
G F♯ Bm A
I've of - ten tried to hold the sea
Dsus2
the sun, the fields, the tide
G F♯ Bm G F♯ Bm
Pay me now lay me down
Gtrs. 1 & 2
Rhy. Fig. 3
End Rhy. Fig. 3
1.
E A5
Gtr. 1
Gtr. 2
(Gtr. 1 cont. in slash)
dist. off
2.
To Coda
Gtrs. 1 & 2: w/ Rhy. Fig. 3
G F♯ Bm C
Gtrs. 1 & 2
(2nd time cont. in notation)
Pay me now pay me now lay me down lay me down lay me down
(lay)
Chorus
Gtrs. 1 & 2: w/ Rhy. Fig. 1, 2 times, simile
G F♯ Bm A Dsus2
All o - ver you, All o - ver me
G F♯ Bm A Dsus2
All o - ver you, All o - ver me

Gtrs. 1 & 2: w/ Rhy. Fig. 3, 3 times
G F♯ Bm
Pay me now
G F♯ Bm G F♯ Bm
lay me down down Pay me now pay me now
C
Gtrs. 1 & 2
(cont. in notation)
lay me down lay me down lay.
(lay)
Interlude
E5 F♯5 Fmaj11 E5 F♯5 Fmaj11
Gtrs. 1 & 2
let ring
E5 F♯5 Fmaj11 E5 F♯5 Fmaj11
play 3 times
let ring
(3rd time cont. in slash)
Verse
Dsus2 A F♯ G A
Gtrs. 1 & 2 (clean)
(Gtr. 2 cont. in notation)
3. Our love is like wa - ter pinned down and a - bused for be - in' strange
D.S. al Coda
(take 2nd ending)
Dsus2 A F♯ G A
Gtr. 1
w/ dist.
Our love is no oth - er than me a - lone, hey, hey, hey.
Gtr. 2
let ring throughout
w/ dist.

Coda
A
G♯
C♯m
Gtrs. 1 & 2
let ring
A
G♯
C♯sus2
let ring
A
G♯
C♯m
Dsus2
G
let ring
F♯
Bm
A
Dsus2
rit.

Back Against the Wall

Words and Music by Jared Champion, Lincoln Parish, Brad Schultz, Matthew Schultz and Daniel Tichenor

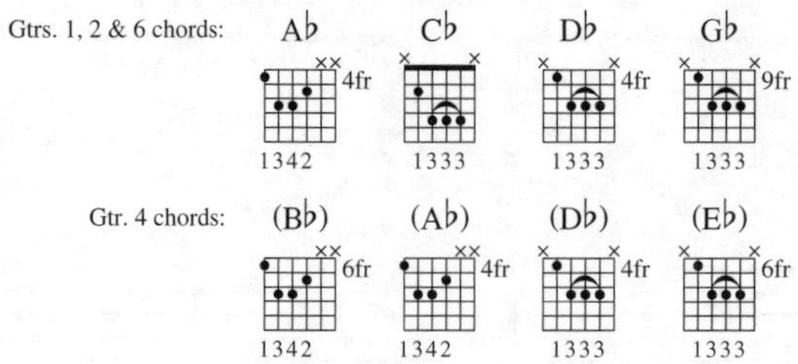

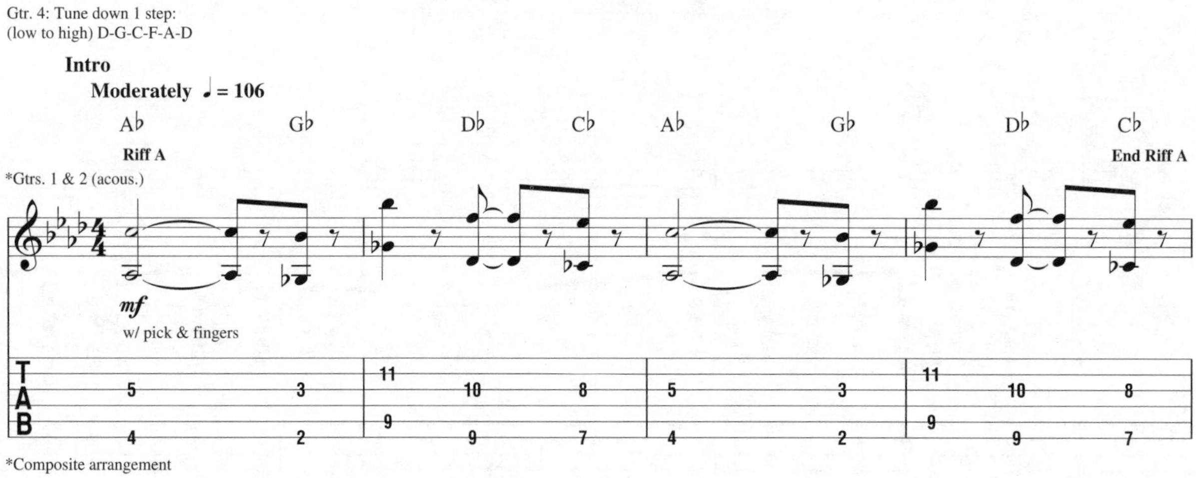

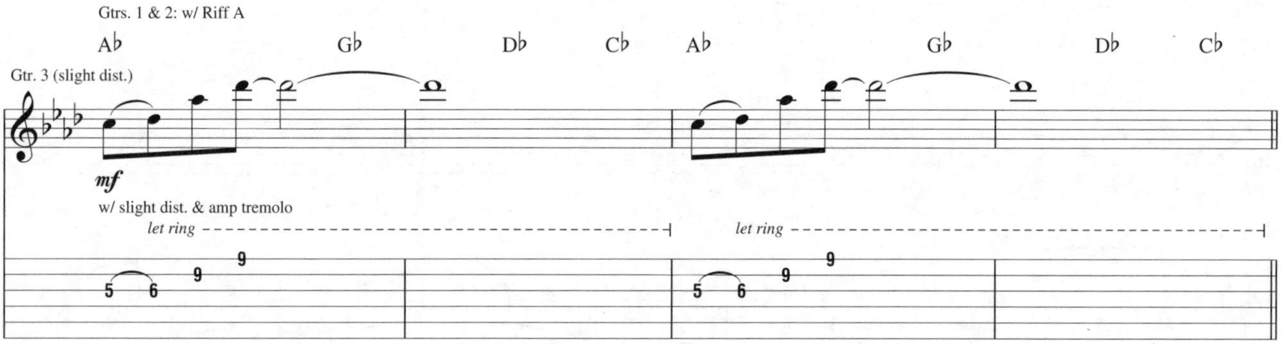

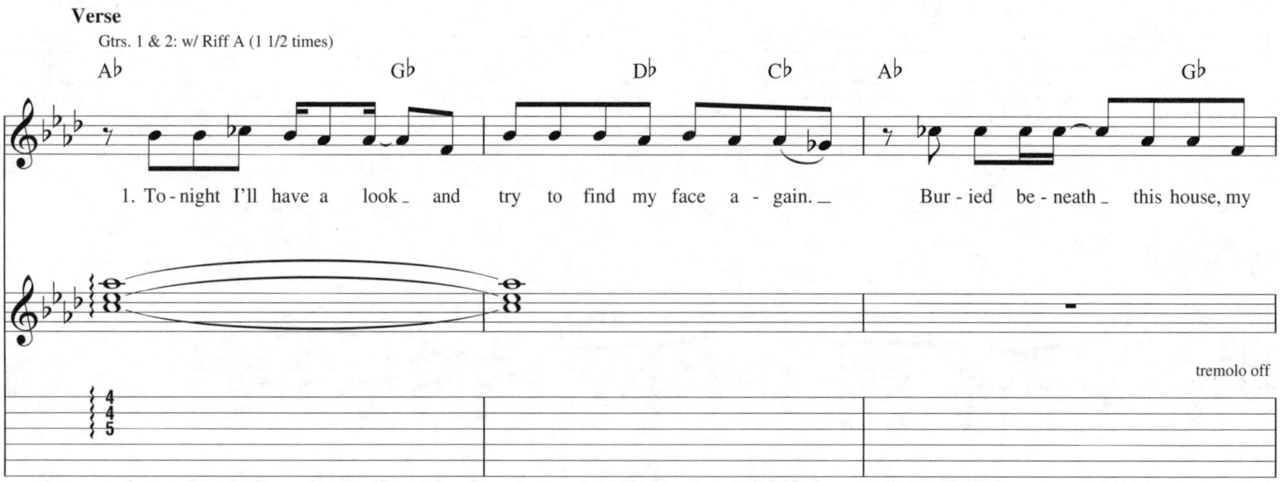

*See top of first page of song for chord diagrams pertaining to rhythm slashes.

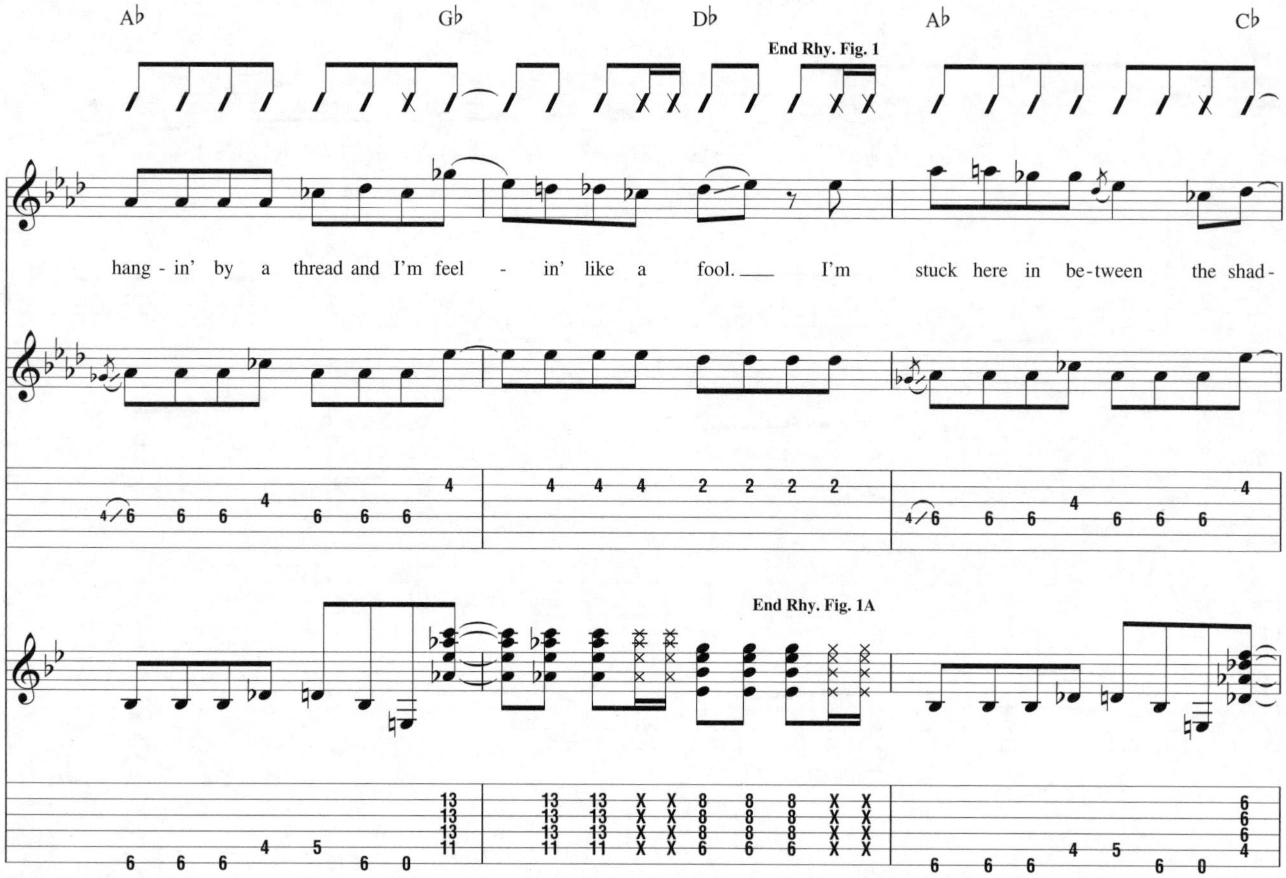
A♭
G♭
D♭
A♭
C♭
End Rhy. Fig. 1
hang - in' by a thread and I'm feel - in' like a fool. I'm stuck here in be-tween the shad-
End Rhy. Fig. 1A

D♭
A♭
G♭
D♭
- ows of my yes - ter - day. I wan na get a - way, I need to get a - way.
let ring -

Verse
Gtrs. 1 & 2: w/ Riff A (2 times)
Gtr. 4 tacet
2nd time, Gtr. 5 tacet
A♭ G♭ D♭ C♭
2. Blan - ket of si - lence makes me wan - na sink my teeth in deep.
3. Deep in the jun - gle cam - ou - flaged by all the fall - en leaves,
Gtr. 5
End Riff B
w/ amp tremolo
let ring
Gtr. 3
*Gtr. 5 tacet
A♭ G♭ D♭ C♭ A♭ G♭
Burn all the ev - i - dence of fab - ri - cat - ed dis - be - lief. Pulled back the cur - tain, took a
a hand holds up the sky while shame ful - ly I make my plea. The al - ter's call - in' but my
Gtr. 3
let ring
*Tremolo off
D♭ C♭ A♭ G♭ D♭ C♭
look in - to your eyes. My tongue has now be - come a plat - form for your lies.
legs won't seem to stand. Guess I'm a cow - ard, scared to face the man I am.
I said, "You
let ring

Pre-Chorus
Gtrs. 1 & 2: w/ Rhy. Fig. 1 (2 times)
Gtr. 4: w/ Rhy. Fig. 1A (2 times)
1st time, Gtr. 5: w/ Riff B
2nd time, Gtr. 5: w/ Riff B (1st 2 meas.)
2nd time, Gtr. 5: w/ Fill 1
A♭ C♭ D♭ A♭ G♭ D♭
*(B♭) (D♭) (E♭) (B♭) (A♭) (E♭)
got me where you want me a - gain __ and I can't turn a-way. _ I'm hang in' by a thread and I'm feel - in' like a fool. _ I'm
*Symbols parentheses represent chord names respective to de-tuned guitar. Symbols above represent actual sounding chords.
2nd time, Gtr. 5: w/ Riff B (last 6 meas.)
A♭ C♭ D♭ A♭ G♭ D♭
(B♭) (D♭) (E♭) (B♭) (A♭) (E♭)
stuck here in be-tween the shad - ows of my yes-ter-day. _ I wan-na get a-way, I need __ to get a-way." _
Chorus
(B♭) (A♭) (D♭) (E♭)
Rhy. Fig. 2A
Gtr. 4
Now you know, yeah, ______ you've got my back a - gainst _ the
Rhy. Fig. 2
**Gtrs. 1, 2 & 6
*Vocals doubled, next 9 meas.
**Gtr. 6 (elec.); played mf, w/ dist. Composite arrangement
(B♭) (A♭) (D♭) (E♭)
End Rhy. Fig. 2A
wall. __ Oh, God, __ I ______ ain't got no oth - er place _ to
End Rhy. Fig. 2
Fill 1
Gtr. 5

To Coda
Gtrs. 1, 2 & 6: w/ Rhy. Fig. 2
Gtr. 4: w/ Rhy. Fig. 2A
A♭ (B♭) G♭ (A♭) C♭ (D♭) D♭ (E♭) A♭ (B♭) G♭ (A♭) C♭ (D♭) D♭ (E♭)
hide. Chained down like a sit-tin' duck just wait-in' for the fall. You know, yeah, you've got my back a - gainst the
Interlude
D.S. al Coda
Gtrs. 1 & 2: w/ Riff A
A♭ G♭ D♭ C♭ A♭ G♭ D♭ C♭
wall.
Gtr. 3
Coda
Guitar Solo
A♭ C♭ D♭ A♭ C♭ D♭
Rhy. Fig. 3
End Rhy. Fig. 3
*Gtrs. 1, 2 & 6
wall.
Gtr. 8 (elec.)
mf
w/ dist.
(cont. on lower staff)
Gtr. 7 (elec.)
f
w/ dist.
(cont. on upper staff)
*Composite arrangement
Gtrs. 1, 2 & 6: w/ Rhy. Fig. 3
A♭ C♭ D♭ A♭ C♭ D♭
Gtr. 7
Gtr. 8
fdbk.
Pitch: C♭

*Vocals doubled till end.

C♭ (D♭) D♭ (E♭) A♭ (B♭) G♭ (A♭)
ain't got no oth - er place to hide. Chained down like a
C♭ (D♭) D♭ (E♭) A♭ (B♭) G♭ (A♭)
sit-tin' duck just wait-in' for the fall. You know, yeah,
(D♭) (E♭) (B♭)
Gtr. 4
you've got my back a - gainst the wall.
Gtr. 7
Gtrs. 1, 2 & 6

Better Days

Words and Music by John Rzeznik

D5
Gsus2
___ need box - es wrapped _ in strings _ and de-sign - er love and emp - ty things, just a chance _
Rhy. Fig. 1
Gtr. 2 (clean)
mf
Asus4
Gsus2
D5
Rhy. Fill 1
End Rhy. Fill 1
*Gtr. 3 (clean)
p
mf
(cont. in notation)
___ that may - be we'll ___ find bet-ter days. ___ So
Gtr. 1
Fill 1
End Fill 1
Gtr. 2
End Rhy. Fig. 1
*Doubled throughout
Chorus
Gtrs. 1 & 2 tacet
Gsus2
Asus4
take these _ words ___ and sing out _ loud ___ 'cause
Gtr. 3
Rhy. Fig. 2
End Rhy. Fig. 2

To Coda 2
Gtr. 3: w/ Rhy. Fig. 2
Gsus2
Asus4
ev - 'ry - one is for - giv - en now. 'Cause to - night's
To Coda 1
Interlude
Bm7
Gsus2
D5
the night the world be - gins a - gain.
Gtr. 2
2. I need some
Verse
Gtr. 2: w/ Rhy. Fig. 1 (2 times)
D5
Gsus2
place sim - ple where we could live. And some - thing on - ly you can give. And that's faith
Riff B
Gtr. 1

Asus4
Gsus2
D5
and trust and peace while we're a - live.
And the one
End Riff B
Gtr. 2: w/ Riff B
Gsus2
poor child who saved this world. And there's ten mil - lion more who prob - a - bly could if we all
D.S. al Coda 1
Gtr. 1: w/ Fill 1
Gtr. 3: w/ Rhy. Fill 1
Asus4
Gsus2
D5
just stopped and said a prayer for them.
So
Coda 1
Interlude
Gtr. 2 tacet
D5
Gsus2
Rhy. Fig. 3
End Rhy. Fig. 3
Gtr. 3
*Gtr. 4
f
*Strings arr. for gtr.
Bm7
Gsus2
D5
Rhy. Fig. 4
End Rhy. Fig. 4
I wish ev -

Bridge
Gtr. 3: w/ Rhy. Fig. 3
Gtr. 4 tacet
D5
Gsus2
- 'ry - one was loved to - night and some - how stop this end - less fight. Just a chance
D.S. al Coda 2
Asus4
Gsus2
D5
that may - be we'll find bet - ter days. So
Gtr. 3
Coda 2
Gtr. 3: w/ Rhy. Fig. 4
Bm7
G5
D5
the night the world be - gins a - gain. 'Cause to - night's
Gtr. 4
Bm7
Gsus2
D5
Gtr. 2
rit.
the night the world be - gins a - gain.
Gtr. 4
rit.
Gtr. 5 (clean)
rit.
mf

Brain Stew (The Godzilla Remix)

from the TriStar Motion Picture GODZILLA

Words by Billie Joe Armstrong
Music by Green Day

Gtr. 2 tacet
F#5 N.C. F5 N.C. E5 N.C. A5 N.C. G5 N.C. F#5 N.C. F5 N.C. E5 N.C.
Verse
Gtr. 1: w/ Rhy. Fig. 1 (3 times)
A5 G5 F#5 F5 E5
Gtr. 4: w/ Rhy. Fig. 2 (3 times)
A5 G5
2., 4. My eyes feel like they're gon-na bleed.
Dried up and bulg - ing out my
*Gtr. 4
Rhy. Fig. 2
End Rhy. Fig. 2
mp
w/ fingers
*String ensemble arr. for gtr.
F#5 F5 E5 A5 G5 F#5 F5 E5
skull.
My mouth is dry,
my face is numb.
To Coda
Interlude
Gtr. 2: w/ Riff A
A5 G5 F#5 F5 E5 A5 N.C. G5 N.C.
Fucked up and spun out in my room.
On my own, here we go.
Gtr. 1
Rhy. Fig. 3
End Rhy. Fig. 3
Rhy. Fig. 4
**Harm.
Harm.
**Random harmonics produced while lightly muting on strings.
Gtr. 1: w/ Rhy. Fig. 4
F#5 N.C. F5 N.C. E5 N.C. A5 N.C. G5 N.C. F#5 N.C. F5 N.C. E5 N.C.
End Rhy. Fig. 4
Harm.
Harm.
Harm.
Verse
Gtr. 1: w/ Rhy. Fig. 1 (3 times)
A5 Gsus2 F#m F Esus4
3. My mind is set on o - ver - drive.
Gtr. 4
Rhy. Fig. 5
End Rhy. Fig. 5

Gtr. 4: w/ Rhy. Fig. 5 (3 times)
A5 Gsus2 F♯m F Esus4 A5 Gsus2 F♯m F Esus2
The clock is laugh - ing in my face. A crook-ed spine, my sens-es dulled.
Gtr. 1: w/ Rhy. Fig. 3
A5 Gsus2 F♯m F Esus4
Past the point of de - lir - i - um. On my own, here we go.
Gtr. 5 (dist.)
mf
Gtr. 6 (dist.) divisi
*Harm.
*Applies to both gtrs.
Interlude
Gtr. 1: w/ Rhy. Fig. 4 (2 times)
Gtr. 2: w/ Riff A
Gtrs. 5 & 6 tacet
A5 N.C. G5 N.C. F♯5 N.C. F5 N.C. E5 N.C. A5 N.C. G5 N.C. F♯5 N.C. F5 N.C. E5 N.C.
*A B♭ C5 A B♭ C5
Riff B
End Riff B
Gtr. 7 (clean)
mp
w/ reverb
let ring throughout
Gtr. 1
Riff C
End Riff C
*Chord symbols reflect basic harmony.
D.S. al Coda
Gtr. 1: w/ Riff C (2 times)
Gtr. 7: w/ Riff B
A B♭ C5 A B♭ C5
Riff D
End Riff D
Gtr. 8 (clean)
mp
let ring throughout

Coda
Outro
Gtr. 2: w/ Riff A
F♯5 F5 E5 A5 G5 F♯5 F5 E5
room.
On my own, here we go.
Gtr. 4
Gtr. 1
Rhy. Fig. 6
End Rhy. Fig. 6
Gtr. 1: w/ Rhy. Fig. 6 (5 times)
A5 G5 F♯5 F5 E5
let ring
A5 G5 F♯5 F5 E5 A5 G5 F♯5 F5 E5
Gtr. 2: w/ Riff A
A5 G5 F♯5 F5 E5 A5 G5 F♯5 F5 E5
8va
*Trem. pick in sixteenth-note rhythm, next 4 meas.
Begin fade
Fade out
Gtr. 4 tacet
Gtr. 8: w/ Riff D (till fade)
A5
Gtr. 1 tacet
N.C.

Break

Words and Music by Three Days Grace and Barry Stock

Verse
*D5
B♭5 A5 G5 F5 G5 A5
1. To - night, my head _ is spin - ning. _ I need some - thing _ to pick me _ up.
fdbk.
pp
Rhy. Fig. 2
End Rhy. Fig. 2
*Chord symbol reflects overall harmony.
Gtr. 1 tacet
Gtr. 2: w/ Rhy. Fig. 2
D5
B♭5 A5 G5 F5 G5 A5
I've tried, but noth - in' _ is work - ing. I won't stop, I won't say _ I've had e - nough.
Pre-Chorus
B♭5
C5 G5
To - night, {I / we} start _ the fire. _ To - night, {I / we} break _ a - way.
Gtr. 1
mf
w/ pick
Gtr. 2
Chorus
Gtr. 1 tacet
Gtr. 2: w/ Rhy. Fig. 1
D5 F5 G5 A5 G5 F5 C5 A5 D5 F5 G5 A5 G5 F5 C5 A5 D5
Break _ a - way from ev - 'ry - bod - y. Break _ a - way from ev - 'ry - thing. If

F5 C/E C5 A5
you can't stand the way this place is,
Gtr. 2
Rhy. Fig. 3
To Coda
D5 F5 G5 A5 G5 F5 C5 A5 D5
take your - self to high - er plac - es.
End Rhy. Fig. 3
Interlude
Dm(add9)
(Oh, oh.)
Gtr. 1
*p mf
*Vol. swell
Gtr. 2
P.M.
let ring
Verse
Gtr. 1 tacet
Gtr. 2: w/ Rhy. Fig. 2 (2 times)
D5 B♭5 A5 G5 F5 G5 A5
2. At night, I feel like a vam - pire. It's not right, but I just can't give it up.

D.S. al Coda
D5
B♭5 A5 G5 F5 G5 A5
I'll try to get my - self high - er. Let's go. We're gon - na light it up.
Coda
Interlude
D5
B♭5 A5 G5 F5 G5 A5
Voc. Fig. 1
End Voc. Fig. 1
(Oo.)
Gtr. 1
fdbk.
P.S.
Gtr. 2
Guitar Solo
Half-time feel
Gtr. 1 tacet
D5 A5 C5 A5 D5 A5 D5 C5 A5 D5 B♭5 A5 G5 F5 G5 A5
*Gtr. 3
(dist.)
8va
*Doubled throughout
**Downstroke
Rhy. Fig. 4
End Rhy. Fig. 4
Gtr. 2
Bkgd. Voc.: w/ Voc. Fig. 1
Gtr. 2: w/ Rhy. Fig. 4
D5 A5 C5 A5 D5 A5 D5 C5 A5 D5 B♭5 A5 G5 F5 G5 A5
8va
Gtr. 3

B♭5 A5 G5 F5 G5 A5 B♭5 A5 G5 F5 G5 A5
If
Gr. 3 loco
Gtr. 2
Bridge
End half-time feel
Gtr. 3 tacet
D5
N.C.
you can't stand the way this place is, take your-self to high - er plac - es.
(Take your-self!)
Chorus
Gtr. 2: w/ Rhy. Fig. 1
D5 F5 G5A5G5 F5 C5 A5 D5 F5 G5A5G5 F5 C5 A5 D5
Break a - way from ev - 'ry - bod - y. Break a - way from ev - 'ry - thing. If

Gtr. 2: w/ Rhy. Fig. 3
F5 C/E C5 A5 D5 F5 G5 A5 G5 F5 C5 A5 D5
you can't stand the way this place is, take your-self to high - er plac - es.
(Take your - self!)
Gtr. 3
Outro
Gtr. 2: w/ Rhy. Fig. 1
D5 F5 G5 A5 G5 F5 C5 A5 D5 F5 G5 A5 G5 F5 C5 A5 D5
High - er plac - es, to high - er plac - es.
(Oh, oh,
Riff A
End Riff A
8va
Gtr. 2: w/ Rhy. Fig. 3
Gtr. 3: w/ Riff A
F5 C/E C5 A5 D5 F5 G5 A5 G5 F5 C5 A5 D5
High - er plac - es, take your-self to high - er plac - es.
oh.)
D5
Gtr. 3
pp
fdbk.
Gtr. 2
Pitch: F♯ C

Breath

Words and Music by Benjamin Burnley and Mark J. Klepaski

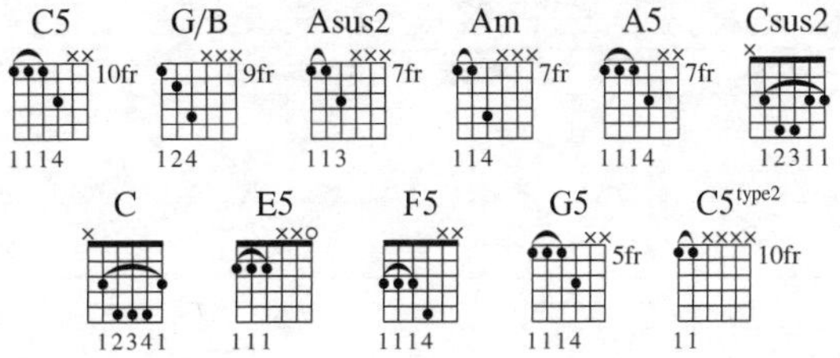

Drop D tuning, down 2 steps:
(low to high) B♭-F-B♭-E♭-G-C

Asus2
Am
C5
G/B
8va
loco
let ring
Verse
A5
Gtrs. 2, 3 & 4 tacet
Am
1. I see noth-ing in your eyes
and the more I see the
Riff A
Gtr. 1
let ring throughout
Gtr. 2
*Roll back vol. 1/2 way.
Fsus2
less I like. Is it o - ver yet?
In my head,
Gtr. 1
End Riff A
Gtr. 3
p

Gtr. 1: w/ Riff A (1st 4 meas.)
Am
oo,
I know noth-ing of your
8va
loco
fdbk.
mf
mp
*Vol. swell
kind
and I won't re - veal your e - vil mind.
Is it o -
Gtr. 3
8va
fdbk.
mp
Fsus2
Am
- ver yet?
I can't win.
Gtr. 1
Fill 1
Gtr. 3

Pre-Chorus
Gtr. 1 tacet
F5
N.C.
Rhy. Fill 1
End Rhy. Fill 1
Gtr. 4
mf
(cont. in notation)
So sac - ri - fice _ your - self and let me have _ what's left. I know that I ___ can
End Fill 1
8va
loco
Gtrs. 3 & 4
mf
*Swell to full vol.
A5
N.C.
A5
E5
A5
B5
F5
find the fire ___ in ___ your eyes. I'm go - ing all the way. _
Gtrs. 3 & 4
To Coda
Chorus
Gtrs. 3 & 4 tacet
Csus2
C
*Gtr. 5
(acous.)
mf
Get a - way _ please. ___ You take the
Riff B
Gtr. 2
wah-wah off
*Doubled throughout

Gtrs. 3 & 4: w/ Rhy. Fill 1
Gtr. 5 tacet
Csus2 C Csus2
A5
Gtrs. 3 & 4
breath right out of me. You left a
E5 F5
(Gtr. 3, cont. in notation)
hole where my heart should be. You got to
G5
(Gtr. 3, cont. in notation)
fight just to make it through 'cause I will
End Riff B

Interlude
Gtr. 1: w/ Riff A (1st 2 meas.)
A5
Verse
Gtr. 1: w/ Riff A
Gtrs. 2 & 4 tacet
Am
Gtr. 4
be the death of __ you. ___
2. This will be all o - ver __
Gtr. 2
Gtr. 3
8va
fdbk.
mf
__ soon. __
Whispered: (This will be all o - ver soon.)
Pour the salt __ in - to __ the o - pen __ wound. __ Is it o -
D.S. al Coda
Gtr. 1: w/ Fill 1
Gtr. 4: w/ Rhy. Fill 1
Fsus2
Am
N.C.
- ver yet? __
Let me __ in. ___
So sac - ri - fice __ your -
Gtr. 3
fdbk.
mf

Coda
Chorus
Gtr. 2: w/ Riff B
C5
G/B
You take the breath right out of me.
A5
E5
You left a hole where my heart should be.
F5
You got - ta fight just to make it through
(cont. in slashes)
G5
Gtrs. 3 & 4
'cause I will be the death of you.
Gtr. 2

Interlude
A5
F5
Gtr. 2
12
Gtr. 6 (elec.)
mf
*w/ dist. & delay
*Delay set for eighth-note regeneration w/ 1 repeat.
Gtr. 2 tacet
G5
F5
Gtr. 6
let ring
Bridge
A5
F5
I'm wait - ing.
I'm pray - ing.
mp
delay off

G5
C5 type2
B
⑥
7 fr.
P.M.
Re - al - ize.
Start hat - ing.
P.M.
Chorus
C5
G/B
A5
You take the breath right out of me.
You left a
Gtr. 6
Riff C
Gtr. 2
End Riff C

Gtr. 2: w/ Riff C
E5
F5
G5
hole where my heart should be.
You got - ta fight just to make it through
Gtr. 6
A5
'cause I will be the death of you.
Gtr. 6
Gtr. 2
divisi
Gtr. 2
Gtr. 1
(cont. on higher staff)
Gtr. 7 (elec.)
mf
w/ clean tone
let ring

Calling All Angels

Words and Music by Pat Monahan, Scott Underwood, James Stafford and Charlie Colin

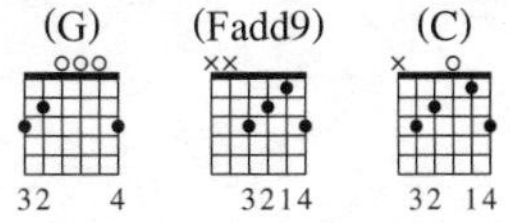

Capo III

Intro

Fade In

Moderately ♩ = 83

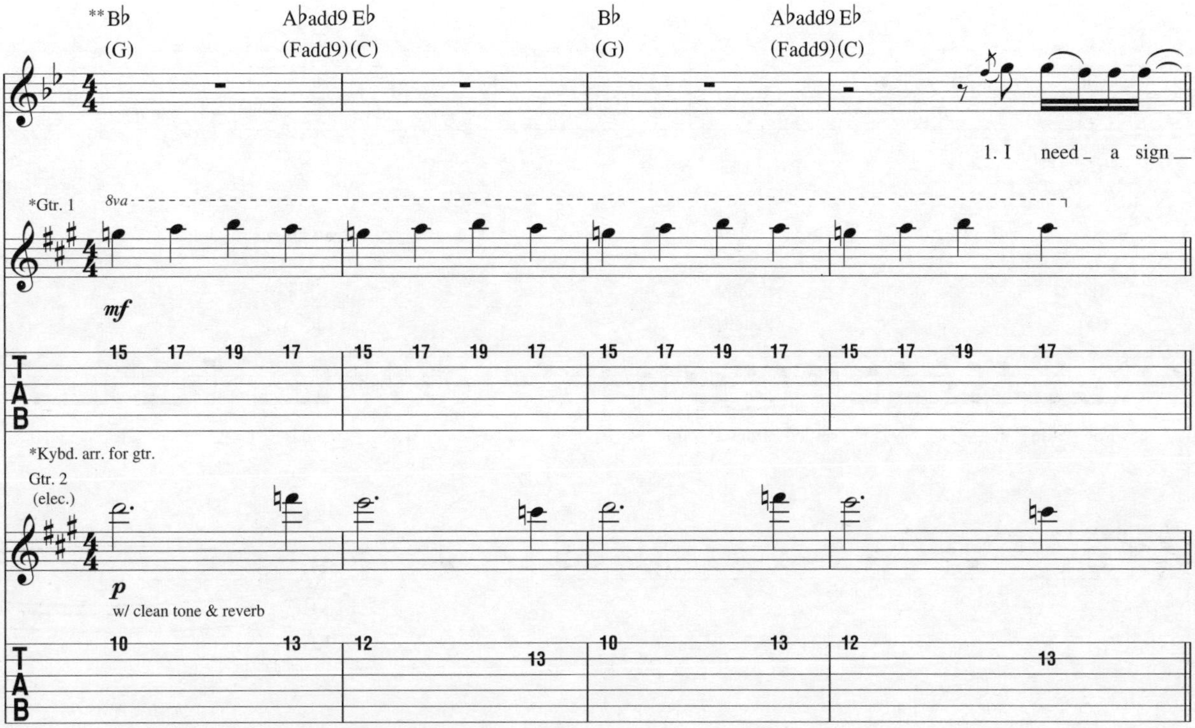

**Chord symbols in parentheses represent chord names respective to capoed guitar. Symbols above represent actual sounding chords. Capoed fret is "0" in tab. Chord symbols reflect overall harmony.

Verse

E♭ (C) B♭ (G) A♭add9 (Fadd9) E♭ (C)
- mo - sphere. I need to know that things are gon - na look up, 'cause I feel us
End Riff A
B♭ (G) A♭add9 (Fadd9) E♭ (C)
Pre-Chorus
Gtr. 3 tacet
drown - ing in a sea spilled from a cup. When there is no place safe and no safe
Gtr. 4 (elec.)
mf
w/ slight dist.
let ring
place to put my head, when you can feel the world shake from the words that I said. And I'm
let ring

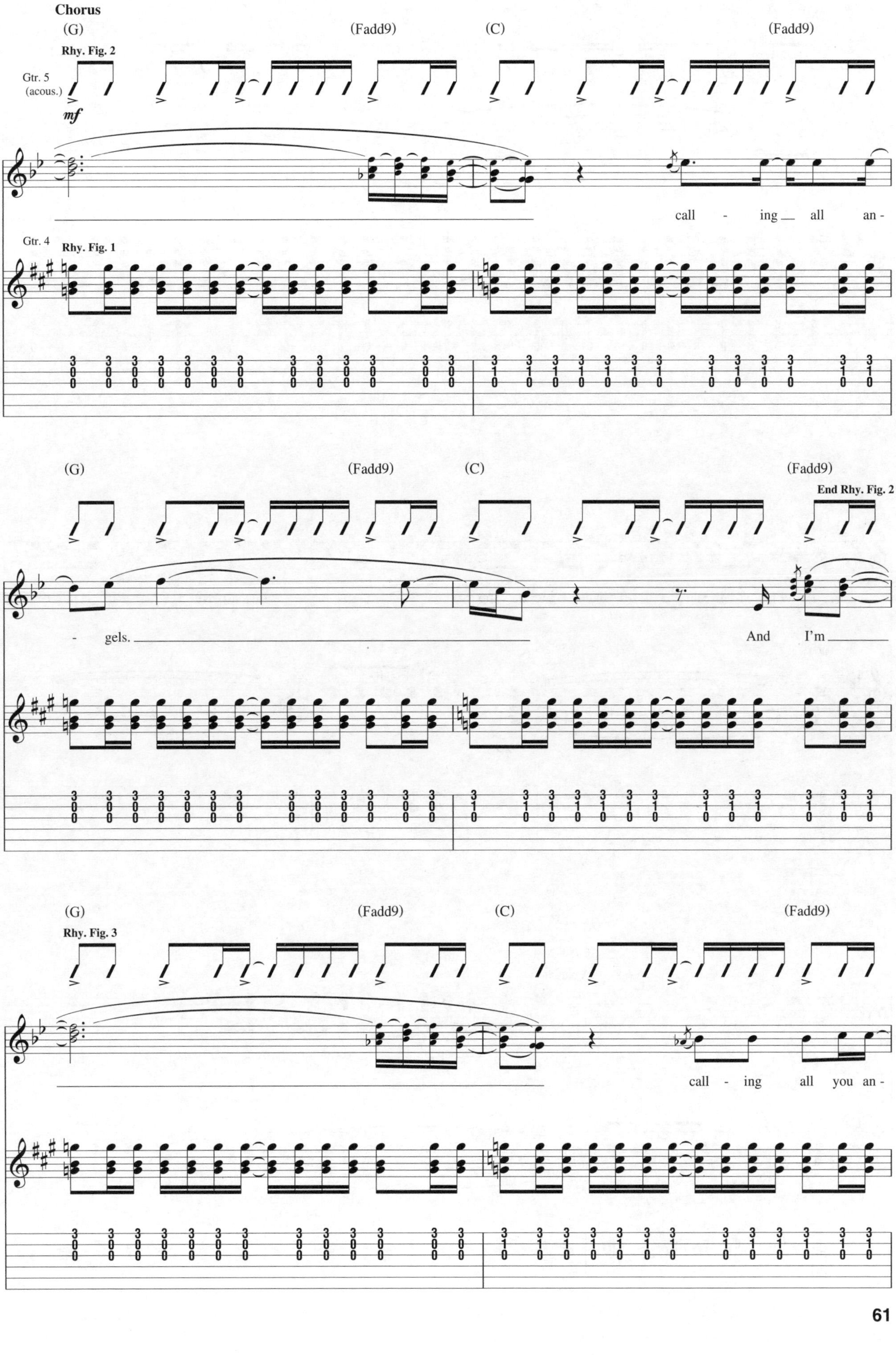
Chorus
(G)
(Fadd9)
(C)
(Fadd9)
Rhy. Fig. 2
Gtr. 5 (acous.)
mf
call - ing all an -
Gtr. 4
Rhy. Fig. 1
(G)
(Fadd9)
(C)
(Fadd9)
End Rhy. Fig. 2
- gels.
And I'm
(G)
(Fadd9)
(C)
(Fadd9)
Rhy. Fig. 3
call - ing all you an -

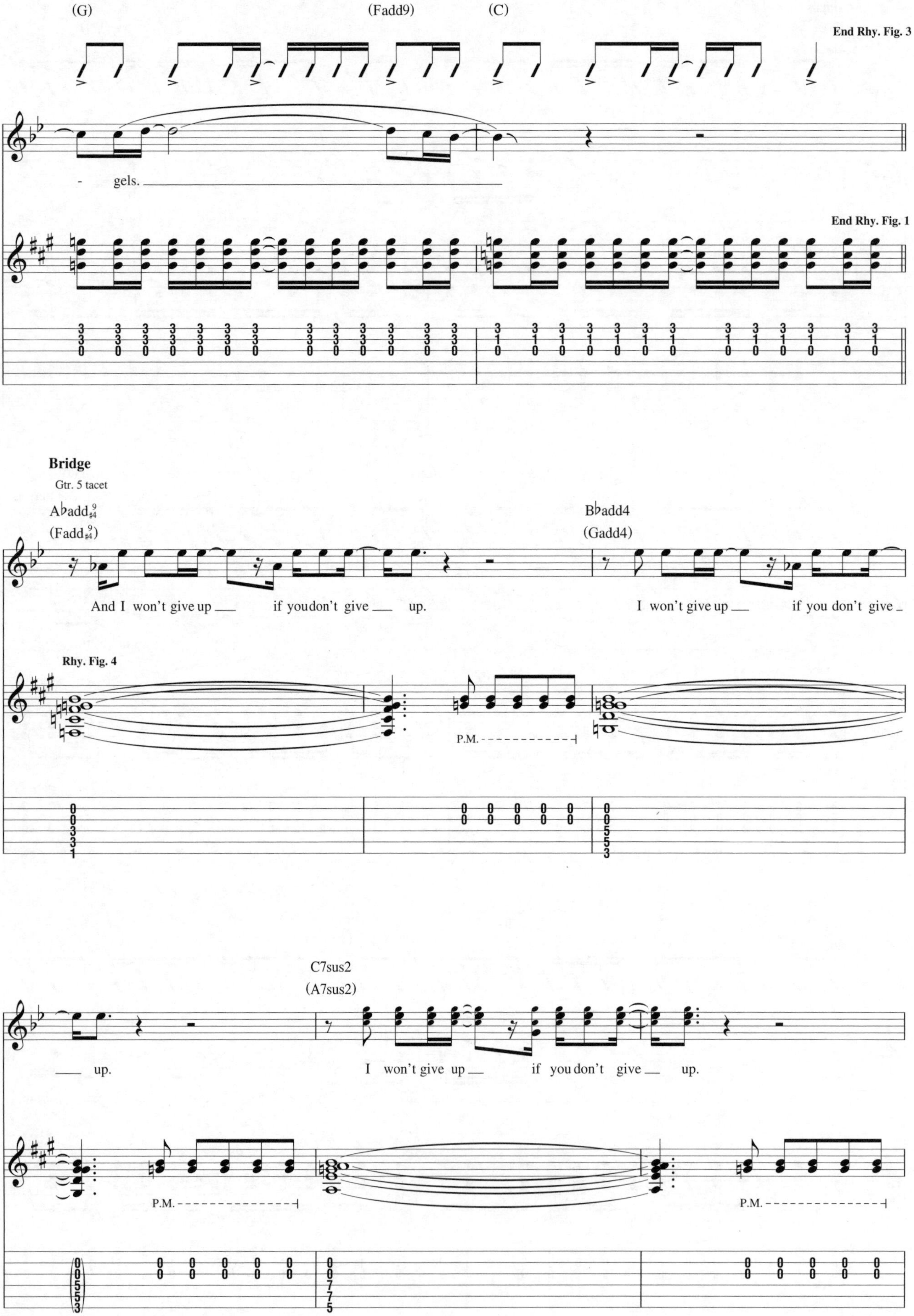
(G)
(Fadd9)
(C)
End Rhy. Fig. 3
- gels.
End Rhy. Fig. 1
Bridge
Gtr. 5 tacet
A♭add♯4 9
(Fadd♯4 9)
B♭add4
(Gadd4)
And I won't give up if you don't give up.
I won't give up if you don't give
Rhy. Fig. 4
P.M.
C7sus2
(A7sus2)
up.
I won't give up if you don't give up.
P.M.
P.M.

D♭6
(B♭6)
I won't give up if you don't give up. 2. I need a sign
End Rhy. Fig. 4
Verse
Gtr. 3: w/ Riff A (2 times)
Gtr. 4 tacet
Gtr. 5: w/ Rhy. Fig. 2 (2 times)
B♭
(G)
A♭add9
(Fadd9)
E♭
(C)
A♭add9
(Fadd9)
to let me know you're here, 'cause my T V set
*Gtr. 6
Riff B
mp
*Kybd. arr. for gtr.
Gtr. 7 (elec.)
mp
**w/ clean tone & delay
w/ fingers
let ring
let ring
1/2
**Delay set for quarter-note regeneration.

B♭ (G) A♭add9 (Fadd9) E♭ (C) A♭add9 (Fadd9)
just keeps it all from be - ing clear. I want a rea -
End Riff B
let ring
1/2
Gtr. 6: w/ Riff B
B♭ (G) A♭add9 (Fadd9) E♭ (C) A♭add9 (Fadd9)
- son for the way things have to be. I need a hand
Gtr. 7 Riff C
let ring
1/2
let ring
B♭ (G) A♭add9 (Fadd9) E♭ (C) A♭add9 (Fadd9)
to help build up some kind of hope in - side of me. And I'm
End Riff C
let ring
let ring
1/2

Chorus

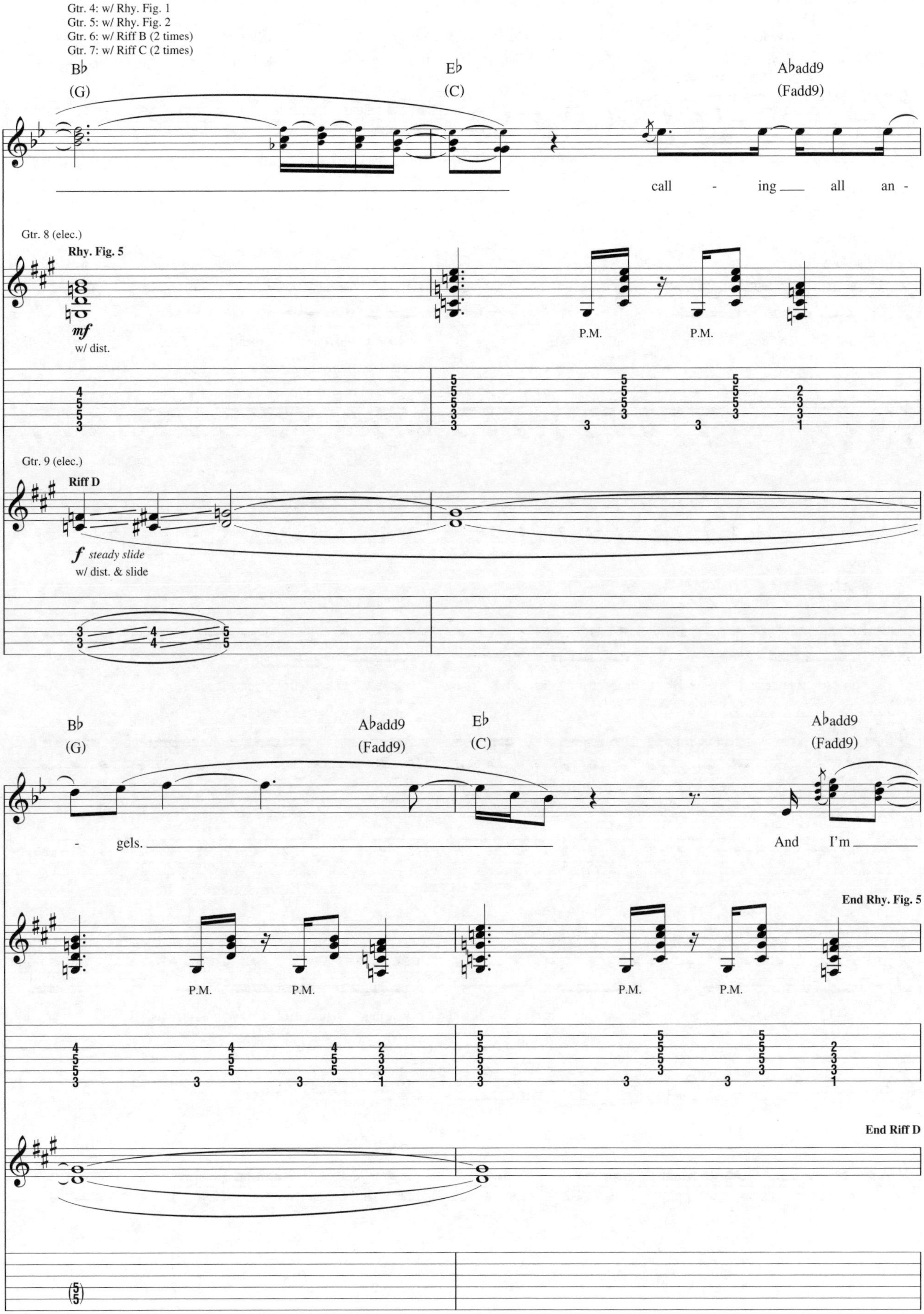
Gtr. 4: w/ Rhy. Fig. 1
Gtr. 5: w/ Rhy. Fig. 2
Gtr. 6: w/ Riff B (2 times)
Gtr. 7: w/ Riff C (2 times)
B♭
(G)
E♭
(C)
A♭add9
(Fadd9)
call - ing all an -
Gtr. 8 (elec.)
Rhy. Fig. 5
mf
w/ dist.
P.M.
Gtr. 9 (elec.)
Riff D
f steady slide
w/ dist. & slide
- gels.
And I'm
End Rhy. Fig. 5
End Riff D

Gtr. 5: w/ Rhy. Fig. 3
Gtr. 8: w/ Rhy. Fig. 5
Gtr. 9: w/ Riff D
B♭ (G)
A♭add9 (Fadd9)
E♭ (C)
A♭add9 (Fadd9)
B♭ (G)
A♭add9 (Fadd9)
E♭ (C)
A♭ (F)
call - ing all you an - gels. When
Bridge
Gtr. 4: w/ Rhy. Fig. 4
A♭add9♯4 (Fadd9♯4)
chil - dren have to play in - side so they don't dis - ap - pear, while
Gtr. 10 (elec.)
mf
w/ dist. & wah-wah
P.M.
B♭add4 (Gadd4)
pri - vate eyes solve mar-riage lies 'cause we don't talk for years. And
P.M.
C7sus2 (A7sus2)
fut - bal teams are kiss - ing queens and los - ing sight of hav - ing dreams, in a
(I won't give up if you don't give up.
P.M.

D♭6
(B♭6)
Gtr. 4
world where what we want is on - ly what we want un - til it's ours.
I won't give up if you don't give up.)
*Gtr. 11 (elec.)
mf w/ slight dist. & reverse delay
P.M.
Gtr. 10
divisi
*Backwards guitar loop arrangement
Interlude
Gtrs. 4 & 10 tacet
B♭7
(G7)
And I'm
Gtr. 11
Outro-Chorus
Gtr. 4: w/ Rhy. Fig. 1 (till fade)
Gtr. 5: w/ Rhy. Fig. 2 (till fade)
Gtr. 6: w/ Riff B (till fade)
Gtr. 7: w/ Riff C (till fade)
Gtr. 8: w/ Rhy. Fig. 5 (till fade)
Gtr. 9: w/ Riff D (till fade)
Gtr. 11 tacet
B♭ A♭add9 E♭ A♭add9 B♭ A♭add9 E♭ A♭add9
(G) (Fadd9) (C) (Fadd9) (G) (Fadd9) (C) (Fadd9)
call - ing all an - gels. And I'm
Voc. Fig. 1
(Call - ing all an - gels.

B♭ (G) A♭add9 (Fadd9) E♭ (C) A♭add9 (Fadd9) B♭ (G) A♭add9 (Fadd9) E♭ (C) A♭add9 (Fadd9)
call - ing all you an - gels. And I'm
End Voc. Fig. 1
Call - ing all you an - gels.)
Bkgd. Voc.: w/ Voc. Fig. 1
B♭ (G) A♭add9 (Fadd9) E♭ (C) A♭add9 (Fadd9)
call - ing all an -
Voc. Fig. 2
(I won't give up if you don't give up.
Gtr. 12 (elec.)
Riff E
mf
*w/ dist. & delay
let ring
let ring
8 8 7 7 8 8 7 7 8 7
8 8 8 8 8 8 8 8 8 8
*Delay set for eighth-note regeneration.
B♭ (G) A♭add9 (Fadd9) E♭ (C) A♭add9 (Fadd9)
- gels. And I'm
End Voc. Fig. 2
I won't give up if you don't give up.)
End Riff E
let ring
let ring
8 12 12 10 10 12 12 10 10 12 10
12 8 8 8 8 8 8 8 8 8 8

Bkgd. Voc.: w/ Voc. Fig. 2 (till fade)
Gtr. 12: w/ Riff E
B♭ (G) A♭add9 (Fadd9) E♭ (C) A♭add9 (Fadd9) B♭ (G) A♭add9 (Fadd9)
call - ing all you an - gels.
Begin fade
Bkgd. Voc.: w/ Voc. Fig. 1 (last 3 meas.)
E♭ (C) A♭add9 (Fadd9) B♭ (G) A♭add9 (Fadd9) E♭ (C) A♭add9 (Fadd9)
Call-ing all you an - gels. Call - ing all you an -
Riff F
Gtr. 12
let ring
let ring
Gtr. 12: w/ Riff F
B♭ (G) A♭add9 (Fadd9) E♭ (C) A♭add9 (Fadd9) B♭ (G) A♭add9 (Fadd9)
- gels. Call - ing all you an - gels.
End Riff F
Fade out
Bkgd. Voc.: w/ Voc. Fig. 1 (till fade)
E♭ (C) A♭add9 (Fadd9) B♭ (G) A♭add9 (Fadd9) E♭ (C) A♭add9 (Fadd9)
Call - ing all you an - gels.

Closer

Words and Music by Caleb Followill, Nathan Followill, Jared Followill and Matthew Followill

Intro

Moderately slow ♩ = 79

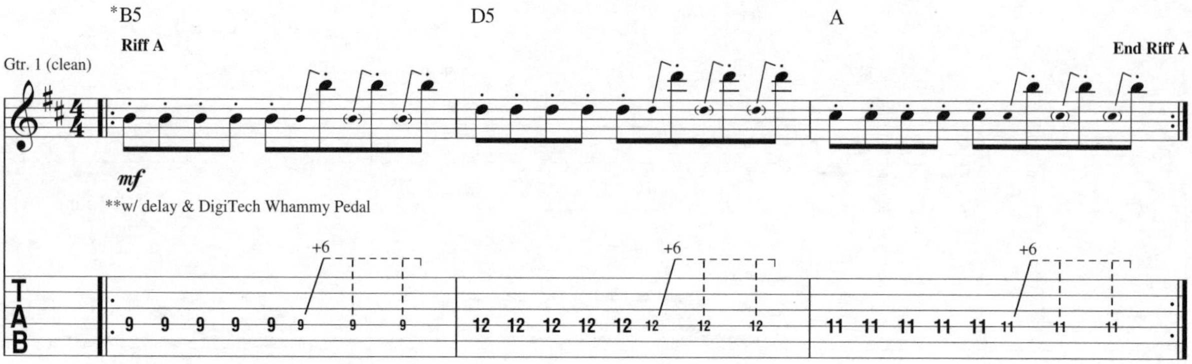

*Chord symbols reflect implied harmony.

**Delay set for eighth-note regeneration w/ 1 repeat.
Whammy pedal set for one octave above.

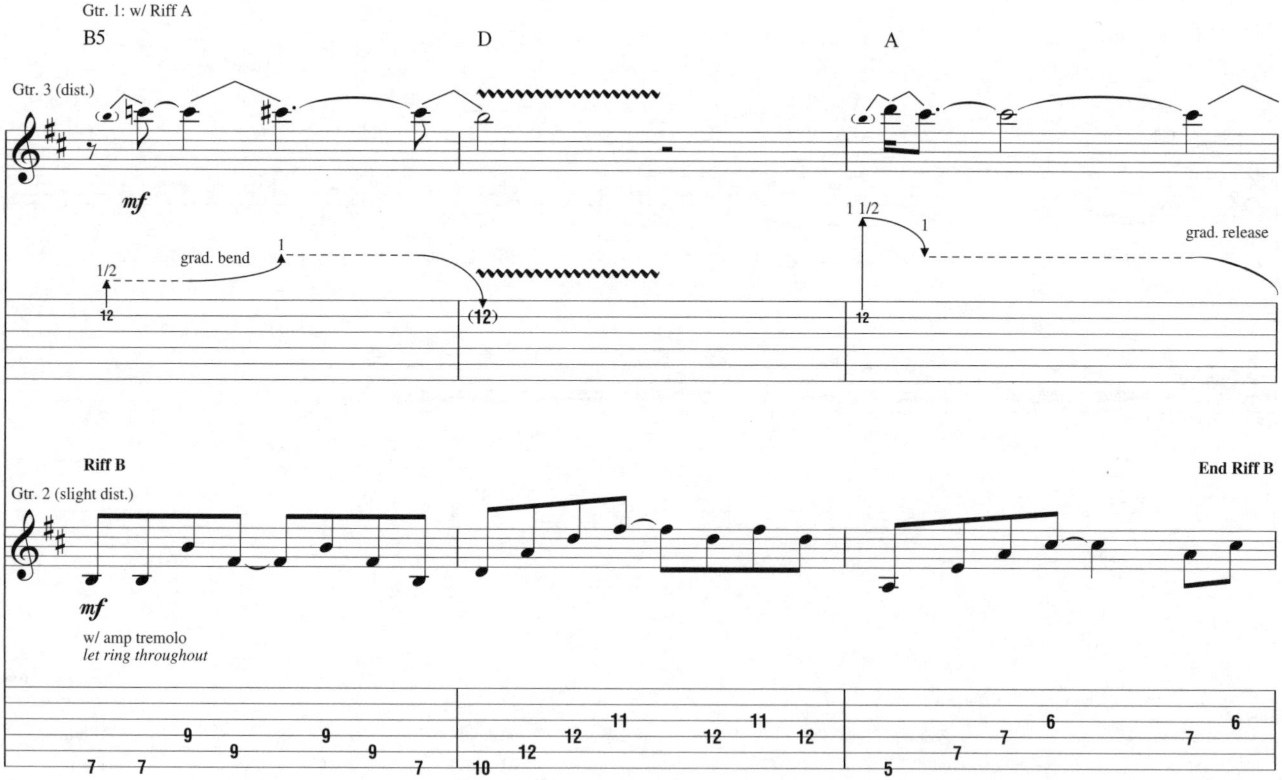

B5
D
A
1. Strand -
Gtr. 3
1
3/4
1/2
grad. release
Riff C
End Riff C
Gtr. 1
Gtr. 2
Verse
Gtr. 3 tacet
B5
D5
A
- ed in the spook - y town.
Stop lights are sway - ing and the phone - lines are down.
Gtr. 1
Gtr. 2
Riff D

B5
D5
A
Floor is crack-ling cold.
She took my heart,
I think she took my soul.
Riff E
Gtr. 1
End Riff E
+6
Gtr. 2
Gtr. 1: w/ Riff E
B5
D5
A
With the moon I run
far from the car - nage of the fier - y sun.
Gtr. 2
End Riff D
Interlude
Gtr. 1: w/ Riff C
Gtr. 2: w/ Riff B (2 times)
B5
D
A
Gtr. 3
3/4
1
grad. release

Gtr. 1: w/ Riff E
B5
D
A
2. Driv -
grad. release
1/2
1
1 1/2
Verse
Gtr. 1: w/ Riff E
Gtr. 2: w/ Riff D
D5
- en by the stran - gle of veins showing no mer -
shim - my shook my bones leav - ing me strand -
- cy. I'd do it a - gain. O - pen up your eyes.
- ed all in love on my own. Do you think of me?
Gtr. 1: w/ Riff C (3 times)
You keep on cry - ing, ba - by, I'll bleed you dry.
Where am I now? Ooh, ba - by, where do I sleep?

B5
D5
The skies, they blink at me. I see a storm
It feels so good but I'm old. Two thou - sand years
1st time, Gtr. 2: w/ Riff D (last 3 meas.)
2nd time, Gtr. 3: w/ Fill 1
2nd time, Gtr. 2: w/ Riff B
A
B5
bub - ling up from the sea.
of chas - ing tak - ing its toll,
D5
A
and it's com - ing clos - er,
Fill 1
Gtr. 3
1 1/2
1
grad. release

Chorus
1st time, Gtr. 1: w/ Riff E
1st time, Gtr. 2: w/ Riff B (2 times)
2nd time, Gtr. 1: w/ Riff C
2nd time, Gtr. 2: w/ Riff B (3 times)
B5
D
A
and it's com - ing clos - er.
Riff F
End Riff F
let ring
Gtr. 1: w/ Riff C
Gtr. 3: w/ Riff F
1.
2.
3.You
And it's com - ing clos - er.
And it's com - ing clos - er.
Gtr. 3
Gtr. 1
Outro
Gtr. 1: w/ Riff C (3 2/3 times)
Gtr. 2: w/ Riff D (3 times)
D5
Riff G
End Riff G

Gtr. 3: w/ Riff G (2 times)
B5
D5
A
B5
D5
A
B5
Gtr. 3
D5
Gtr. 4
mf
w/ amp tremolo & chorus
Gtr. 2
Gtrs. 3 & 4 tacet
A
Bsus2
Gtr. 1
Gtr. 2

Crack the Skye

Words and Music by Brann Dailor, William Hinds, William Kelliher and Troy Sanders

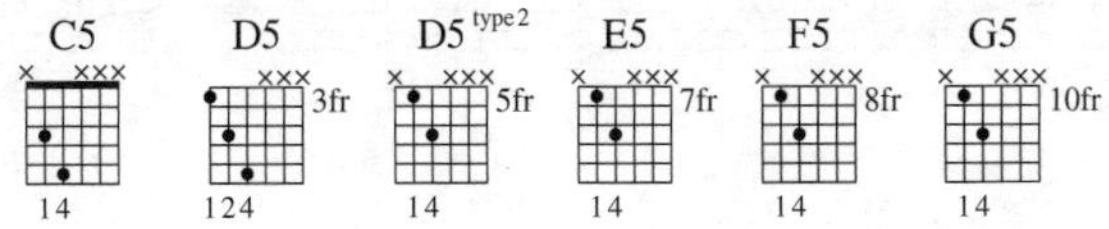

Drop B tuning, down 1 step:
(low to high) A-G-C-F-A-D

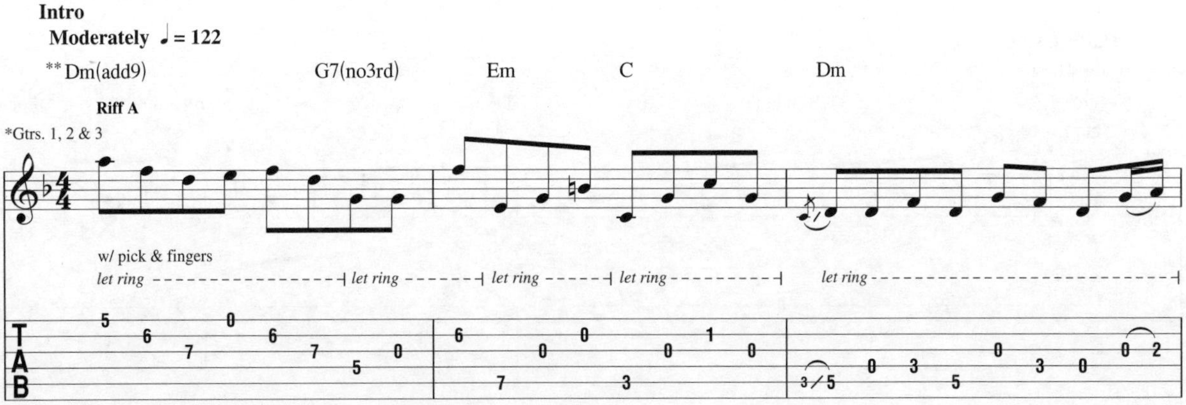

*Gtr. 1 (acous.), played *mf*. Gtrs. 2 & 3 (elec.) w/ dist., played *f*. Composite arrangement

**Chord symbols reflect basic harmony.

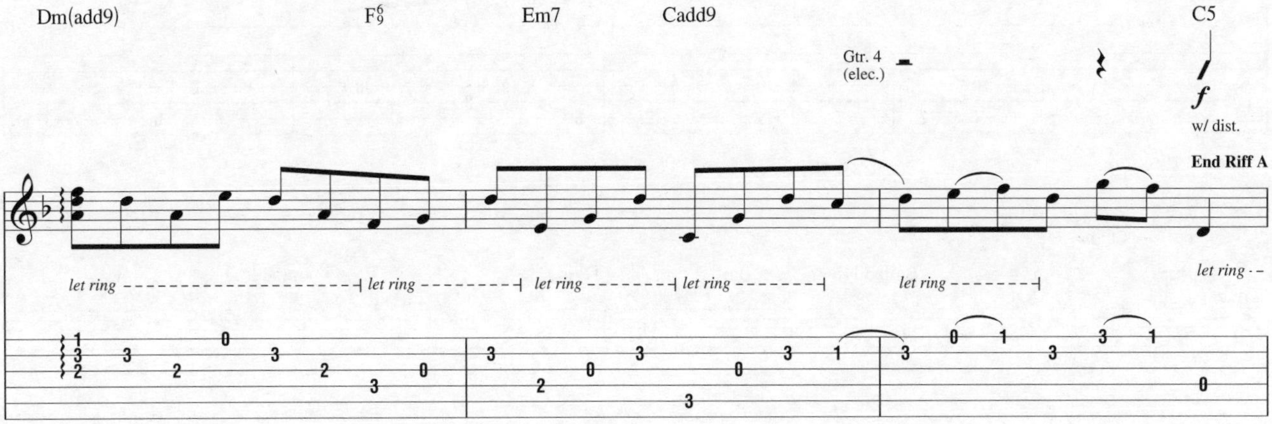

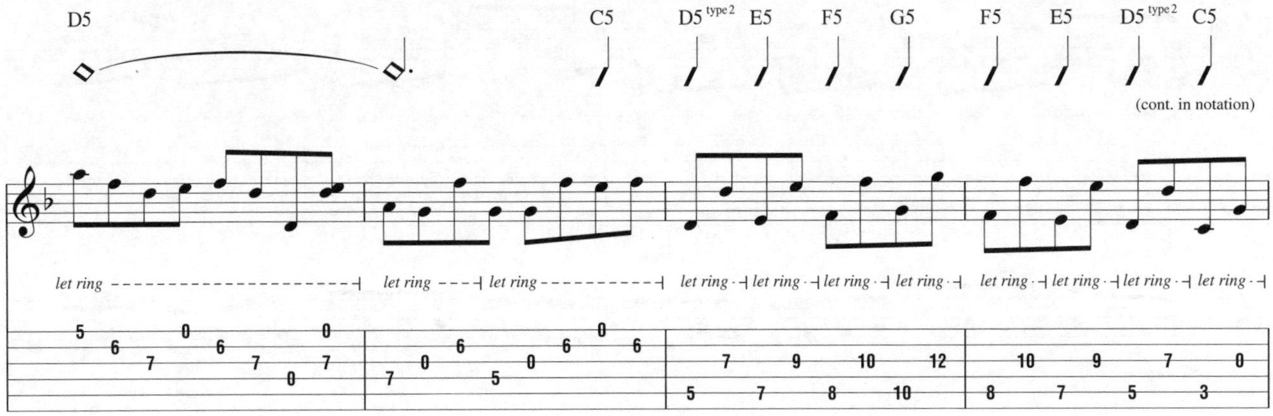

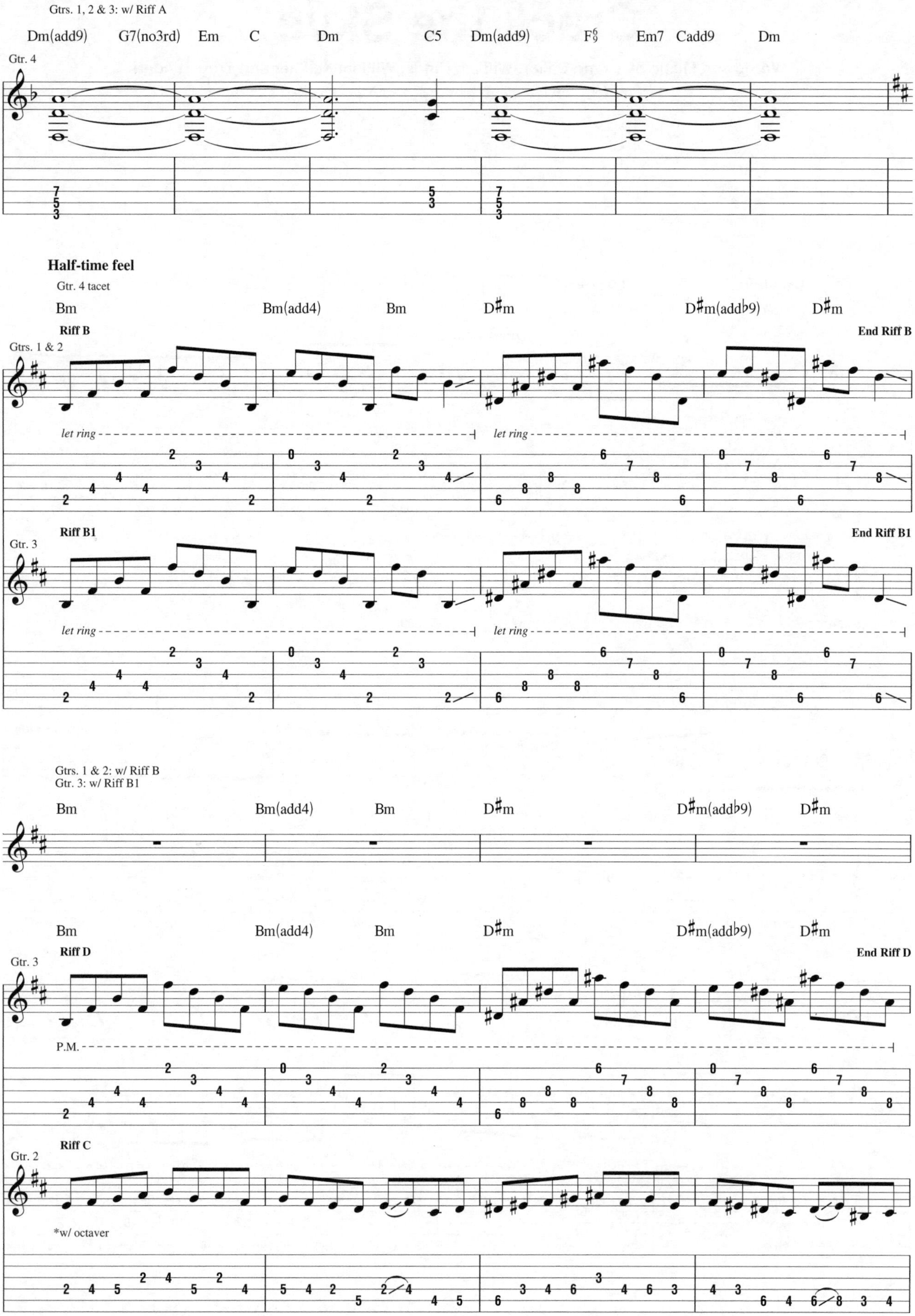

*Set for one octave above.

Gtr. 3: w/ Riff D
Bm
Bm(add4)
Bm
D♯m
D♯m(add♭9)
D♯m
Gtr. 2
End Riff C
Verse
B5
D♯5
1. Bless - ed vi - sion - ar - y, cut me
2. The ves - sel forged in - side of me
Rhy. Fig. 1
*Gtrs. 2 & 3
P.M.
let ring
*Gtr. 2: octaver off
B5
with your sun. The riv - ers ran in blood,
watch - es o - ver
D♯5
spark fueled to fi - re.
like the death of the moon.
End Rhy. Fig. 1

B5
G
Deep with - in this end - less
Strike the shep - herd, sheep will
Riff E1
*Gtr. 5 (elec.)
mf
w/ dist.
*9-str. gtr. (Top 3 strings are doubled).
Rhy. Fig. 2
**Gtr. 6 (elec.)
mf
w/ dist.
**Two gtrs. arr. for one.
Riff E
Gtrs. 2 & 3
Gtr. 6: w/ Rhy. Fig. 2
B5
void, search - ing for a
scat - ter. Moun - tains of de -
End Rhy. Fig. 2

Chorus
Gtr. 5 tacet
G
D♯5 E5 F♯5 G5 D♯5 D
sign.
spair.
I can
Gtr. 5
End Riff E1
12 12 12 12 12 12 12 12 14 14 14 14 14 14 14 14 16 16 16 16 16 16 16 16 19 19 19 19 19 19 19 19
Gtrs. 2 & 3
End Riff E
Rhy. Fig. 3
let ring
D♯5 E5 F♯5 G5 D♯5 D
see the pain, it's writ - ten all o - ver your face.
Gtrs. 2 & 3
End Rhy. Fig. 3
let ring
let ring
Verse
Gtrs. 2 & 3: w/ Rhy. Fig. 1
B5
D♯5
*Voc. Fig. 1
End Voc. Fig. 1
3. The scream-ing ar - rows tear through my soul.
(Oo.)
*Refers to upstemmed voc. only
Bkgd. Voc.: w/ Voc. Fig. 1
B5
D♯5
In the dawn your face is haunt - ing while ghost - ly dreams of

*Composite arrangement

Gm7
C♯m7
let ring
hold bend
C♯m7add♯4
Gtrs. 1 & 2: w/ Riff B (2 times)
Gtr. 3: w/ Riff B1 (2 times)
Bm
Bm(add4)
Bm
Vocoder:
Gtr. 7
let ring
(cont. on lower staff)
mf
* w/ dist. fdbk.
Riff G
Gtr. 8
Gtr. 8 (elec.)
Gtr. 2
divisi
End Riff F1
Pitch: F♯
*Vol. swell
End Riff F
Gtrs. 1 & 3
Gtr. 7
let ring

D♯m
D♯m(add♭9)
D♯m
Bm
Gtr. 8
Gtr. 7
Bm(add4)
Bm
D♯m
D♯m(add♭9)
D♯m
End Riff G
Gtrs. 1 & 3: w/ Riff F
Gtr. 2: w/ Riff F1
Gtr. 8 tacet
Dmaj9
B♭m7♭5
Gtr. 7
let ring
hold bend

Gm7
C♯m7
let ring
C♯m7add♯4
Gtrs. 1 & 2: w/ Riff B (2 times)
Gtr. 3: w/ Riff B1 (2 times)
Gtr. 8: w/ Riff G
Bm
Bm(add4)
Bm
Vocoder:
let ring
D♯m
D♯m(add♭9)
D♯m
Bm
Bm(add4)
Bm
D♯m
D♯m(add♭9)
D♯m

Interlude

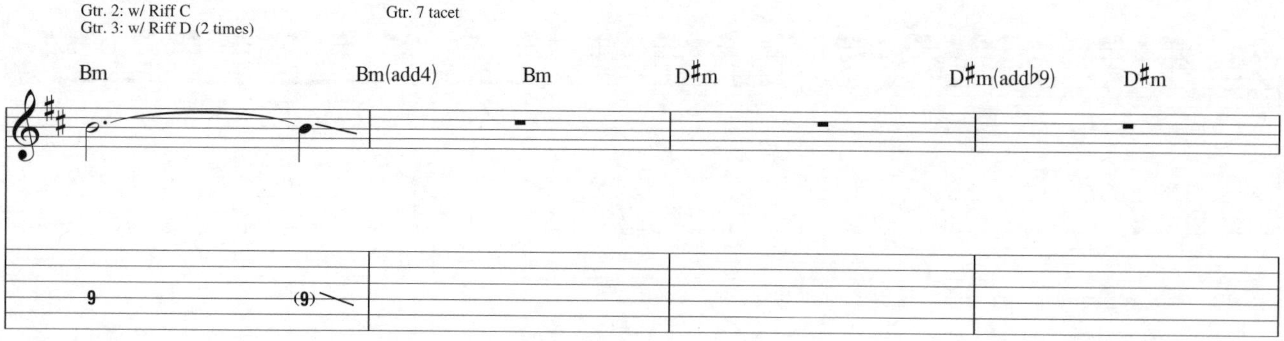

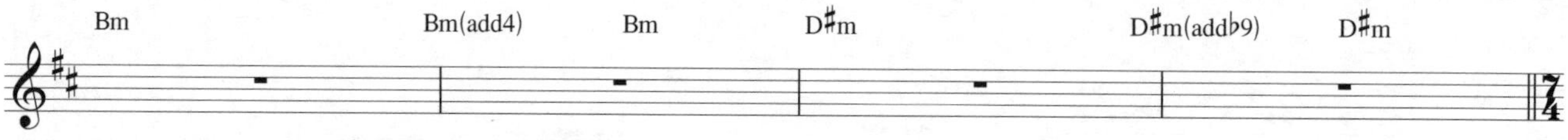

Guitar Solo

Gtr. 2: w/ Rhy. Fig. 4
B5 C#5 B5 C#5 B5 C#5 B5 C#5 D5 C#5 B5 A#5 B5 C#5 B5 C#5 B5 C#5 B5 C#5 D5 E5 F#5 G5
Gtr. 9
8va
let ring
Gtr. 8
Gtr. 3
*Vol. swell
Pre-Chorus
Gtrs. 2 & 3: w/ Riff E
Gtr. 5: w/ Riff E1
Gtr. 6: w/ Rhy. Fig. 2 (2 times)
Gtrs. 8 & 9 tacet
B5 G B5
Des - per - ate hea - thens flock to si - rens. Guard your heart - ache
Verse
Bkgd. Voc.: w/ Voc. Fig. 1
Gtrs. 2 & 3: w/ Rhy. Fig. 1
G B5 D#5
well. 4. Mom - ma, don't let them take her,
B5 D#5
don't let 'em take her down...
Pre-Chorus
Gtrs. 2 & 3: w/ Riff E
Gtr. 5: w/ Riff E1
Gtr. 6: w/ Rhy. Fig. 2 (2 times)
B5 G
Please tell Lu - ci - fer he can't have

End half-time feel
B5
G
this one, her spir - it's too strong.
(Strong.)
Chorus
Gtrs. 2 & 3: w/ Rhy. Fig. 3 (2 times)
D♯5 E5 F♯5 G5 D♯5 D D♯5 E5 F♯5 G5 D♯5 D
I can see the pain, it's writ - ten all o - ver your face.
D♯5 E5 F♯5 G5 D♯5 D D♯5 E5 F♯5 G5 D♯5 D
I can see the pain, you can make it all go a - way.
Outro
Dm(add9) G7(no3rd) Em C Dm C5 Dm(add9) F6/9
*Gtrs. 1, 2 & 3
let ring
*Composite arrangement
Gtr. 4
Em7 Cadd9 Dm C5 D5
rit.
fdbk.

Death of Me

Words and Music by Jasen Rauch and Rob Graves

Drop D tuning, down 2 steps:
(low to high) B♭-F-B♭-E♭-G-C

Gtr. 4 tacet
So go a-head and take an-oth-er piece of me now, while we all bow down to you.
Riff B
Gtrs. 2 & 3
End Riff B
Chorus
Half-time feel
3rd time, Gtrs. 2 & 3 tacet
D5 F5 B♭5 F/A
You tear me down and then you pick me up. You take it all and still it's not e-nough.
Riff C
Gtr. 4
End Riff C
octaver off
Rhy. Fig. 2
Gtr. 1
End Rhy. Fig. 2
To Coda 1
To Coda 2
End half-time feel
Gtr. 1: w/ Rhy. Fig. 2
Gtr. 4: w/ Riff C
D5 F5 B♭5 F/A
You try to tell me you can heal me but I'm still bleed-ing and you'll be the death of me.
Interlude
Gtr. 1: w/ Rhy. Fig. 1
D5 C5 E♭5 D5 B♭5 F5 D5 C5 E♭5 D5 B♭5 F5
Verse
Gtrs. 2 & 3: w/ Riff A
D5
2. How can you help my af-flic-tion if you're the sick-ness and

Gtrs. 2 & 3: w/ Riff B
not the cure?
For too long now I've
Gtr. 4
8va
loco
P.M.
Harm.
Pitch: D A
D.S. al Coda 1
faked this ad - dic - tion,
an - oth - er sac - ri - fice to make us pure.
Coda 1
Gtr. 1: w/ Rhy. Fig. 2 (2 times)
Gtr. 4: w/ Riff C (2 times)
D5 F5 B♭5 F/A
You tear me down and then you pick me up. You take it all and still it's not e - nough.
Voc. Fig. 1
End Voc. Fig. 1
(Oh, oh.)
Bkgd. Voc.: w/ Voc. Fig. 1
You try to tell me you can heal me but I'm still bleed - ing and you'll be the death of me.
Bridge
D5 N.C.
Whispered:
I won't for - get, I can - not for - get this. I won't for - get, I'll nev - er for - get this.
Gtr. 1

D5 N.C. D5 F5 A♭5 D5 N.C. D5 F5 A♭5
I won't for - get, I can - not for - get this. I won't for - get, I'll nev - er for - get this.
Gtr. 1
Half-time feel
D5 A♭5 D5 A♭5
I won't for - get, I can - not for - get this! I won't for - get, I'll nev - er for - get this!
Rhy. Fig. 3
End Rhy. Fig. 3
Gtr. 1: w/ Rhy. Fig. 3
D5 A♭5 D5 A♭5
I won't for - get, I can - not for - get this! I won't for - get, I'll nev - er for - get!
Verse
*Gtr. 5: w/ Riff A (1 1/2 times)
D5
Spoken: 3. I know I can never prove this il - lu - sion. You aren't the one that I
*Gtr. 5 (elec.) w/ dist., played f.
thought you were. And so I learned to em - brace this de - lu - sion.
Gtr. 2
Gtr. 3
divisi

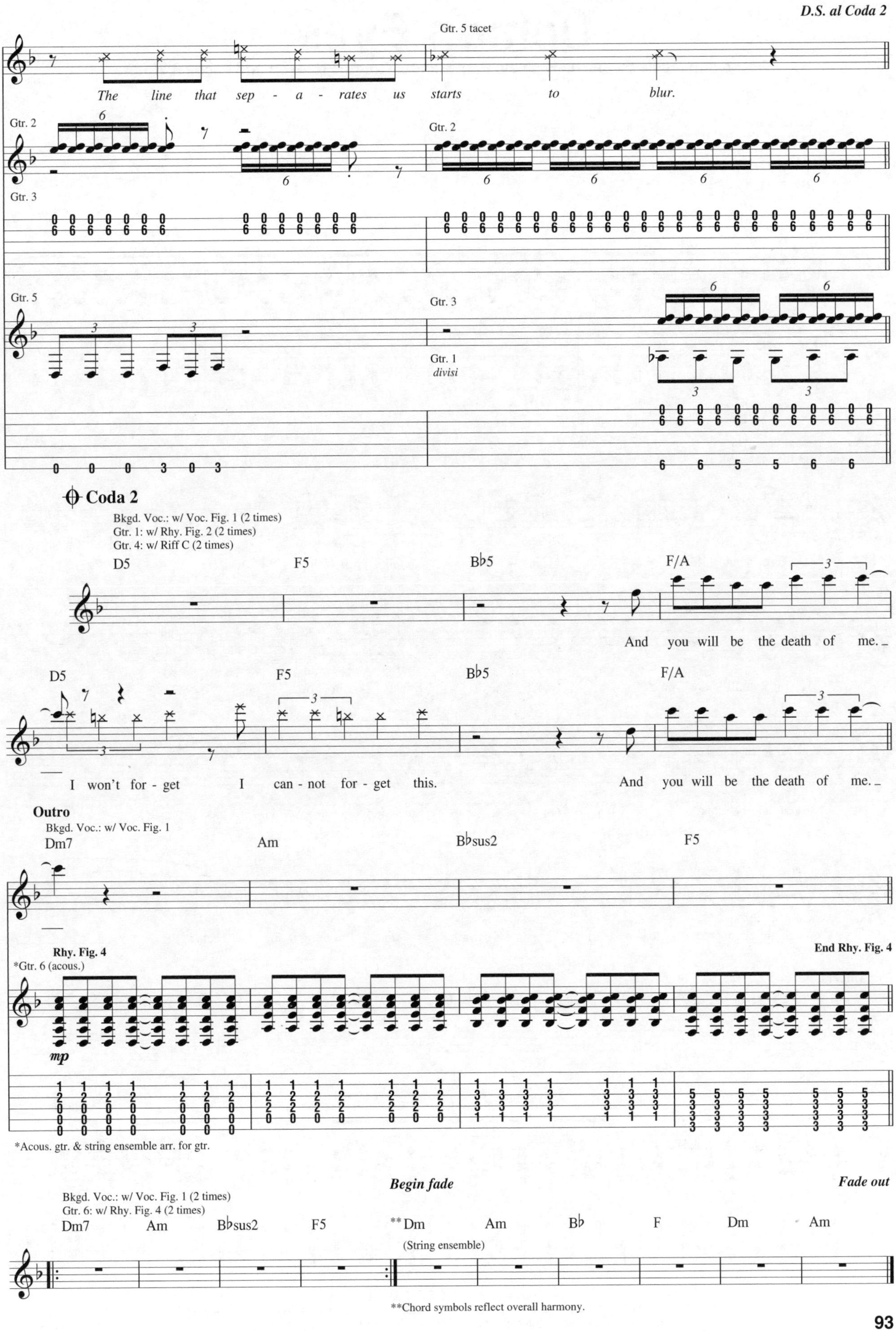
D.S. al Coda 2
Gtr. 5 tacet
The line that sep - a - rates us starts to blur.
Gtr. 2
Gtr. 3
Gtr. 5
Gtr. 1
divisi
Coda 2
Bkgd. Voc.: w/ Voc. Fig. 1 (2 times)
Gtr. 1: w/ Rhy. Fig. 2 (2 times)
Gtr. 4: w/ Riff C (2 times)
D5 F5 B♭5 F/A
And you will be the death of me.
D5 F5 B♭5 F/A
I won't for - get I can - not for - get this. And you will be the death of me.
Outro
Bkgd. Voc.: w/ Voc. Fig. 1
Dm7 Am B♭sus2 F5
Rhy. Fig. 4
End Rhy. Fig. 4
*Gtr. 6 (acous.)
mp
*Acous. gtr. & string ensemble arr. for gtr.
Begin fade
Fade out
Bkgd. Voc.: w/ Voc. Fig. 1 (2 times)
Gtr. 6: w/ Rhy. Fig. 4 (2 times)
Dm7 Am B♭sus2 F5 **Dm Am B♭ F Dm Am
(String ensemble)
**Chord symbols reflect overall harmony.

Demon Eyes

Words and Music by James Heatley, Paul Mahon, Cormac Neeson and Michael Waters

Bb G Bb G Bb G F5 G Bb G Bb G Bb G C G Bb G
let ring
Verse
G G5
2. So take a look a-cross your desk, you tell me why I'm here.
let ring
You been mak-in' all that mon-ey prey - in' on the fear.
Bb G C G Bb G
Rhy. Fig. 2
End Rhy. Fig. 2
Bb G Bb G Bb G F5 G Bb G Bb G Bb G C G Bb G
I can see your de-mon eye, the tar - get has been set.
Rhy. Fig. 3
End Rhy. Fig. 3
Gtr. 1: w/ Rhy. Fig. 1
Bb G Bb G Bb G Bb G Bb G Bb G Bb C Bb G
Take a shot for old time's sake, you've done no dam-age yet. The

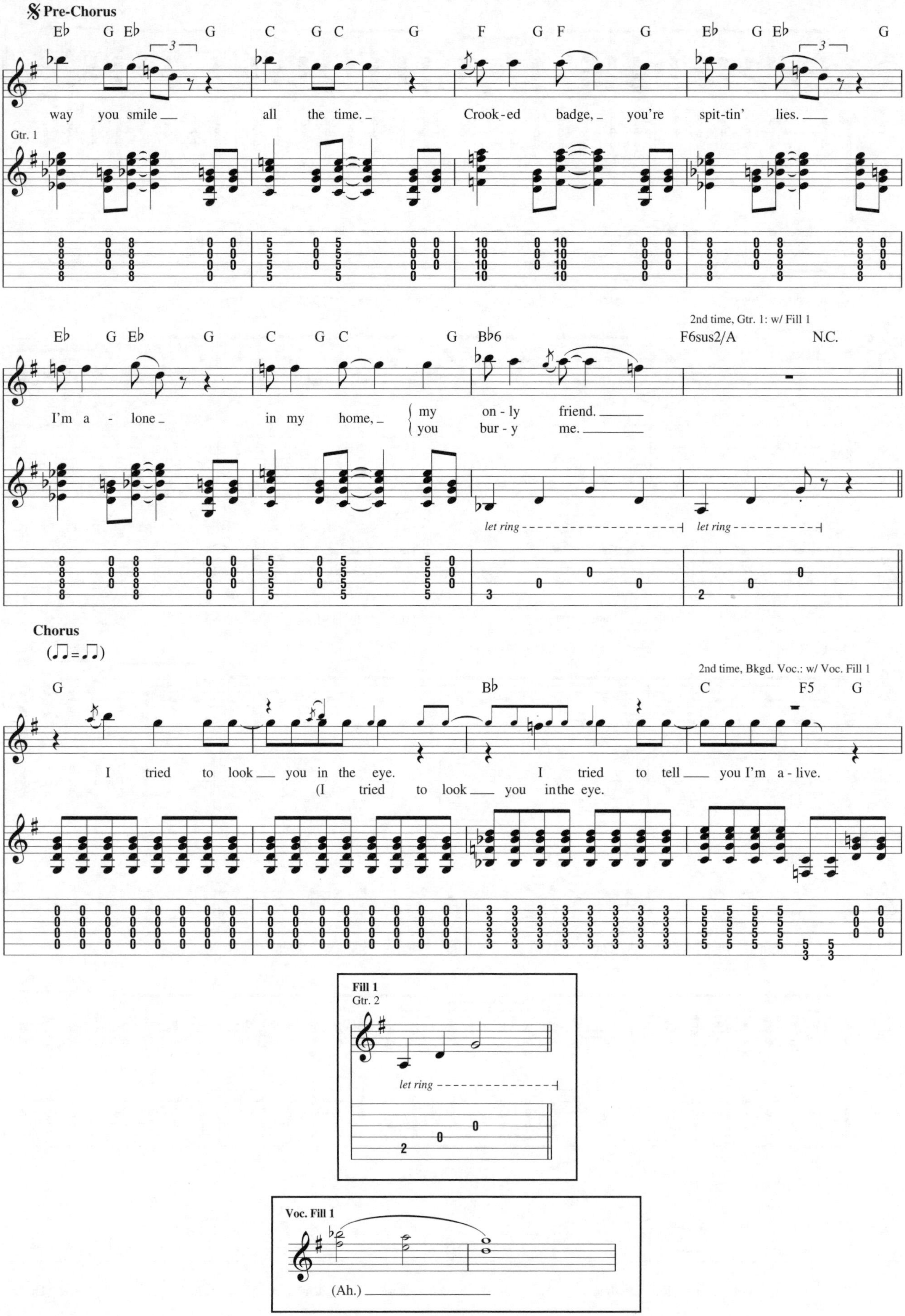
Pre-Chorus
Eb G Eb G C G C G F G F G Eb G Eb G
way you smile all the time. Crook-ed badge, you're spit-tin' lies.
Gtr. 1
Eb G Eb G C G C G Bb6 F6sus2/A N.C.
2nd time, Gtr. 1: w/ Fill 1
I'm a - lone in my home, my on - ly friend.
you bur - y me.
let ring
let ring
Chorus
2nd time, Bkgd. Voc.: w/ Voc. Fill 1
G Bb C F5 G
I tried to look you in the eye. I tried to tell you I'm a - live.
(I tried to look you in the eye.
Fill 1
Gtr. 2
let ring
Voc. Fill 1
(Ah.)

B♭ G *F5/C **C/E G
I tried, I tried to tell ya. When there's
I tried, to tell ya. Oh.)
*Bass plays F. **Bass plays E.
Half-time feel
C/G G5 C/G G B♭ C B♭6/F G
just no med - i - cine for the lies of mine. I'm
Rhy. Fig. 4
To Coda
End half-time feel
C/G G C/G G B♭ C B♭5/F
ter - ri - fied what I might find what you hide be - hind these de - mon
Interlude
G5
eyes.

Verse
G5
3. Why'd you take the time you're tak - in' to un - der - mine my name?
T A B
Gtr. 1: w/ Rhy. Fig. 2
A, does it help you sleep at night to play that right - eous game?
Gtr. 1: w/ Rhy. Fig. 3 (2 times)
B♭ G C G B♭ G B♭ G B♭ G B♭ G F5 G
Why'd you say those things you said,
B♭ G B♭ G B♭ G C G B♭ G B♭ G B♭ G
words that you don't mean? A, two fac - es
D.S. al Coda
B♭ G F5 G B♭ G B♭ G B♭ G C G B♭ G
tell - in' lies, tell - in' lies at me. The
Coda
G5 N.C. G N.C. G5 N.C. G
eh, eh, eyes, yeah.
Gtr. 1

Guitar Solo
Gtr. 2
G Bb G Bb G Bb G Bb G Bb G Bb G Bb G F5 G
semi-P.H.
Gtr. 1
Gtr. 1: w/ Rhy. Fig. 1
Bb G Bb G Bb G Bb G Bb G Bb G
Gtr. 1: w/ Rhy. Fig. 3 (2 times)
Bb G C G Bb G Bb G Bb G Bb G F5 G
P.H.
Pitch: D
Bb G Bb G Bb G C G Bb G Bb G Bb G
Bb G F5 G Bb G Bb G Bb G C G Bb G
8va

Interlude
B♭5
C5
F5
G5
8va
Gtr. 2
20
(20)
Gtr. 1
0
X
3
5
3
5
B♭5
C5
F5
G5
8va
(20)
(20)
steady gliss.
3
5
3
5
Bridge
Half-time feel
Gtr. 2 tacet
B♭6
C5
Fsus2
G5
You love to look me in the eye, to tell me you're a - live.
Riff B
End Riff B
Gtr. 1
let ring
let ring
let ring
let ring
3
0
0
5
0
3
0
0
0
0

Gtr. 1: w/ Riff B (2 times)
B♭6 C5 Fsus2 G5
You love to look me in the eye, to tell me you're a - live.
B♭6 C5 Fsus2 G5
You love, you love to look me in the eye, to tell me you're a - live.
End half-time feel
B♭6 C5 Fsus2 G5 N.C.
You love, you love to look me in the eye, to tell me you're a - live.
Gtr. 1
let ring
B♭ C B♭5/F G
You love to look me in the eye, to tell me you're a - live. You've got the de-mon eyes.
B♭ C B♭5/F G F6
Oh, oo, yeah.

G F6 B♭ C F6 G
You got - ta know I tried, you got - ta know I,
Outro-Chorus
Half-time feel
Gtr. 1: w/ Rhy. Fig. 4
C/G G C/G G B♭ C B♭6/F G
I tried, I tried to look you in the eye to tell you I'm a - live.
(I tried.)
C/G G C/G G B♭ G *F5/C C/E
I tried I tried to tell you. When there's
(I tried.)
Gtr. 1
*As before
Gtr. 1: w/ Rhy. Fig. 4
C/G G C/G G B♭ C B♭6/F G
just no med - i - cine for the lies of mine. Still
C/G G C/G G B♭ C B♭6/F G5 N.C.
ter - ri - fied what I might find what you hide be - hind those de - mon eyes.
Gtr. 1

Dirty Little Secret

Words and Music by Tyson Ritter and Nick Wheeler

*Symbols in parentheses represent chord names respective to capoed gtr. Symbols above reflect actual sounding chords. Capoed fret is "0" in tab.

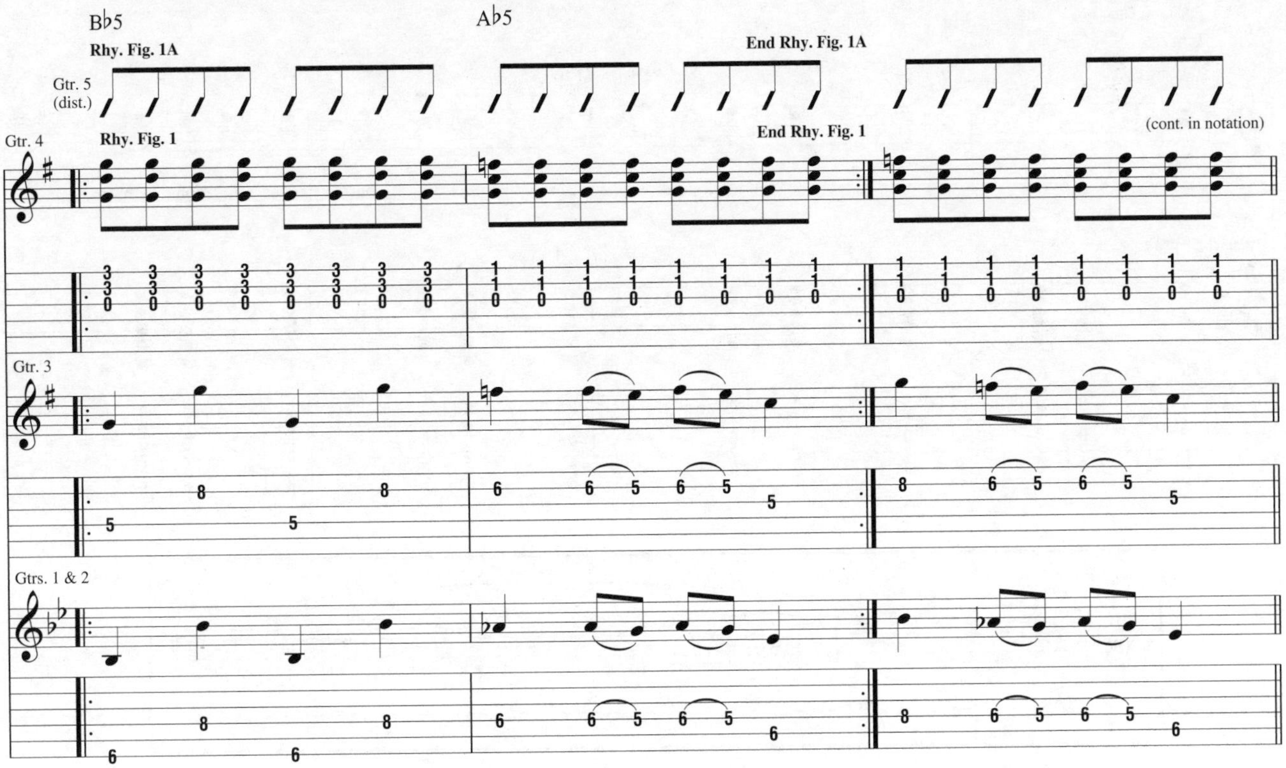

Verse
Gtrs. 3 & 4 tacet
Gtrs. 1 & 2 tacet
*B♭5
F
G5
E♭
1. Let me know that I've done wrong when I've known this all a - long.
Rhy. Fig. 2
Gtr. 5
End Rhy. Fig. 2
mf
Gtrs. 1 & 2
*Chord symbols reflect implied harmony.
Gtr. 5: w/ Rhy. Fig. 2
B♭5
F
G5
E♭
I go a - round a time or two just to waste my time with you.
Pre-Chorus
2nd time, Bkgd. Voc.: w/ Voc. Fig. 1
2nd time, Gtrs. 1 & 2 tacet
Cm7
(Am7)
Gm
(Em)
Tell me all that you've thrown a - way, find out games you don't wan - na play.
Gtr. 6 (slight dist.)
mf
Voc. Fig. 1
(Ah, ah.)

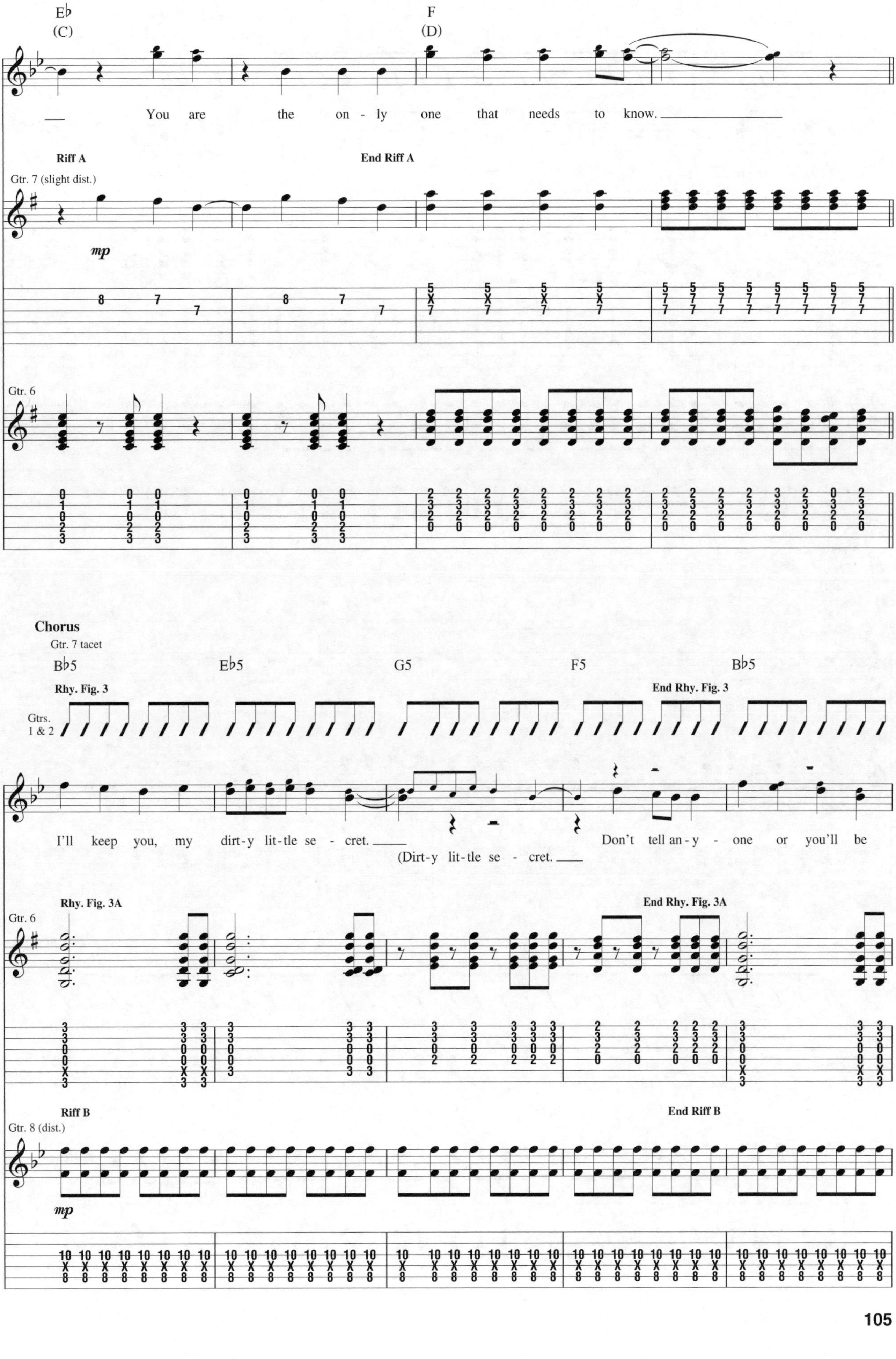
E♭
(C)
F
(D)
You are the on-ly one that needs to know.
Riff A
End Riff A
Gtr. 7 (slight dist.)
mp
Gtr. 6
Chorus
Gtr. 7 tacet
B♭5
E♭5
G5
F5
B♭5
Rhy. Fig. 3
End Rhy. Fig. 3
Gtrs. 1 & 2
I'll keep you, my dirt-y lit-tle se-cret. Don't tell an-y - one or you'll be
(Dirt-y lit-tle se - cret.
Rhy. Fig. 3A
End Rhy. Fig. 3A
Gtr. 6
Riff B
End Riff B
Gtr. 8 (dist.)
mp

To Coda
E♭5
G5
F5
E♭5
just an-oth-er re - gret.
Just an-oth-er re - gret, hope that you can keep it...)
My dirt-y lit-tle se - cret. 2. Who has to know,
Verse
Gtr. 8 tacet
B♭5
when we live such frag-ile lives?
It's the best way we sur - vive.
Gtr. 6
mf
P.M.
D.S. al Coda
B♭5
F5
G5
E♭5
P.M.
I go a - round a time or two just to waste my time with you.
P.M.

Coda
Bridge
Half-time feel
Gtrs. 6 & 8 tacet
G5
E♭5
(cont. in notation)
The way she feels in - side, those thoughts I
Who has to know?
(In - side.
Gtrs. 1 & 2
G5
E♭5
can't de - ny. These sleep - ing dogs won't lie, and now I
De - ny. Won't lie.)
End half-time feel
B♭/D
(G/B)
Cm7
(Am7)
try to lie. It's eat - ing me a - part. Trace this line
Gtr. 6
Gtrs. 1 & 2

Interlude
Gtrs. 1 & 2 tacet
Gtrs. 4 & 5: w/ Rhy. Figs. 1 & 1A (4 times)
Gtr. 6 tacet
B♭5 (G5)
A♭5 (F5)
B♭5 (G5)
back.
Gtr. 3
A♭5 (F5)
B♭5 (G5)
A♭5 (F5)
B♭5 (G5)
A♭5 (F5)
Gtr. 3
Chorus
Gtr. 3 tacet
B♭5 (G5)
E♭5 (C5)
Gm (Em)
F (D)
I'll keep you, my dirt - y lit - tle se - cret.
Don't tell an - y -
Whispered: (Dirt - y lit - tle se - cret.)
Gtr. 4

Gtr. 7: w/ Riff A
B♭5 E♭5 G5 F Fsus4
Gtrs. 1 & 2
P.M.
one or you'll be just an-oth-er re - gret.
(Just an-oth-er re - gret.)
P.M.
Chorus
Gtrs. 1 & 2: w/ Rhy. Fig. 3 (2 times)
Gtr. 6: w/ Rhy. Fig. 3A (2 times)
Gtr. 8: w/ Riff B (2 times)
B♭5 E♭5 G5 F5
I'll keep you, my dirt - y lit - tle se - cret.
(Dirt - y lit - tle se - cret.)
Don't tell an - y -
B♭5 E♭5 G5 F5
one or you'll be just an - oth - er re - gret.
(Just an - oth - er re - gret, hope that you can keep it...)
My
E♭5 F5 G5 A♭5
Gtrs. 1 & 2
(Gtr. 2, cont. in notation)
dirt - y lit - tle se - cret, dirt - y lit - tle se - cret, dirt - y lit - tle se - cret.
Who has to know?
Gtr. 6
Gtr. 8

Outro

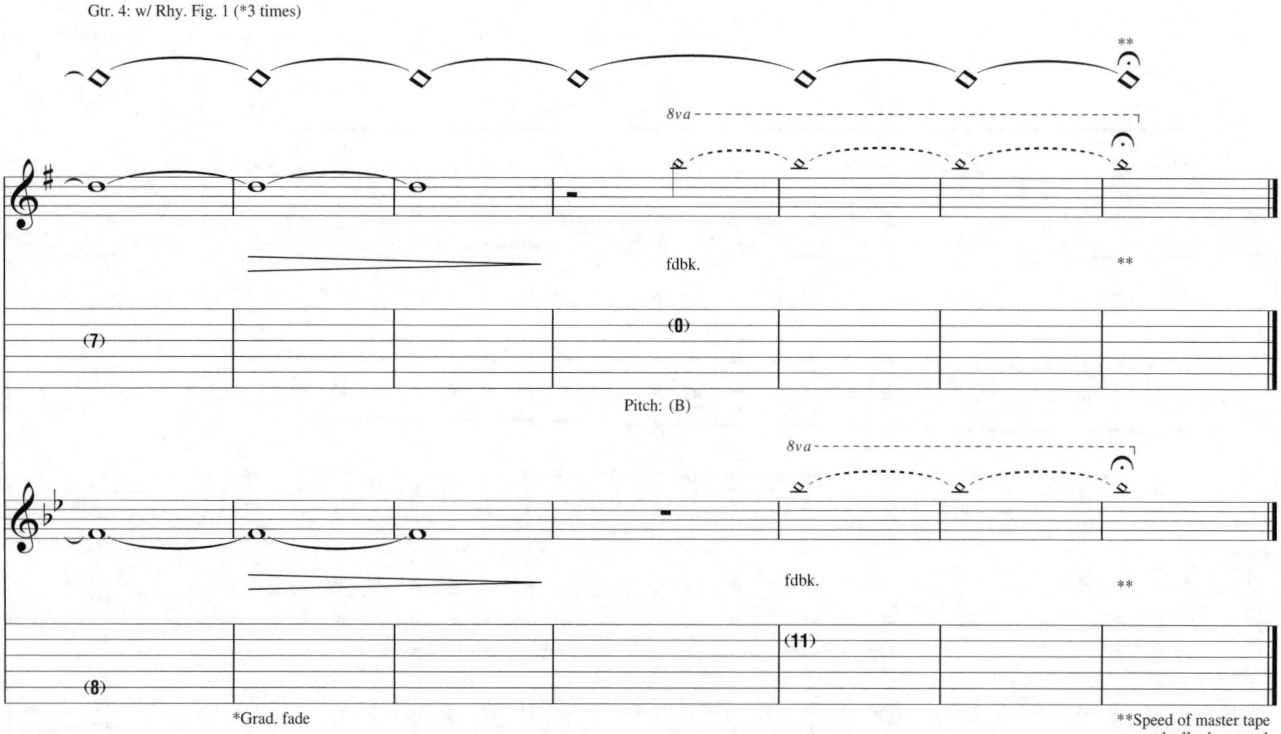

*Grad. fade

**Speed of master tape gradually decreased.

Everyday

Words and Music by Glen Ballard and David J. Matthews

Gtr. 1: w/ Rhy. Fig. 1 (2 3/4 times)
C/F C C/F C C/F C
Pay no mind to taunts or ad - vanc - es. I take my chanc - es on
Pay no mind to taunts or ad - vanc - es. I'm gon-na take my chanc - es on
B♭sus2 C C/F C C/F C
ev - er - y day. Left to right, up and down, love,
ev - er - y day. Left to right, up and up and in - side out right,
Gtr. 3 (acous.)
mf
let ring throughout
C/F C B♭sus2 C
2nd time, Gtr. 5: w/ Fill 1
C/F C
I push up love, love, ev - er - y day. Jump in the mud, oh,
good love fight for ev - er - y day. Jump in the mud, mud,
Fill 1
Gtr. 5 (elec.)
mf
w/ semi-clean tone & wah-wah
1/2

C/F
C
C/F
C
get your hands dirt - y with...
get your hands filth - y, love.
Love it up, oh,
Give it up, love,
Chorus
Bb sus2
C
Am
G/A
ev - er - y day.
ev - er - y day.
All you need is,
Gtr. 1
*Gtr. 4
mf
(cont. in lower staff)
Gtr. 3
**Gtrs. 1 & 3
*Violin arr. for gtr.
**Composite arrangement
Fmaj7
G
Am
G/A
all you want is,
all you need is
***T
***T = Thumb on 6th string

*Last note of Rhy. Fig. 1 is played by Gtr. 1 only.

2.
Gtr. 4 tacet
Bridge
G
Bbsus2
Db/Ab
Absus2
C5
C5/G
love.
Oo.
What you've got,
Rhy. Fig. 2
*Gtr. 5 (elec.)
End Rhy. Fig. 2
mf
w/ dist.
Rhy. Fig. 2A
End Rhy. Fig. 2A
*Two gtrs. arr. for one.
Gtrs. 1 & 3: w/ Rhy. Fig. 2A (2 1/2 times)
Gtr. 5: w/ Rhy. Fig. 2 (2 1/2 times)
lay it down on me.
What you've got,
D.S. al Coda
lay it down on me.
Gtr. 5
Gtrs. 1 & 3
Coda
Gtrs. 1 & 3: w/ Rhy. Fill 2
Gtr. 4: w/ Fill 2
Gtrs. 1 & 2: w/ Rhy. Fill 1
**Gtrs. 1 & 2: w/ Rhy. Fig. 1 (last 3 meas.)
C/F
C
love.
Oo,
ev - 'ry day,
ev - 'ry
**Last note of Rhy. Fig. 1 is played by Gtr. 1 only.

Outro
w/ Bkgd. Voc. ad lib (till end)
Gtr. 1: w/ Rhy. Fig. 1 (6 3/4 times)
C/F
C
B♭sus2
day.
Oh, ev - 'ry day.
Mm, mm, pick me up, love.
Pick me up, love, hey, oh,
Voc. Fig. 1
(Pick me up, love.
Mm, lift me up, love, oh, oh, to,
oo, ev - er - y day.
Lift me up, love.
Pick me up, love,
w/ Lead Voc. ad lib (till end)
Bkgd. Voc.: w/ Voc. Fig. 1 (till end)
to the top ev - er - y day.
Come on, come on, come on, ev - er - y - day.
End Voc. Fig. 1
ev - er - y day.
Gtr. 5
1/2

Bbsus2
C
C/F
C
C/F
C
C/F
C
Bbsus2
C
C/F
C
C/F
C
C/F
C
Bbsus2
C
C/F
C
C/F
C
C/F
C
Bbsus2
C
C/F
C
C/F
C
C/F
C
Bbsus2
C
Gtr. 1

Feel Good Drag

Words and Music by Stephen Arnold, Joseph Milligan, Deon Rexroat and Nathan Young

Gtr. 3 tacet
A♭/D♭
E♭5
Fm
Fill 1
End Fill 1
semi-harm.
End Rhy. Fig. 1
semi-harm.
Verse
Gtrs. 2 & 3 tacet
*Fm
E♭
D♭
1. "I'm here for you," she said, "and we can stay for a - while. My boy - friend's gone,
Gtr. 1
w/ delay
P.M.
*Chord symbols reflect overall harmony.
E♭
Fm
E♭
we can just pre - tend." Lips that need no in - tro - duc - tion. Now who's the great - er sin?
P.M.

D♭
E♭
A♭5 E♭5 F5
Your drab eyes seem to in - vite. Tell me dar-ling, where do we be - gin?
Gtr. 1
P.M.
grad. bend
Gtr. 3
mp
Gtr. 2
Fill 2
End Fill 2
Chorus
Gtr. 2: w/ Rhy. Fig. 1 (1st 4 meas.)
Gtr. 3 tacet
E♭5 F5
E♭
A♭/D♭
Was this o - ver be - fore... Your kiss, your calls, your
Be - fore it ev - er be - gan?
Riff B
let ring
Gtr. 2: w/ Rhy. Fig. 1
2nd time, Gtr. 2: w/ Rhy. Fig. 1 (1st 4 meas.)
E♭5
F5
crutch. Like the dev-il's got your hand. Be - fore it ev - er be - gan.
This was o - ver be - fore...
End Riff B
semi-harm.

To Coda
Gtr. 1: w/ Riff B (last 2 meas.)
Gtr. 1: w/ Fill 1
Ab/Db
Eb5
Fm
Your lips, your lies, your lust. Like the dev-il's in your hands.
Verse
Fm
Eb
Db
2. Ev - 'ry - one in this town is see - ing some-bod - y else. Ev - 'ry - bod-y's tired of some-
Gtr. 1
*w/ delay
P.M.
*Set for eighth-note regeneration w/ 1 repeat.
Eb
Fm
Eb
one. Our eyes wan - der for help. Prayers that need no an - swer now 'cause I'm tired of who I am.
P.M.
D.S. al Coda
Gtr. 2: w/ Fill 2
Db
Eb
Ab5
Eb5
F5
You were my great - est mis - take. I fell in love with your sin your lit - tl - est sin.
Gtr. 1
P.M.
1/2
Gtr. 3

Coda
Gtr. 1: w/ Riff A
N.C.
Bridge
Gtr. 1: w/ Riff A (2 times)
F5
hands.
Fail - ure is your dis - ease.
Gtr. 2
Eb5
Ab/Db
Eb5
You want my out - line drawn.
You were my great - est fail - ure.
Dis-course your sav - ing song.
Gtr. 4 (dist.)
f
*w/ delay
*Set for half-note regeneration w/ 1 repeat.
Gtr. 2
steady gliss.
Guitar Solo
F5 Eb5 F5 C5 Eb5 F5 Eb5 F5 C5 Eb5 Ab/Db
delay off

Eb5
8va
loco
F5 Eb5 F5 C5 Eb5 F5 Eb5 F5 C5 Eb5
P.H.
1 1/2
Pitch: Ab F
Ab/Db
Eb5
F5
Eb5
let ring
hold bend
*Using a guitar with Les Paul style electronics, set lead volume to 0 and rhythm volume to 10. Strike the strings while the pickup selector switch is in the lead position, then flip the switch in the rhythm indicated to simulate the re-attack.
semi-harm.
P.M.
Chorus
Gtr. 1: w/ Riff B (2 times)
Gtr. 4 tacet
F5 Eb Ab/Db Eb5
Was this o ver be-fore...
Be-fore it ev - er be-gan?
Your kiss, your calls, your crutch.
Like the dev-il's got your
Gtr. 2
P.M.
semi-harm.

Gtr. 2: w/ Rhy. Fig. 1 (1st 4 meas.)
F5
E♭
A♭/D♭
E♭5
hand.
Be-fore it ev - er be - gan.
This was o - ver be - fore...
Your lips, your lies, your lust. Like the dev - il's in your
F5
hands.
Gtr. 3
w/ wah-wah
wah off
Gtr. 3
semi-harm.
Outro
Gtrs. 1 & 3: w/ Riffs A & A1 (1 1/2 times)
Gtr. 2: w/ Rhy. Fig. 2 (1st 3 meas.)
E♭5 F5
E♭5
A♭/D♭
E♭5
Gtr. 1
15ma
Harm.
Gtr. 3
15ma
Harm.
Gtr. 2
15ma
Harm.

Fell on Black Days

Words and Music by Chris Cornell

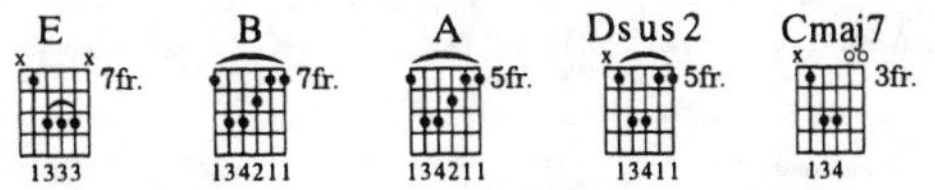

E5 B5 N.C. C E5 B5 N.C. C
— Just when ev - 'ry - day seemed to greet me with a
E5 B5 N.C. C E5 B5 C
smile, sun - spots have fad - ed, now I'm do - ing time.
w/Rhy. Fill 2A (Gtr. II)
E5 B5 N.C. C E5 B5 E5 B5
Now I'm do - ing time.
Rhy. Fill 2 (Gtr. I)
9 7 7 9 7 7 9 7 7 9 7 7 × 9 7 7 × 9 9 7
A5 D5 Cmaj7
'Cause I fell
(end Rhy. Fill 2)
sl.
(9) (9) (7) 7 7 5 7 7 5 7 7 5 0 0 0 0 2 3 0 0 0 0 2 3 (0) (0) (0) (0) (2) (3)
Rhy. Fill 2A (Gtr. I)
sl.
9 7 9 7 9 9 7 (9) (9) (7) 7 7 5 7 7 5 7 7 5 0 0 0 0 2 3 0 0 0 0 2 3 (0) (0) (0) (0) (2) (3)

on black days. I fell
w/Rhy. Fill 1 (Gtrs. I & II)
E5 B5 N.C. C E5 B5 N.C. C
on black days.
2nd Verse
w/Rhy. Fig. 1 (9 times) (Gtrs. I & II)
E5 B5 N.C. C E5 B5 N.C. C
Whom - so - ev - er I've cured I've sick - ened now.
And whom - so - ev - er I've cra - dled, I've put you down.
I'm a search light soul they say, but I can't see it in the
night. I'm on - ly fak - ing when I get it right,
w/Rhy. Fill 2 (Gtr. II)
when I get it right.
Gtr. II
Full
A5 Dsus2 Cmaj7
'Cause I fell

Chorus
w/Rhy. Fig. 1 (2 times) (Gtrs. I & II)
E5 B5 N.C. C E5 B5 N.C. C
on black days. I fell
E5 B5 N.C. C E5 B5 N.C. C D5
on black days. How would I
Rhy. Fig. 2
Gtrs. I & II
(end Rhy. Fig. 2)
1/2
P.M.
E5 B5 N.C. C E5 B5 N.C. C D5
know that this could be my fate? How would I
E5 B5 N.C. C E5 B5 N.C. C
know that this could be my fate?
Rhy. Fill 3
(end Rhy. Fig. 3)

Interlude
N.C.
(D)
Ooh.
Gtrs. I & II
sl.
H P
3.
3rd Verse
w/Rhy. Fig. 1 (8 times) (Gtrs. I & II)
E5 B5 N.C. C
To what you want - ed to see good, has made you blind.
And what you want - ed to be yours, has made it mine.
So don't you lock up some - thing that you want - ed to see
Gtr. III
fly. Hands are for shak - ing, no, not ty - ing,
*Trem. pick muted 1st stg.

w/Rhy. Fig. 3 (Gtr. I)
Rhy. Fig. 3A (Gtr. III)
E B E B A Dsus2 Cmaj7
no, not ty - ing. I
Gtr. II
*vib. w/wah wah
w/Rhy. Fig. 3A (2 times)
(end Rhy. Fig. 3)
sure don't mind a change. I
sure don't mind a change. Yeah, I
grad. release
Rhy. Fig. 3 (Gtr. I)
1.2.3.
4.

w/Rhy. Fig. 3A (1st 2 bars only)
E B E B A Dsus2 Cmaj7
sure don't mind, — sure don't mind — a change.
Fdbk.
Full
(Gtr. III) Freely
I sure don't mind a change.
'Cause I fell
w/Fdbk.
A tempo
Chorus
w/Rhy. Fig. 1 (2 times) (Gtrs. I & II)
E5 B5 N.C. C E5 B5 N.C. C
on black days. I fell
Gtr. III
sl.
w/Rhy. Fig. 2 (4 times) (Gtrs. I & II)
E5 B5 N.C. C E5 B5 N.C. C D5
on black days. How would I

E5 B5 N.C. C E5 B5 N.C. C D
know— that this could be— my fate?— How would I
Riff A (Gtr. III)
(end Riff A)
sl.
w/Riff A (2 times)
E5 B5 N.C. C E5 B5 N.C. C D5 E5 B5 N.C. C
know— that this could be— my fate?— How would I know that this could be my—
w/Rhy. Fill 3 (Gtrs. I & II)
E5 B5 N.C. C D5 E5 B5 N.C. C E5 B5 N.C. C
fate?— How would I know that this could be my- fate?—
Gtr. III
w/Rhy. Fig. 3 (1st 2 bars only) (Gtrs. I & II)
E5 B5 E5 B5 A5 Dsus2 Cmaj7
Gtr. II
Full
H P
Freely
(Gtrs. I & III)
I sure don't mind a change.—
w/Fdbk.

Float On

Words and Music by Isaac Brock, Eric Judy and Dann Gallucci

A♯m
F♯sus2
A♯m7/E♯
he just drove off, some-times life's O. K.
I ran my mouth off a bit
too much, oh, what did I say?
Bmaj7
A♯m
F♯sus2
Well, you just laughed it off, it was all O. K.
Gtr. 2
A♯m7/E♯
Bmaj7
A♯m
Chorus
F♯
A♯m6/E♯
1st time, Gtr. 2 tacet
2nd time, Gtr. 2: w/ Fill 1
Bmaj7
And we'll all float on O. K.
And we'll
Gtr. 2
Gtr. 1
Fill 1
Gtr. 2

To Coda
A♯m
F♯
A♯m6/E♯
all float on O. K. And we'll all float on O. K.
Gtr. 1
Verse
Gtr. 1: w/ Rhy. Fig. 1 (4 times)
Bmaj7
A♯m
F♯sus2
And we'll all float on an - y - way. 2. Well, a fake Ja - mai - can took ev -
A♯m7/E♯
Bmaj7
- 'ry last dime with that scam. It was
Gtr. 2
P.H.
Pitch: D♯ E D♯ E D♯ E D♯ E D♯ E D♯ C𝄪
A♯m
F♯sus2
worth it just to learn some sleight of hand. Bad news comes, don't you wor - ry e -
Pitch: D♯ C𝄪

A♯m7/E♯
Bmaj7
A♯m
- ven, and, when it lands.
Good news will work its way to all them
8va
loco
P.H.
1/2
Harm.
Pitch: D♯ E D♯ G
F♯sus2
A♯m7/E♯
Bmaj7
plans. We both got fired on (ex-)act - ly the same day.
Well,
P.M.
A♯m
F♯sus2
A♯m7/E♯
we'll float on, good news is on the way.
Mumbled: Please come, please come good news, good news,
P.M.
D.S. al Coda
Bmaj7
A♯m
good news, good news, good news com - ing.
Go - ing to, how well? I can't tell.

Coda
Bridge
Gtr. 1: w/ Rhy. Fig. 1 (2 times)
Bmaj7
A#m
F#sus2
And we'll all float on. Al - right already, we'll all
Gtr. 2
A#m7/E#
Bmaj7
A#m
float on. No, don't you worry we'll all float on. Al -
F#sus2
A#m7/E#
Bmaj7
right al - read - y, we'll all float on. Al - right, don't wor - ry we'll
Interlude
Gtrs. 1 & 2 tacet
A#m
F#
N.C.(F#)
all float on.
Gtr. 1
Gtr. 2
divisi
*w/ echo repeat.
**Gtr. 1 to left of slash in tab.

Gtrs. 3 & 4 tacet
And we'll all float on. Al -
(Al - right al - read - y.)
Gtr. 3 (dist.)
mf
A.H.
T T T
16 17 16
Gtr. 4 (dist.)
mf
6 4 4
*Gang vocals next 13 meas.
right al - read - y, we'll all float on. Al - right, don't wor - ry e - ven
if things end up a bit too heav - y. We'll all float on. Al -
w/ Voc. ad lib. (next 8 meas.)
Gtr. 1: w/ Rhy. Fig. 1 (2 times)
F#sus2
A#m7/E#
Bmaj7
right al - read - y, we'll all float on. Al - right al - read - y, we'll all
Gtr. 2

A♯m
F♯sus2
float on O. K. Don't wor - ry, we'll all
A♯m7/E♯
Bmaj7
A♯m
float on. E - ven if things get heav - y, we'll all float on. Al -
F♯
Gtr. 1
Gtrs. 1 & 2 tacet
N.C.
right al - read - y, we'll all float on all.... Don't you wor - ry, we'll
(All, al - right.
Gtr. 2
F♯
N.C.
all float on. We'll all float on.
Al - right.)
Gtr. 1
pp

Forever

Words and Music by Tobin Esperance, Jerry Horton, Jacoby Shaddix and David Buckner

D5
F5
C5
B♭5
Take these mem - o - ries that are haunt - ing me of a pa - per man cut in - to shreds
by his own pair of scis - sors. He'll nev - er for - give her, he'll nev - er for - give her.
Be - cause
Gtr. 2
Riff B
End Riff B
Gtr. 3 (slight dist.)
mf
*w/ delays
*One set for quarter-note regeneration w/ 1 repeat, one set for eighth-note regeneration w/ 1 repeat.
Gtrs. 4 & 5 (dist.)
f

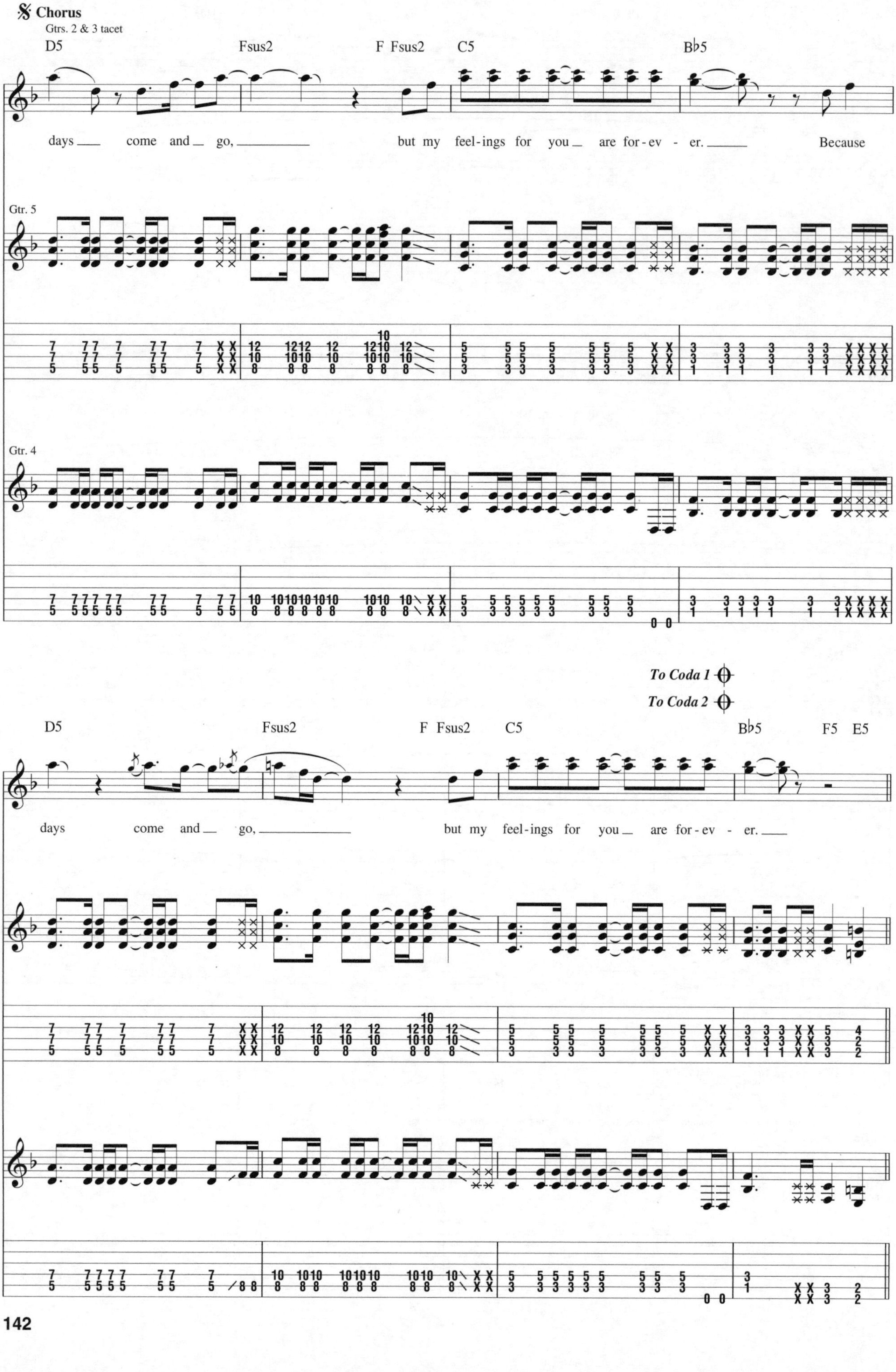
Chorus
Gtrs. 2 & 3 tacet
D5 Fsus2 F Fsus2 C5 B♭5
days come and go, but my feel-ings for you are for-ev - er. Because
Gtr. 5
Gtr. 4
To Coda 1
To Coda 2
D5 Fsus2 F Fsus2 C5 B♭5 F5 E5
days come and go, but my feel-ings for you are for-ev - er.

Interlude
Gtrs. 4 & 5 tacet
*Dm F C B♭
2. Sit - tin' by
Gtr. 5
Gtr. 4
divisi
pp
**
3 2 0 0/0 0
*Chord symbols reflect overall harmony.
**Gtr. 5 to left of slash in tab.
Verse
Dm F C B♭
a fire __ on a lone - ly night, ____ hang - in' o - ver from an - oth - er good time with an - oth -
Dm F C B♭ B♭/C
er girl, __ lit - tle dirt - y girl. ____ You should lis - ten __ to __ this sto - ry __ of __ a life. __
Dm F C B♭ B♭/C
____ You're my her - o - ine. In this mo - ment I'm lone - ly, ful - fill - ing my dark - est dreams. __
Gtr. 3
Riff C
End Riff C
12 10 10 10 12 10 12 15 14 13 14 15 14 10 12 13 12 10 12 10 8 10 11 10 8 10 8
Gtr. 3: w/ Riff C
Dm F C B♭
__ All these drugs, __ all these wom - en. I'm nev - er for - giv - en, this bro - ken heart __ of mine. __
D.S. al Coda 1
Gtr. 3: w/ Riff B
Dm F C B♭ N.C.
__ Be - cause
Gtrs. 4 & 5
f

Coda 1
Bridge
B♭5 F5 E5 D5 F5 C/E C5 F5 E5
er. One last kiss be-fore I go. Dry your
Rhy. Fig. 1A
Rhy. Fig. 1
B♭5 F5 C/E G5 F5 G5 A5 F5 C/E
tears, it is time to let you go. One last
End Rhy. Fig. 1A
End Rhy. Fig. 1
Gtrs. 4 & 5: w/ Rhy. Figs. 1 & 1A
D5 F5 C/E C5
*Voc. Fig. 1
kiss be - fore I go.
(One last kiss be - fore I
*Refers to upstemmed voc. only.
F5 E5 B♭5 F5 C/E
End Voc. Fig. 1
Dry your tears, it is time
go. Dry your tears.)

D.S. al Coda 2
G5
A5
N.C.
to let you go be - cause
Gtr. 5
Gtr. 4
Coda 2
Outro
Bkgd. Voc.: w/ Voc. Fig. 1
B♭5
F5 E5
D5
F Fsus2
F Fsus2 C5
B♭5
er. One last kiss be-fore I go. Dry your

D5 F Fsus2 F Fsus2 C5 B♭5 F5 E5
tears, it is time to let you go. One last
D5 F5 C5 B♭5
kiss before I go. Dry your
Gtr. 5
Gtr. 4
divisi
*Gtr. 5 to left of slash in tab.
D5 F5 C5 B♭5 D5
tears, it is time to let you go. One last kiss.
pp

Forever in Your Hands

Words and Music by All That Remains

Tune down 1 1/2 steps:
(low to high) C♯-F♯-B-E-G♯-C♯

Intro
Moderately fast ♩ = 185

*Chord symbols reflect overall harmony.

Am9
Fmaj7/A
Fmaj9/A
Gadd2
Fmaj7
Fmaj7/E
Cmaj7
End Riff B
P.M.
Half-time feel
Am(add9)
Fmaj7/A
Gtr. 3
Rhy. Fig. 1
Gtr. 1
Rhy. Fig. 1A
Gtr. 2
Gtr. 3 tacet
Em7/A
E
End Rhy. Fig. 1
End Rhy. Fig. 1A

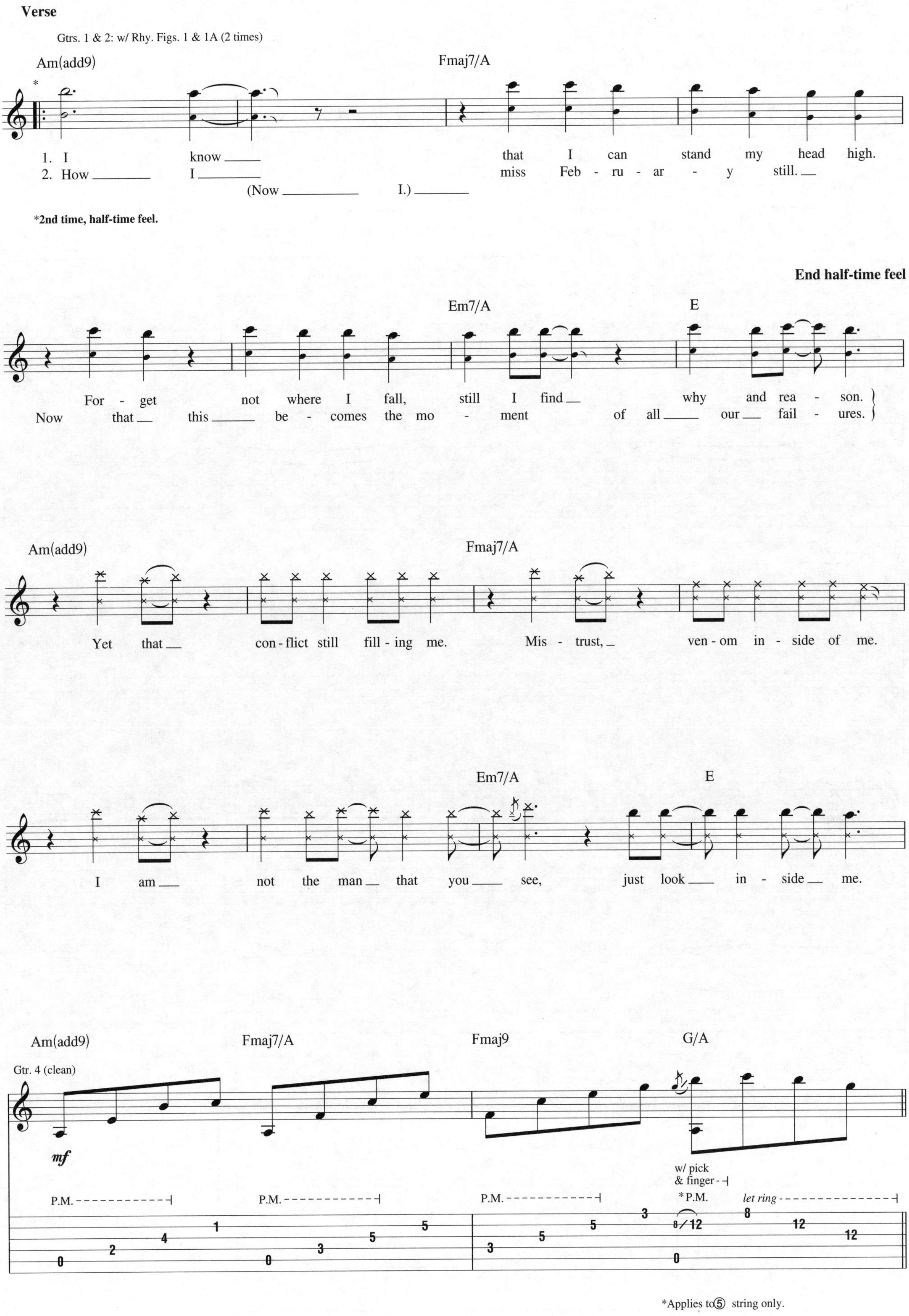
Verse
Gtrs. 1 & 2: w/ Rhy. Figs. 1 & 1A (2 times)
Am(add9)
Fmaj7/A
1. I know that I can stand my head high.
2. How I miss Feb - ru - ar - y still.
(Now I.)
*2nd time, half-time feel.
End half-time feel
Em7/A
E
For - get not where I fall, still I find why and rea - son.
Now that this be - comes the mo - ment of all our fail - ures.
Am(add9)
Fmaj7/A
Yet that con - flict still fill - ing me. Mis - trust, ven - om in - side of me.
Em7/A
E
I am not the man that you see, just look in - side me.
Am(add9)
Fmaj7/A
Fmaj9
G/A
Gtr. 4 (clean)
mf
P.M.
w/ pick & finger
*P.M.
let ring
*Applies to ⑤ string only.

Chorus
Half-time feel
Gtr. 4 tacet
3rd time, Gtr. 5: w/ Fill 1
F5
E5
Trust in me the way I trust - ed you.
Riff C
Gtr. 3
P.M.
Gtrs. 1 & 2
G/B
A5
I know we could have done this to - geth - er. (If you) be -
(Done this to - geth -
End Riff C
P.M.

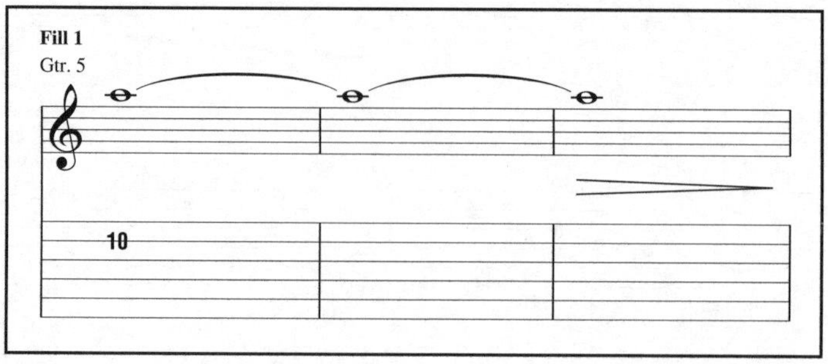
Fill 1
Gtr. 5

Gtr. 3: w/ Riff C
F5
E5
lieved in me like I be - lieved in you,
er.)
Gtrs. 1 & 2
let ring
To Coda
End half-time feel
G5
my heart would be for - ev - er in your hands.
P.M.
Interlude
1st time, Gtr. 3: w/ Riff A (2 times)
A5 F5 C5 F5/C G5/D E5 F5/C A5/E E5 F5 G5/D E5/B
Rhy. Fig. 2
A5 F5 C5 F5/C G5/D E5/B F5/C A5/E E5 F5 G5/D E5/B
End Rhy. Fig. 2

Guitar Solo

Gtrs. 1 & 2: w/ Rhy. Fig. 2 (2 times)
A5 F5 C5 F5/C G5/D E5 F5/C A5/E E5
Gtr. 5 (dist.)
8va
loco
f
P.M.
P.H.
Pitch: B
F5 G5/D E5/B A5 F5 C5 F5/C G5/D E5/B F5/C A5/E E5
8va
loco
P.H.
Pitch: B
F5 G5/D E5/B A5 F5 C5 F5/C G5/D E5
8va
F5/C A5/E E5 F5 G5/D E5/B A5 F5 C5
8va
loco
F5/C G5/D E5/B F5/C A5/E E5 F5 G5/D E5/B

Interlude
Gtr. 1: w/ Riff A
Gtr. 2: w/ Riff B
Am9
Fmaj7/A
Fmaj9/A
Gadd2
Fmaj7
Fmaj7/E
Cmaj7
P.M.
D.S. al Coda
Am9
Fmaj7/A
Fmaj9/A
Gadd2
Fmaj7
Fmaj7/E
Cmaj7
P.M.
Coda
Gtrs. 1 & 2: w/ Rhy. Figs. 1 & 1A (1 5/8 times)
Am(add9)
Fmaj7/A
1.
Em7/A
E
For - ev - er in your hands.
2.
Gtr. 1
Em7
N.C.
E
N.C.
P.M.
P.M.
P.M.
Gtr. 2
P.M.
P.M.

Hand in My Pocket

Lyrics by Alanis Morissette
Music by Alanis Morissette and Glen Ballard

sane but I'm o - ver - whelmed, I'm lost but I'm hope - ful, ba -
brave but I'm chick - en - shit, I'm sick but I'm pret - ty, ba -
Pre-Chorus
Gtr. 3: w/ Rhy. Fill 2, 2nd time
Gtr. 3: w/ Rhy. Fill 3, 2 times, 2nd time
Gtr. 4: w/ Rhy. Fig. 4, 2nd time
G/F
Cadd9
Rhy. Fig. 2A
Gtr. 2 (dist.)
mf
- by. And what it all comes down to
- by. And what it all comes down to
is that ev - 'ry-thing gon-na be
is that no one's real-ly got it fig-ured
End Rhy. Fig. 1
Rhy. Fig. 2
w/ delay
Rhy. Fill 2
Gtr. 3
slight P.M.
Rhy. Fill 3
Gtr. 3
slight P.M.

Chorus
Gtr. 3: w/ Riff A, 1st time; w/ Rhy. Fill 4, 2nd time
Gtr. 3: w/ Rhy. Fill 3, 2 times, 2nd time
G
G D G F G/F A B
3fr 3fr open 1fr open 2fr
End Rhy. Fig. 2A
Rhy. Fig. 3A
fine, fine, fine,
out just yet
'cause I've got a one hand in my pock - et and the
End Rhy. Fig. 2
Rhy. Fig. 3
* w/ bar
To Coda
Gtr. 3: w/ Riff A
C G5/D G type2 G D C B
3fr 3fr 3fr 1fr open
End Rhy. Fig. 3A
oth-er one is giv-in' a high five.
play-in' a pi - an - o.
2. I feel
End Rhy. Fig. 3
Verse
Gtr. 1: w/ Rhy. Fig. 1
G
B C
2fr 3fr
drunk but I'm so - ber, I'm young and I'm un - der - paid. I'm
Gtr. 4 (slight dist.)
Riff B
End Riff B
mf
let ring
let ring
Rhy. Fill 4
Gtr. 3
slight P.M.
Riff A
Gtr. 3 (slight dist.)
mf w/ delay

Gtr. 4: w/ Riff B, 3 times
Gtr. 3: w/ Riff A
tired but I'm work - in', a - yeah.
I care but I'm rest - less, I'm
here but I'm real-ly gone.
I'm wrong and I'm sor - ry, ba - by.
And what it all comes down to
Pre-Chorus
Gtrs 1 & 2: w/ Rhy. Figs. 2 & 2A, simile
Gtr. 3: w/ Riff A
is that ev-'ry-thing's gon-na be quite al - right.
Gtr. 4
Rhy. Fig. 4
let ring
Chorus
Gtrs. 1 & 2: w/ Rhy. Figs. 3 & 3A
'cause I've got-a one hand in my pock-et and the oth-er one is flick-in' a cig-a-rette.
End Rhy. Fig. 4
Rhy. Fig. 5
End Rhy. Fig. 5
let ring

Solo
Gtr. 1: w/ Rhy. Fig. 1
G
G type2
E
2fr
G type2
Gtr. 2
Gtr. 5
8va
* Harmonica arr. for gtr.
Gtr. 3
Gtr. 4
let ring
G/B
C
G type2
E
2fr
D
open
D
open
C
8va

G/B
E
4
2fr
Gtype2
C
Gtype2
And what it all comes down
8va
let ring
Pre-Chorus
Gtr. 5 tacet
Gtrs. 1 & 2: w/ Rhy. Figs. 2 & 2A
Gtr. 4: w/ Rhy. Fig. 4
G/F
Cadd9
to
is that I have - n't got it all fig - ured
Gtr. 3
let ring
Gtr. 3 tacet
G
Chorus
Gtrs. 1 & 2: w/ Rhy. Figs. 3 & 3A
Gtr. 4: w/ Rhy. Fig. 5
G/F
out just yet
'cause I've got - a one hand in my pock - et and the
C
G5/D
G
D.S. al Coda
oth - er one is giv - in' a peace sign.
3. I'm

Coda
Pre-Chorus
Gtr. 3: w/ Rhy. Fill 1
Gtr. 3: w/ Rhy. Fill 2
Gtr. 4: w/ Rhy. Fig. 4
Gtype3
G/F
Gtr. 2
And what it all comes down to my friends, yeah,
Gtr. 1
Cadd9
Gtype3
is that ev-'ry-thing's just fine, fine, fine. 'Cause I've got-a
Gtr. 4: w/ Rhy. Fig. 5
F G/F
C Cadd9 G
Gtype2
1fr
3fr
one hand in my pock - et and the oth-er one is hail-ing a tax - i - cab.
Outro
Gtype3
play 7 times
Gtype3

Hearts Burst into Fire

Words and Music by Matthew Tuck, Jason James, Michael Paget and Michael Thomas

17
A♭5 (B♭5)
A♭maj7 (B♭maj7)
A♭5 (B♭5)
A♭maj7 (B♭maj7)
C5 (D5)
Elec. Gtr. 1
Elec. Gtr. 2
w/ dist.
P.M.
Elec. Gtr. 3
P.M.
20
A♭5 (B♭5)
A♭maj7 (B♭maj7)
A♭5 (B♭5)
A♭maj7 (B♭maj7)
C5 (D5)
B♭5 (C5)
P.M.
P.M.

♩ = 190
E♭5 (F5)
E♭maj7 (Fmaj7)
E♭5 (F5)
E♭maj7 (Fmaj7)
E♭5 (F5)
Cm7 (Dm7)
Elec. Gtr. 1
6fr
Elec. Gtr. 2
P.M.
Elec. Gtr. 3
Cm11 (Dm11)
Cm7 (Dm7)
Cm11 (Dm11)
E♭5 (F5)
w/ feedback

33
E♭maj7 (Fmaj7)
E♭5 (F5)
E♭maj7 (Fmaj7)
E♭5 (F5)
1. I'm coming home, I've been gone for far too long,
2. You're not alone, I know I'm far from home,
Elec. Gtr. 2
P.M.
Fig. 2
TAB
Elec. Gtr. 3
P.M.
Fig. 3
TAB
37
Cm11 (Dm11)
Cm7 (Dm7)
Cm11 (Dm11)
E♭5 (F5)
do you re-mem-ber me at all?
do you re-mem-ber me at all?
P.M.
Fig. 2
TAB
P.M.
Fig. 3
TAB

E♭maj7 (Fmaj7) E♭5 (F5) E♭maj7 (Fmaj7) E♭5 (F5)
I'm leav - ing, have I fucked things up a - gain?
I'm leav - ing, do you wait for me a - gain?
Elec. Gtr. 3
P.M.
Elec. Gtr. 2 plays Fig. 2
Cm11 (Dm11) Cm7 (Dm7) Cm11 (Dm11) A♭5 (B♭5)
I'm dream - ing, too much time with - out you spent.
I'm scream - ing, no more days with - out you spent.
B♭5 (C5) C5* (D5*) B♭5 (C5) A♭5 (B♭5)
It hurts, wounds so sore,
Elec. Gtrs. 2 + 3
P.M.

53
now I'm torn,
now I'm torn.
Elec. Gtr. 1
full
P.M.
57
Elec. Gtr. 3
I've been far a - way.
Elec. Gtr. 1
Elec. Gtr. 2

Elec. Gtr. 3
B♭5 (C5) A♭5 (B♭5) E♭5* (F5*) B♭5 (C5) A♭5 (B♭5) B♭5 (C5) C5* (D5*)
P.M.
61
When I see your face, my heart
Elec. Gtr. 1
Elec. Gtr. 2
full
C5* (D5*) A♭5 (B♭5) B♭5 (C5) A♭5 (B♭5) B♭5 (C5) C5* (D5*)
C5* (D5*) B♭5 A♭5 (C5) (B♭5) C5* B♭5 (D5*) (C5) A♭5 (B♭5) B♭5 (C5) C5* (D5*)
65
bursts in - to fire, hearts

1.
2.
To Coda
A♭5 (B♭5)
B♭5 (C5)
B♭oct (Coct)
E♭5 (F5)
Elec. Gtr. 3
P.M.
69
burst in - to fire.
Elec. Gtr. 2
C5 (D5)
Elec. Gtrs. 2 + 3
74
Ac. Gtr.
My bed's so cold, so lone - ly, no
79
arms, just sheets to hold me. Has this

A♭5 (B♭5) B♭5 (C5) C5 (D5)
84
world stopped turn - ing?
A♭5 (B♭5) B♭5 (C5) E♭5 (F5)
87
Are we for - ev - er to be a - part,
Elec. Gtr. 1 feedback
cont. sim.
15fr
E♭5 (F5) E♭maj7 (Fmaj7) E♭5 (F5) E♭maj7 (Fmaj7) E♭5 (F5) E♭maj7 (Fmaj7) E♭5 (F5)
90
for - ev - er to be a - part?
Elec. Gtr. 2 & Ac. Gtr.
P.M.
Fig. 4
T
A
B

D.S. al Coda
94
E♭maj7 (Fmaj7)
E♭5 (F5)
N.C.
A♭5 (B♭5)
Elec. Gtr. 2
P.M.
Coda
Elec. Gtr. 3
B♭oct (Coct)
E♭5 (F5)
E♭maj7 (Fmaj7)
98
(I'm
Elec. Gtr. 2
Elec. Gtr. 1
w/ echo
Elec. Gtr. 2 plays Fig. 4
100
com - ing home.)
I've been gone for far too long,

Ebmaj7 (Fmaj7)
Eb5 (F5)
103
do you re - mem - ber me at all?
(I'm com - ing home.)
full
Elec. Gtr. 3 tacet
Elec. Gtr. 4
w/ echo
107
(Sing small notes 2° only)
(I'm leav - ing, I'm scream - ing,
Elec. Gtrs. 1 & 4
Elec. Gtr. 3
P.M.
Elec. Gtr. 2 plays Fig. 2

1.
Cm11 (Dm11)
Cm7 (Dm7)
Cm11 (Dm11)
E♭5 (F5)
111
Do you re - mem - ber me at all?
P.M.
P.M.
P.M.
P.M.
P.M.
P.M.
P.M.
P.M.
T
A
B

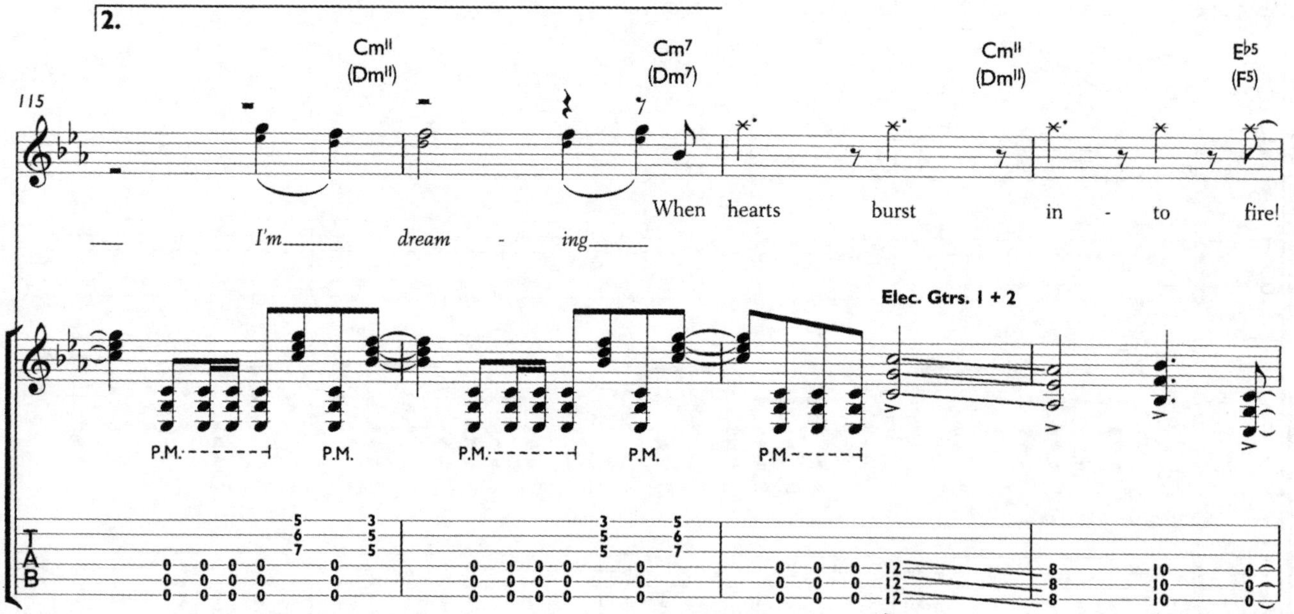
2.
Cm11 (Dm11)
Cm7 (Dm7)
Cm11 (Dm11)
E♭5 (F5)
115
When hearts burst in - to fire!
I'm dream - ing
Elec. Gtrs. 1 + 2
P.M.
P.M.
P.M.
P.M.
P.M.
T
A
B

C5
(D5)
Elec. Gtrs. 2 & 3
119
Elec. Gtr. 1
Elec. Gtr. 4
Repeat section x8
(Guitar parts slowly
get out of sync.)
w/ feedback
rit. (from 4°)
123

Hella Good

Words and Music by Pharrell Williams, Chad Hugo, Gwen Stefani and Tony Kanal

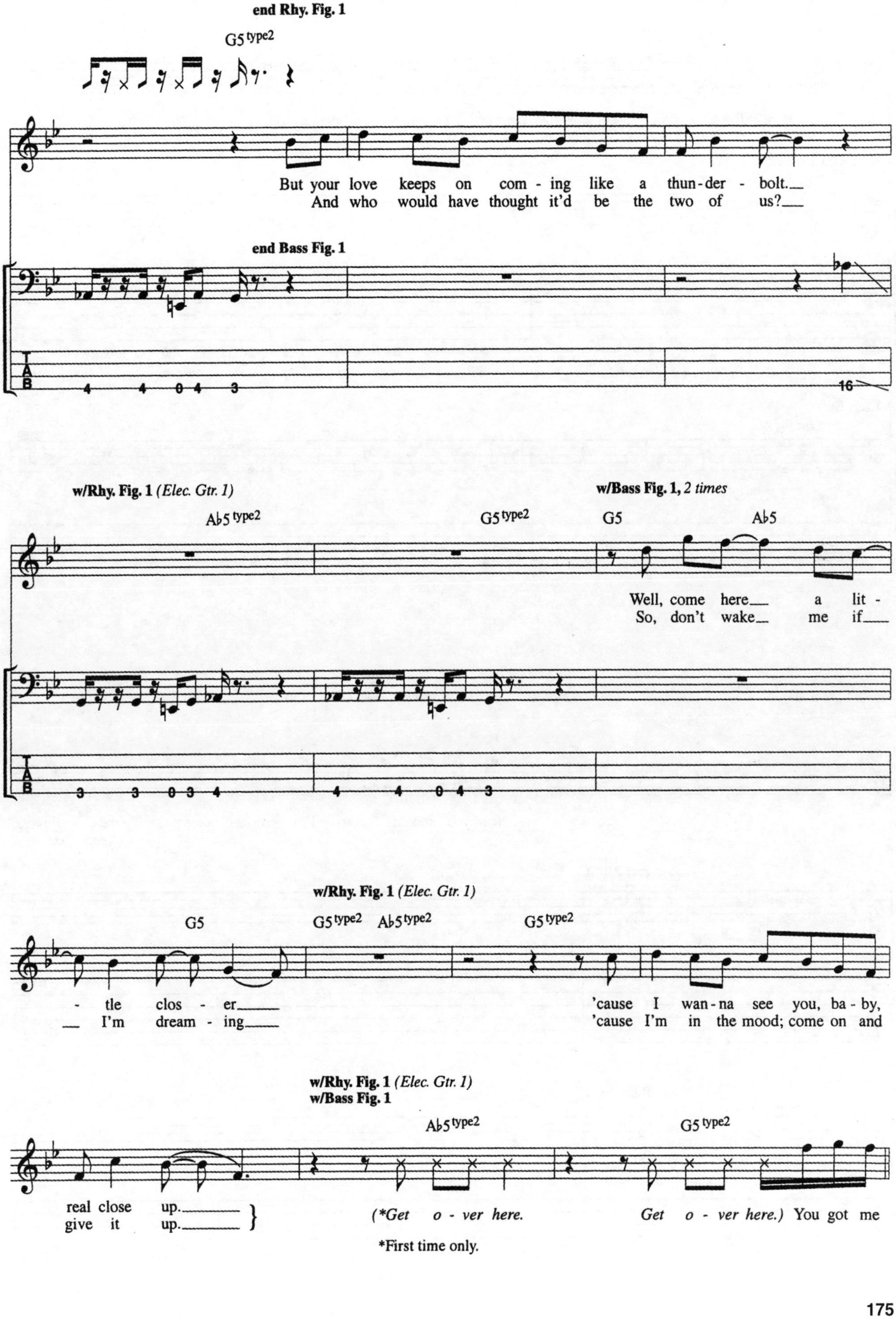
end Rhy. Fig. 1
G5 type2
But your love keeps on com - ing like a thun - der - bolt.
And who would have thought it'd be the two of us?
end Bass Fig. 1
T
A
B
4 4 0 4 3
16
w/Rhy. Fig. 1 (Elec. Gtr. 1)
w/Bass Fig. 1, 2 times
Ab5 type2
G5 type2
G5
Ab5
Well, come here a lit -
So, don't wake me if
3 3 0 3 4
4 4 0 4 3
w/Rhy. Fig. 1 (Elec. Gtr. 1)
G5
G5 type2
Ab5 type2
G5 type2
- tle clos - er
I'm dream - ing
'cause I wan - na see you, ba - by,
'cause I'm in the mood; come on and
w/Rhy. Fig. 1 (Elec. Gtr. 1)
w/Bass Fig. 1
Ab5 type2
G5 type2
real close up.
give it up.
(*Get o - ver here. Get o - ver here.) You got me
*First time only.

Chorus:
G5 Ab5 G5 Ab5
feel - ing hell - a good,_ so let's just keep on danc - ing.
Elec. Gtr. 2 (w/dist.)
Riff A
f
Elec. Bass
Bass Fig. 2
f
Elec. Gtr. 2 & Elec. Bass cont. simile
G5 Ab5 G5
You hold me like you should_ so I'm gon - na keep on danc - ing.__
(Keep on
end Riff A
end Bass Fig. 2

1.
2.3.
Ab5
G5
dance - ing.)
2. A per -
You got me
feel - ing hell - a good so let's just keep on danc - ing.
You hold me like you should so I'm gon - na keep on danc - ing.
(Keep on
To Coda
Bridge:
Ebmaj7
danc - ing.)
Ooh, yeah, yeah.
*Elec. Gtr. 3 (w/dist.)
*w/octave pedal set one octave lower.
Elec. Bass

B♭maj7
Gm
A♭maj7(♯11)
E♭maj7
B♭maj7
Gm
Ooh, yeah, yeah.
Elec. Gtr. 3 out

Drums & Keyboard only
Abmaj7(#11)
*G5 Ab5 G5 Ab5 N.C.
Elec. Bass out
T
A
B
4 4 4 4 × 18
*Harmony implied by keyboard.
D.S. % al Coda
G5 Ab5 N.C. G5 Ab5 N.C.
You got me
Coda
Outro:
Keyboard only
G5 Ab5 G5
Uh, uh, uh.
Ab5 G5 Ab5
Uh, uh, uh.
G5 Ab5 G5
Uh, uh, uh.
w/Riff A (Elec. Gtr. 2)
w/Bass Fig. 2
Ab5 G5 Ab5 G5
Keep on danc - ing.
Ab5 G5 Ab5 N.C.

I Dare You

Words and Music by Brent Smith, Brad Stewart and Tony Battaglia

Tune down 1/2 step:
(low to high) E♭-A♭-D♭-G♭-B♭-E♭

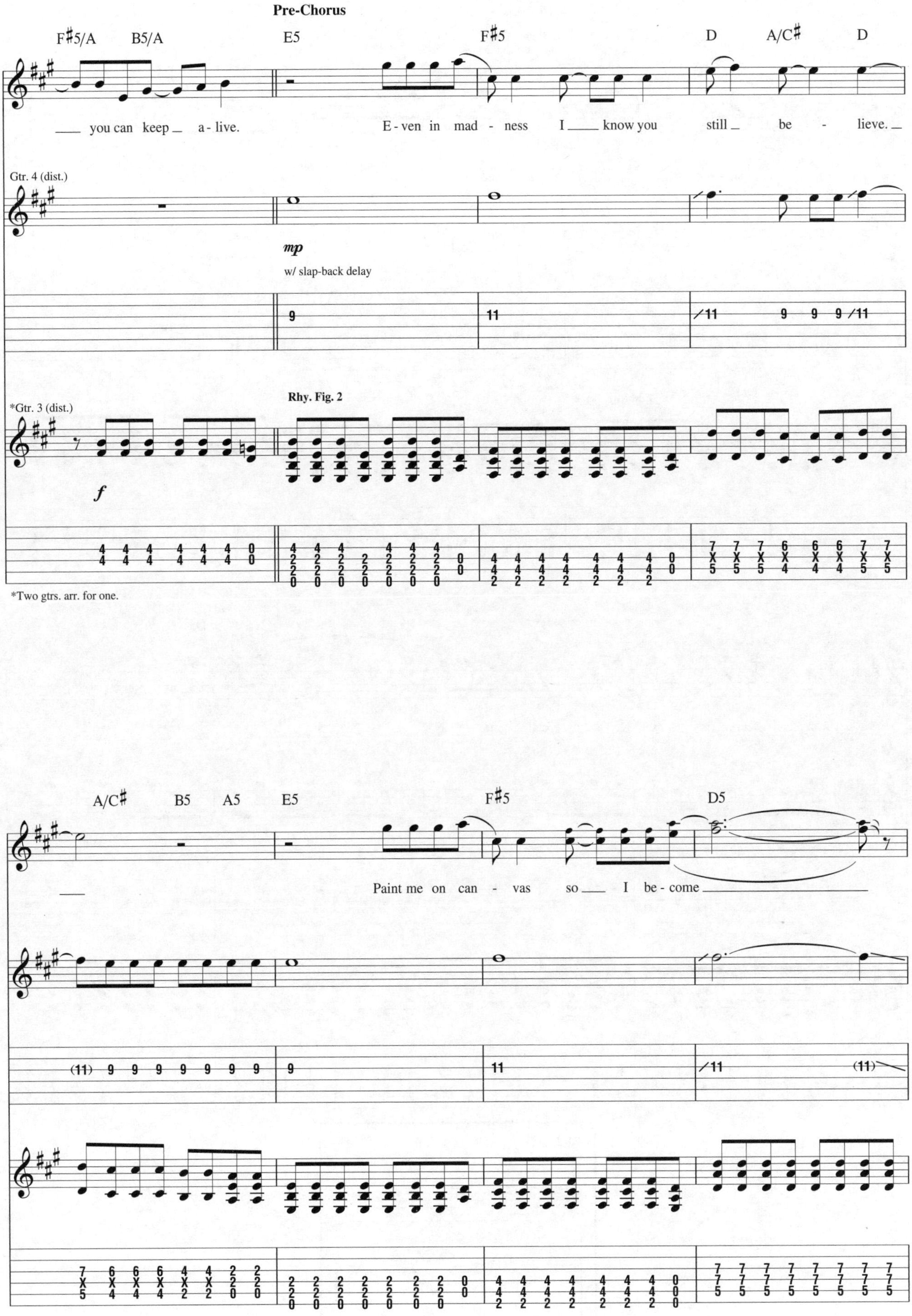
Pre-Chorus
F♯5/A B5/A E5 F♯5 D A/C♯ D
__ you can keep __ a - live. E - ven in mad - ness I ___ know you still __ be - lieve. __
Gtr. 4 (dist.)
mp
w/ slap-back delay
Rhy. Fig. 2
*Gtr. 3 (dist.)
f
*Two gtrs. arr. for one.
A/C♯ B5 A5 E5 F♯5 D5
__ Paint me on can - vas so __ I be - come ___

Chorus
Gtr. 4 tacet
2nd time, Gtr. 6: w/ Fill 1
3rd time, Gtr. 6 tacet
N.C. B5 N.C. B5 A5 C♯5 D5
what you could nev - er be. I dare you to tell me to walk through fi -
Gtr. 5 (slight dist.)
p
let ring
Gtr. 3
End Rhy. Fig. 2
A5 C♯5 D5 B5 C♯5 D5
- re, wear my soul and call me a li - ar.
let ring
Fill 1
Gtr. 6

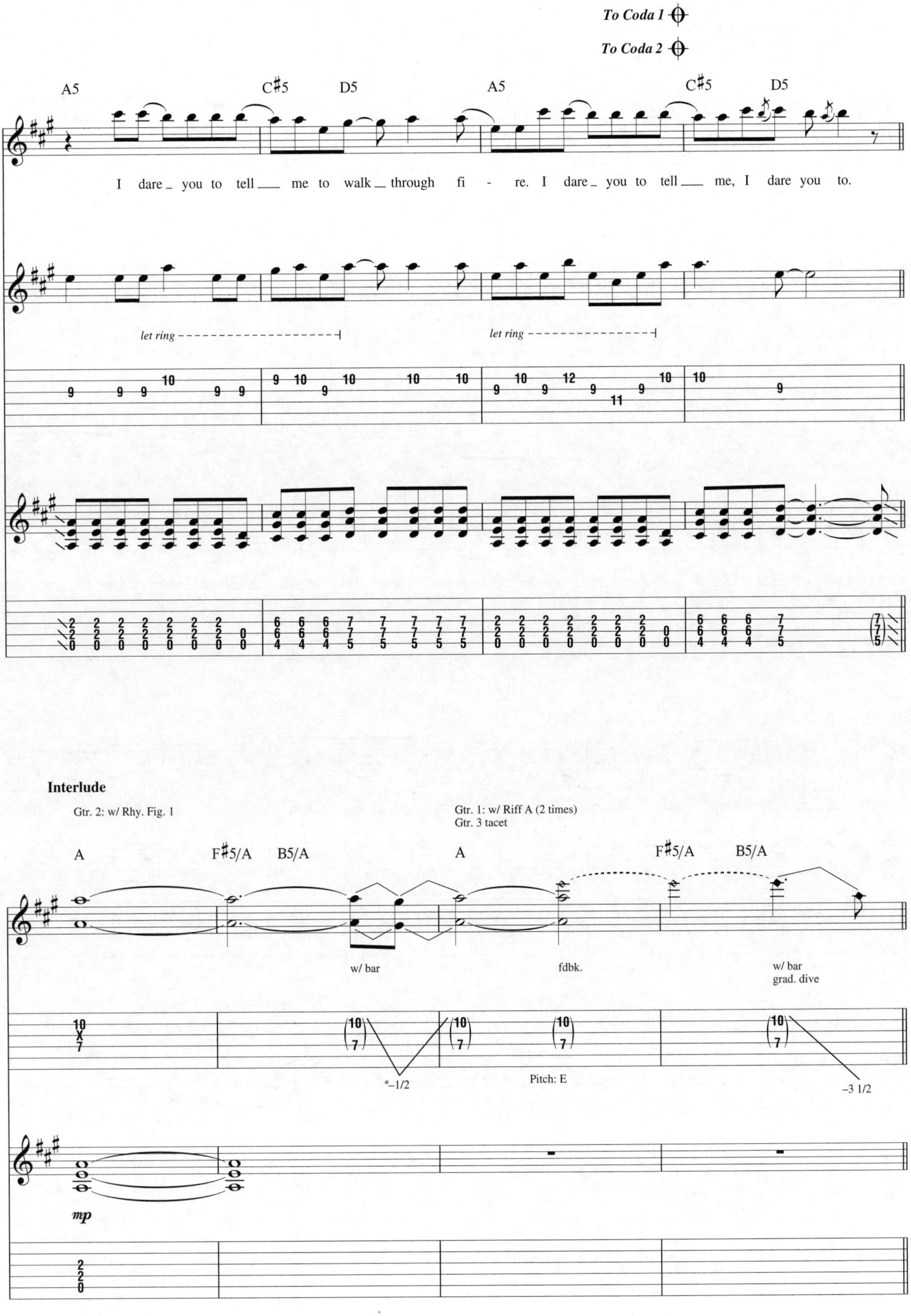
To Coda 1
To Coda 2
A5
C♯5
D5
A5
C♯5
D5
I dare _ you to tell ___ me to walk _ through fi - re. I dare _ you to tell ___ me, I dare you to.
let ring
let ring
Interlude
Gtr. 2: w/ Rhy. Fig. 1
Gtr. 1: w/ Riff A (2 times)
Gtr. 3 tacet
A
F♯5/A
B5/A
A
F♯5/A
B5/A
w/ bar
fdbk.
w/ bar
grad. dive
*–1/2
Pitch: E
–3 1/2
mp

Verse

Gtr. 1: w/ Riff A (12 times)
Gtr. 2: w/ Rhy. Fig. 1 (3 times)
Gtr. 5 tacet
A
F♯5/A
B5/A
A
2. Hel - lo.
Are you still chas - ing
Gtr. 4
let ring
F♯5/A
B5/A
A
F♯5/A
B5/A
the mem - o - ries
in shad - ows?
let ring
A
F♯5/A
B5/A
A
Some stay young,
some grow old.
Come a - live.
let ring
Gtr. 3: w/ Rhy. Fig. 1 (last meas.)
F♯5/A
B5/A
A
F♯5/A
B5/A
There are thoughts un - clear you can nev - er hide.
let ring

Pre-Chorus
Gtr. 3: w/ Rhy. Fig. 2
Gtr. 4 tacet
E5
F#5
D
A/C#
D
A/C#
B5
A5
E - ven in mad - ness I ___ know you still ___ be - lieve. ___
Gtr. 6 (dist.)
mf
Gtr. 5
let ring
let ring
D.S. al Coda 1
E5
F#5
D5
N.C. B5
N.C. B5
Paint me on can - vas so ___ I be - come ___ what you could nev - er be.
let ring
let ring
let ring

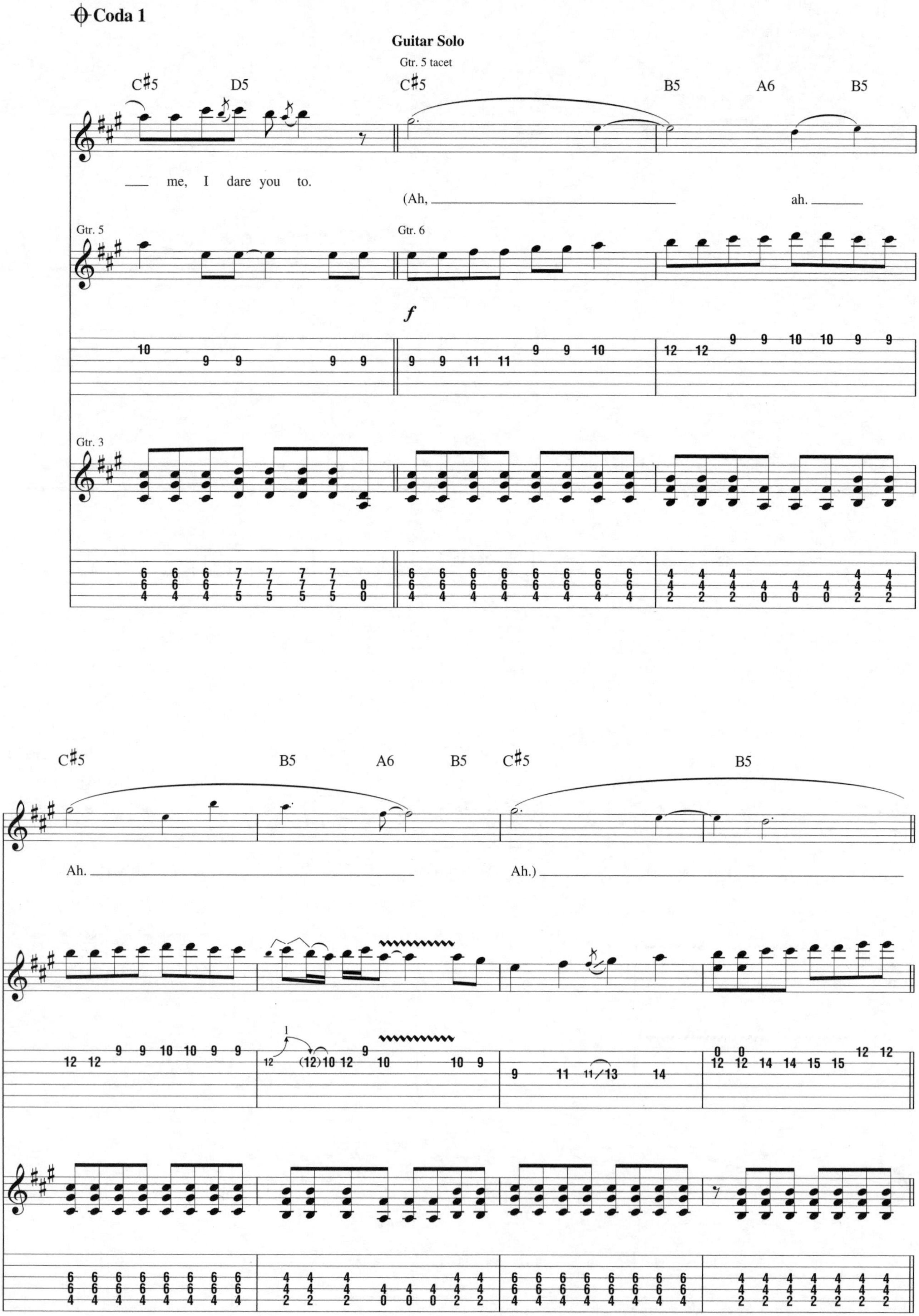
Coda 1
Guitar Solo
Gtr. 5 tacet
C♯5 D5 C♯5 B5 A6 B5
me, I dare you to.
(Ah, ah.
Gtr. 5
Gtr. 6
f
Gtr. 3
C♯5 B5 A6 B5 C♯5 B5
Ah. Ah.)

D.S. al Coda 2
Interlude
Gtr. 2: w/ Rhy. Fig. 1
Gtr. 1: w/ Riff A (2 times)
A
F♯5/A
B5/A
Hel - lo.
fdbk.
mp
mf
Coda 2
C♯5
D5
A5
me, I dare you to.
Hel-lo.
Gtr. 6
Gtr. 5
Gtr. 3
let ring
1/2
1

C♯5 D5 A5 C♯5 D5
I dare you to tell me, I dare you to.
8va
loco
1/2
1
let ring
A5 C♯5 D5
I dare you to tell me, I dare you to.
fdbk.
Pitch: C♯
let ring
fdbk.
Pitch: E
B

I Stand Alone

Words and Music by Sully Erna

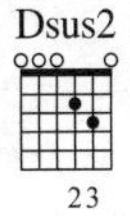

Drop D tuning, down 1 step:
(low to high) C-G-C-F-A-D

Intro

Moderately slow ♩ = 84

N.C.

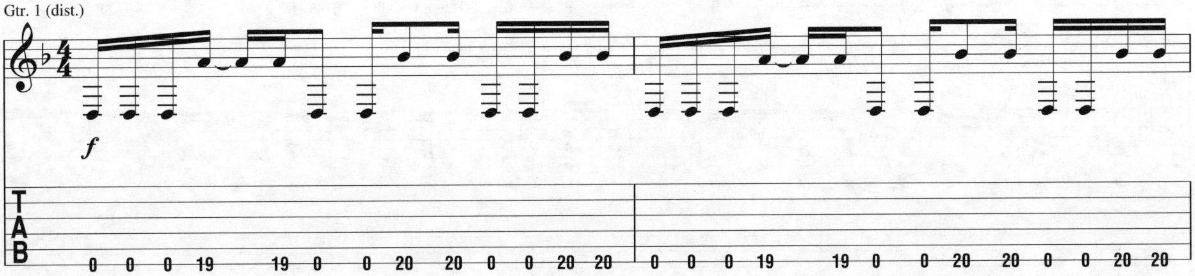

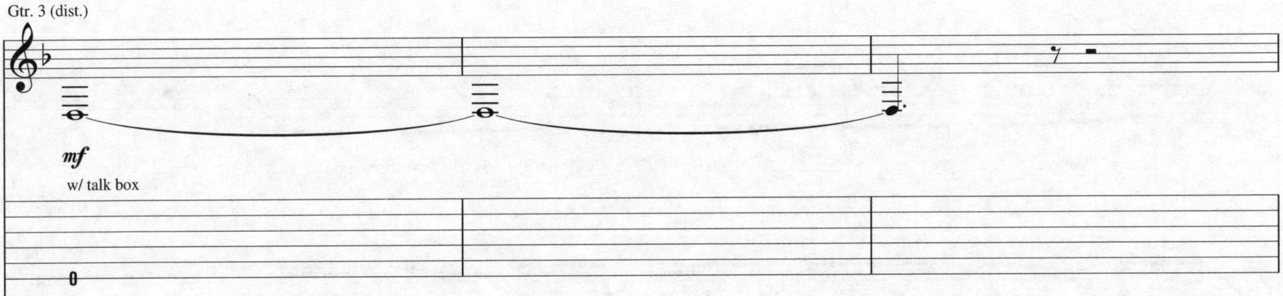

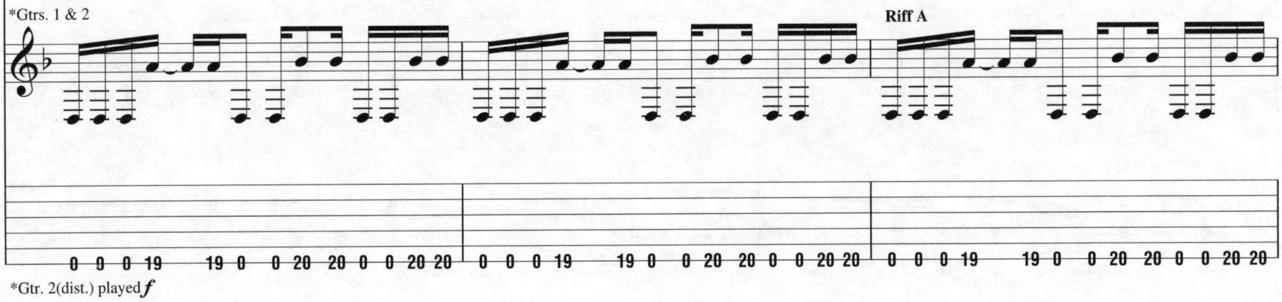

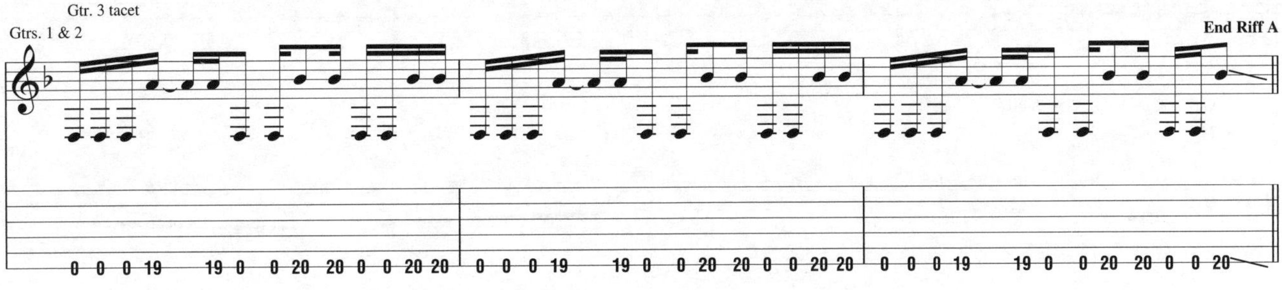

Verse
D
Ab5
D
G5 F5
1. I've told you this once be - fore, can't con - trol me.
Gtr. 1
Rhy. Fig. 1
P.M.
Gtr. 2
Rhy. Fig. 1A
P.M.
D
Ab5
D
N.C.
If you try to take me down you're gon - na break.
End Rhy. Fig. 1
P.M.
End Rhy. Fig. 1A
P.M.
Gtrs. 1 & 2: w/ Rhy. Figs. 1 & 1A (1st 2 meas.)
D
Ab5
D
G5 F5
And I feel your ev - 'ry noth - ing that you're do - ing for me.

D
A♭5
A♭6/9
And I'm think - ing you ought to make your own way.
Gtr. 3
f
Rhy. Fig. 2
Gtr. 1
End Rhy. Fig. 2
P.M.
P.M.
Rhy. Fig. 2A
Gtr. 2
End Rhy. Fig. 2A
P.M.
P.M.
Chorus
Gtrs. 1 & 2: w/ Riff A
Gtr. 3 tacet
N.C.
I stand a - lone in - side. I stand a - lone.
Whispered: (I. I.)
*w/ echo set for half-note regeneration w/ 2 repeats.
Verse
Gtrs. 1 & 2: w/ Rhy. Fig. 1 (1 1/2 times)
D
A♭5
D
G5 F5
D
A♭5
2. You're al - ways hid - ing be - hind your so - called god - dess. So what? You don't think
D
N.C.
D
A♭5
D
G5 F5
that we can see your face? Res - ur - rect - ed back be - fore the fi - nal fall - ing.

Gtrs. 1 & 2: w/ Rhy. Figs. 1 & 1A (1st 2 meas.)
D A♭5 D G5 F5
And I'll nev - er rest un - til I can make my own
G5 B♭sus2 E♭5
way. I'm not a - fraid of fad - ing.
Gtr. 1
let ring
let ring
Gtr. 2
Chorus
Gtrs. 1 & 2: w/ Riff A (last 2 meas.)
N.C.
I stand a - lone. Feel - ing your
Whispered: (I.)
G5 B♭5
sting down in - side me, I'm not dy - ing for it.
Rhy. Fig. 3
End Rhy. Fig. 3
Gtrs. 1 & 2

Gtrs. 1 & 2: w/ Riff A (last 2 meas.)
N.C.
I stand a - lone. Ev - er - y -
(I.)
G5
B♭5
E♭5
thing that I be - lieve is fad - ing.
Rhy. Fig. 4
Gtrs. 1 & 2
End Rhy. Fig. 4
Gtrs. 1 & 2: w/ Riff A (1st 2 meas., 2 times)
N.C.
I stand a - lone in - side. I stand a - lone.
(I. I. I.)
*w/ echo set for half-note regeneration w/ 2 repeats.
Bridge
Dsus2
Gtrs. 1 & 2
Gtrs. 1 & 2 tacet
Fsus2
And now it's my time,
(And now it's my
Gtr. 3
Riff B
let ring
let ring

Gtr. 3: w/ Riff B (3 times)
N.C.
D5
it's my time to dream,
dream of the
time,
it's my time to dream,
End Riff B
Gtr. 1
let ring
mf
P.S.
Gtr. 1 tacet
Fsus2
N.C.
skies.
dream of the skies.)
Make me be-
Dsus2
lieve that this place is - n't plagued by the poi - son in
Gtr. 2
mf
Gtr. 1
w/ amp tremolo
let ring

Fsus2
N.C.
me.
Help me de -
f
tremolo off
string noise
Gtr. 1 tacet
D5
cide if my fire will burn out be - fore you can
Gtr. 2
let ring
Fsus2
N.C.
breathe,
breathe in - to
Gtrs. 1 & 2
f

Guitar Solo
Gtrs. 1 & 2: w/ Rhy. Figs. 1 & 1A (1st 2 meas.)
D
A♭5
D
G5 F5
me.
Gtr. 3
f
Gtrs. 1 & 2: w/ Rhy. Figs. 2 & 2A
D
A♭5
A♭6/9
Chorus
Gtrs. 1 & 2: w/ Riff A
Gtr. 3 tacet
N.C.
I stand a - lone in - side. I stand a - lone. Feel - ing your
Whispered: (I. I.)
Gtrs. 1 & 2: w/ Rhy. Fig. 3
G5
B♭5
sting down in - side me, I'm not dy - ing for it.
Gtrs. 1 & 2: w/ Riff A (last 2 meas.)
N.C.
I stand a - lone. Ev - er - y -
(I.)

Gtrs. 1 & 2: w/ Rhy. Fig. 4
G5
B♭5
E♭5
thing that I believe is fad - ing.
Gtrs. 1 & 2: w/ Riff A (1st 2 meas., 2 times)
N.C.
I stand a - lone in - side. I stand a - lone in - side.
(I. I.
I stand a - lone in - side.
I.
Riff C
Gtr. 1
End Riff C
Gtr. 2
Riff C1
End Riff C1
Gtrs. 1 & 2: w/ Riffs C & C1
I stand a - lone in - side.
I.)
Gtr. 3
mf

I'm Amazed

Words and Music by Jim James

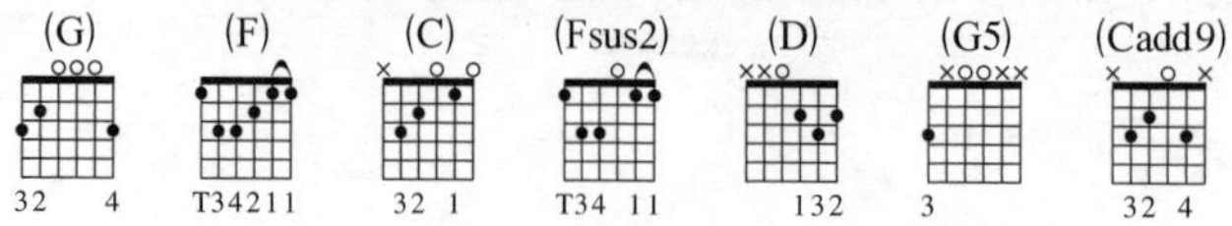

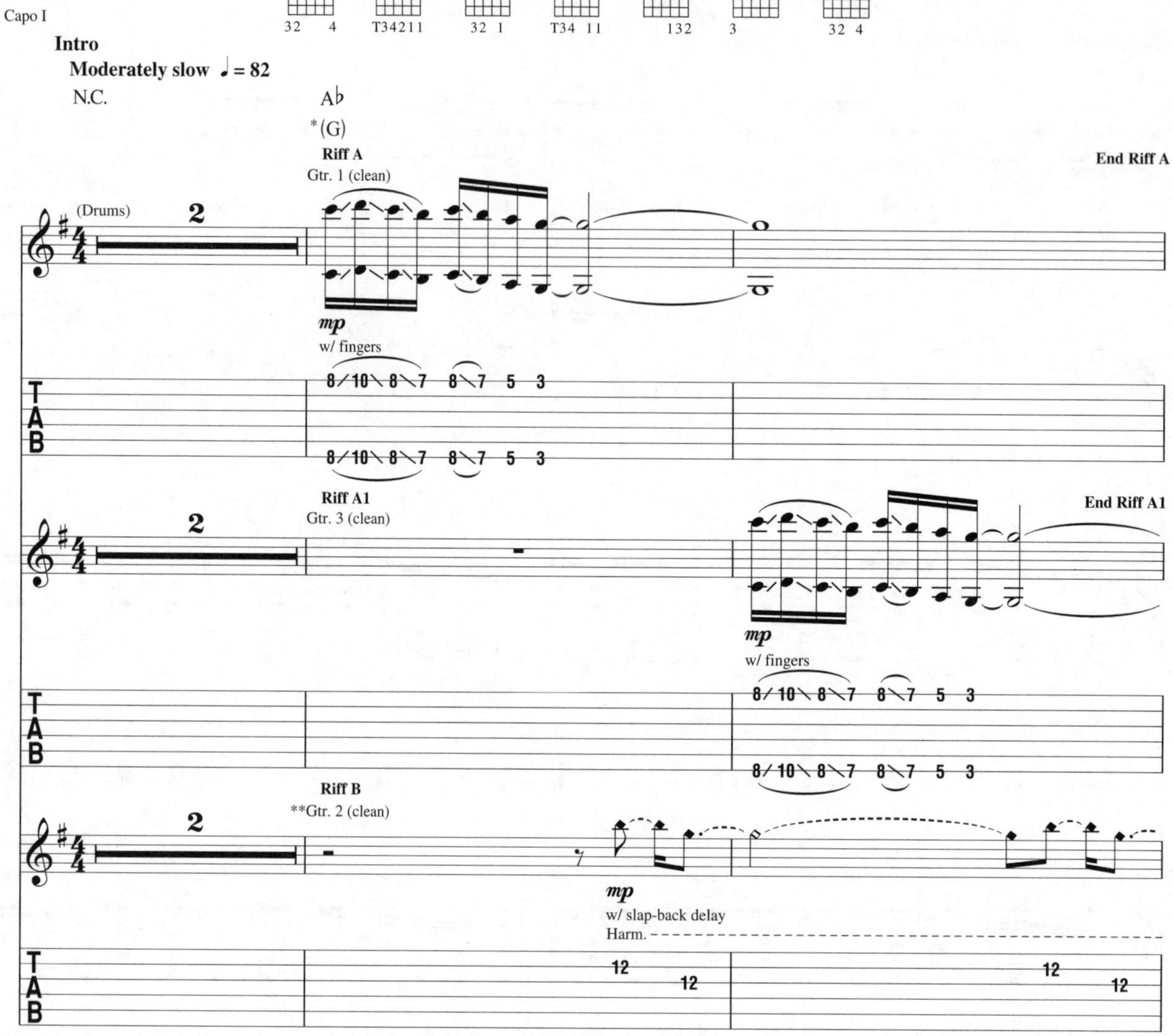

*Symbols in parentheses represent chord names respective to capoed guitar. Symbols above represent actual sounding chords. Capoed fret is "0" in tab. Chord symbols reflect overall harmony.

**Two gtrs. arr. for one.

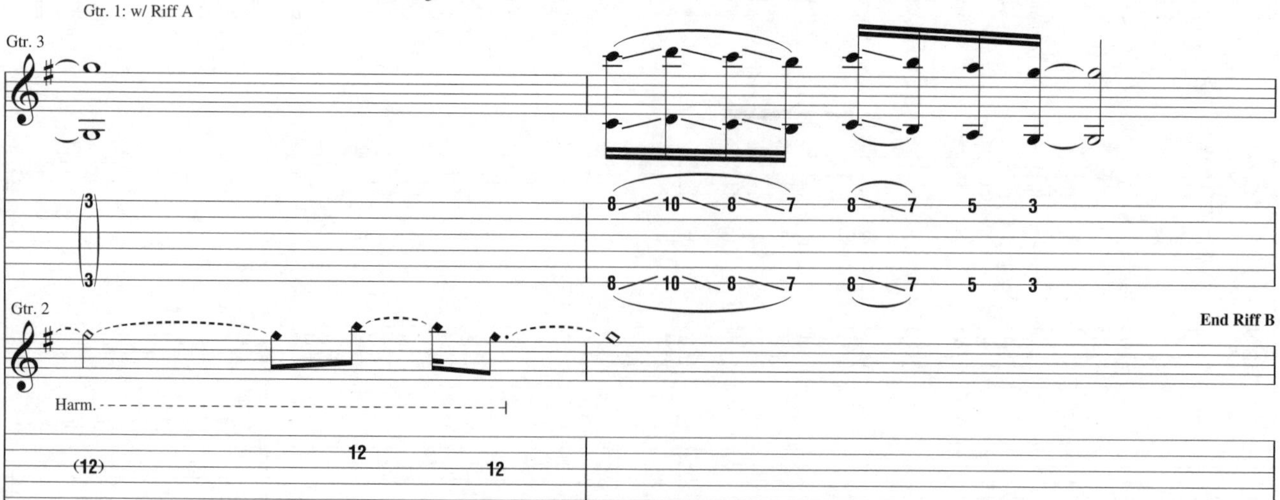

Gtrs. 1, 2 & 3 tacet
(G)
(F)
(C)
Gtr. 4 (dist.)
mf
Gtr. 5 (dist.)
mf
w/ fingers
(G)
(F)
(Fsus2) (F)
(C)
1. I'm a - mazed
w/ pick
Verse
Gtr. 5 tacet
(G)
Rhy. Fig. 1
at a qui - et o - cean.
I'm a - mazed
Gtr. 6 (dist.)
Riff C
mp

(C)
(G)
(C)
End Rhy. Fig. 1
(cont. in notation)
at your warm de-vo-tion.
I'm a-mazed
Ab
(G)
at what the peo-ple say-in'.
I'm a-mazed
Gtr. 4
Gtr. 6
Db
(C)
Ab
(G)
by a di-vid-ed na-tion.
Like the
(cont. in slashes)
End Riff C

Gtr. 6 tacet
(D)
(C)
Gtr. 4
* Voc. Fig. 1
End Voc. Fig. 1
rhy - thm of the Earth, I get dis - rupt -
(Ah.)
Gtr. 5
*Refers to upstemmed voc. only
(G)
(C)
- ed.
2. I'm a - mazed
Verse
Gtr. 4: w/ Rhy. Fig. 1
Gtr. 5 tacet
Gtr. 6: w/ Riff C
A♭
(G)
at all there has been.
I'm a - mazed
D♭
(C)
A♭
(G)
N.C.
D♭
(C)
at all there'll be.
I'm a - mazed

A♭
(G)
Gtr. 4
at the T V sta - tions.
I'm a - mazed
D♭
(C)
A♭
(G)
what they want me to be - lieve.
Af - ter
(cont. in slashes)
Bkgd. Voc.: w/ Voc. Fig. 1
(D)
(C)
Gtr. 4
(cont. in notation)
all is said and done,
where is the jus -
Gtr. 5
Riff D
End Riff D
Interlude
Gtr. 1: w/ Riff A (2 times)
Gtr. 2: w/ Riff B
Gtr. 3: w/ Riff A1
A♭
(G)
A♭
(G)
- tice?
Gtrs. 4 & 5

Gtrs. 4 & 5 tacet
(G)
(C)
Gtr. 4
3. I'm a - mazed
Gtr. 3
Verse
Gtr. 3 tacet
Gtr. 4: w/ Rhy. Fig. 1
Gtr. 6: w/ Riff C
A♭
(G)
at lack of ev - o - lu - tion.
I'm a - mazed
D♭
(C)
A♭
(G)
N.C.
D♭
(C)
at the lack of faith.
I'm a - mazed
A♭
(G)
at the love we re - ject - ing.
I'm a - mazed
Gtr. 4
D♭
(C)
A♭
(G)
what we ac - cept in its place.
Like the

Bkgd. Voc.: w/ Voc. Fig. 1 (3 times)
Gtr. 5: w/ Riff D (2 times)
E♭
(D)
D♭
(C)
rhy - thm of the Earth, and the
E♭
(D)
D♭
(C)
rhy - thm of the ag - es, like the
E♭
(D)
D
(C♯)
D♭
(C)
rhy - thm. I get dis - rupt -
Gtr. 5
f
Gtr. 4
(cont. in slashes)

Guitar Solo

(G5)
Gtr. 4
- ed.
Ow!
Gtr. 5
(Cadd9)
(G)
(C)
(cont. in notation)
Ah,
hold bend
rake
A♭
(G)
woo!
Gtr. 5
P.M.
Gtr. 4
P.M.

D♭
(C)
A♭
(G)
I'm a - mazed.
1/2
1/2 hold bend
let ring
(cont. on lower staff)
(cont. on upper staff)
Bridge
A♭
(G)
G♭
(F)
D♭
(C)
I'm a - mazed.
Gtr. 4
1/2
1/2
Gtr. 5

A♭
(G)
G♭
(F)
D♭
(C)
A♭
(G)
G♭
(F)
D♭
(C)
Ah.

A♭
(G)
G♭
(F)
Ah.
let ring
D♭
(C)
Outro
A♭
(G)

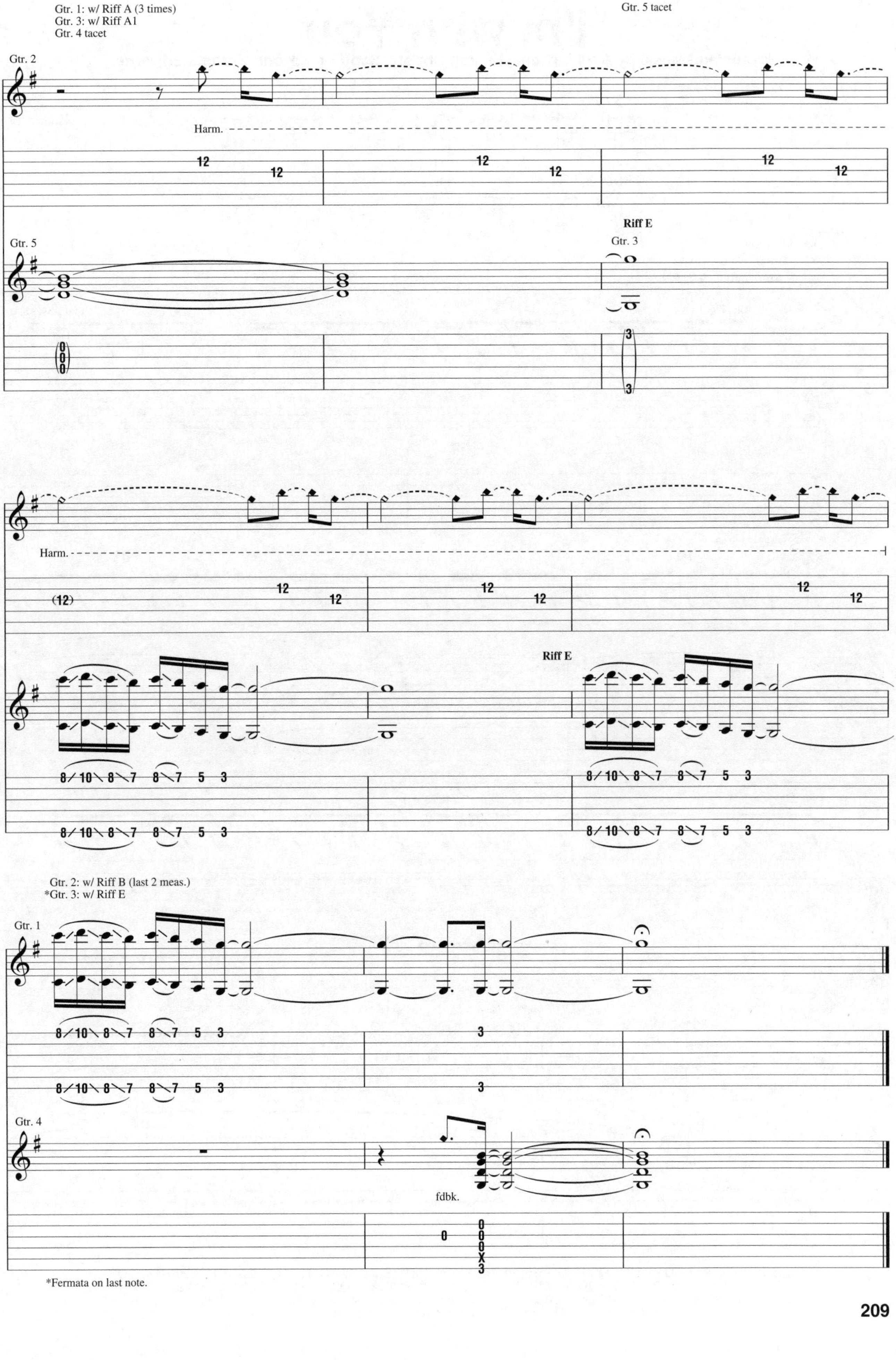

*Fermata on last note.

I'm with You

Words and Music by Avril Lavigne, Lauren Christy, Scott Spock and Graham Edwards

Verse
Gtr. 4 tacet
F♯5
D5open
Rhy. Fig. 2
Gtrs. 1 & 2
P.M.
stand - in' on the bridge, I'm wait - in' in the dark. I
Gtr. 3
fdbk.
(9)
(9)
Pitch: B
F♯5
D5open
Gtrs. 1 & 2
P.M.
thought that you'd be here by now. There's
Gtr. 3
(9)
Gtr. 4
Harm.
12
Gtr. 4 tacet
F♯5
D5open
End Rhy. Fig. 2
P.M.
noth - in' but the rain, no foot - steps on the ground. I'm
1/2
6
7
6
(6)
(12)

F♯5
Gtr. 3 tacet
D5open
Gtrs. 1 & 2
P.M.
(cont. in notation)
lis - ten - ing but there's no sound.
Gtr. 3
(6)
Pre-Chorus
Esus2
E
Is - n't an - y - one try - in' to find me?
Gtrs. 1 & 2
let ring
Gtr. 4
Gtr. 5 (elec.)
mp
w/ clean tone
P.M.
P.M.

Dsus2
Won't some - bod - y come take me home? It's a
let ring
(cont. in slashes)
P.M.
Chorus
Gtr. 4 tacet
Asus2
Bsus4
D6sus2
Rhy. Fig. 3
Gtrs. 1 & 2
damn cold night, I'm try - in' to fig - ure
Gtr. 3
w/ slight dist.
Gtr. 5
let ring

Asus2
Bsus4
D6sus2
out this life. Won't you
let ring
Gtr. 3 tacet
Asus2
Bsus4
D6sus2
Gtrs. 1 & 2
take me by the hand, take me some - where new? I don't
Gtr. 4
let ring
Gtr. 5
let ring

Gtrs. 1 & 2: w/ Rhy. Fig. 2 (1st 4 meas.)
Gtr. 5 tacet
F♯m7add4
E
Dsus2
End Rhy. Fig. 3
F♯5
know who you are but I, I'm with you.
let ring
*Neck pickup
Gtr. 3
dist. off
w/ bar
D5
F♯5
D5
I'm with you.
Mm.
2. I'm
Gtr. 4
w/ bar
let ring
Gtr. 3
w/ bar
Verse
Gtr. 1: w/ Rhy. Fig. 2
Gtrs. 3 & 4 tacet
F♯5
D5
look - in' for a place,
I'm search - in' for a face.
Is
Gtr. 2
P.M.

F♯5
D5
an - y - bod - y here I know? 'Cause
P.M.
noth - in's go - in' right, and ev - 'ry - thing's a mess, and
Gtr. 3
mp
w/ slight dist.
w/ bar
Gtr. 2
D5 open
Gtr. 1
(cont. in notation)
no one likes to be a - lone.
mf

Pre-Chorus
E5
E
Is - n't an - y - one try - in' to find me?
Gtr. 3
Gtr. 1
let ring
Gtr. 2
*Gtrs. 4 & 5
let ring
*Composite arrangement
D6sus2
won't some - bod - y come take me home? It's a
let ring
let ring

Chorus
Gtrs. 1 & 2: w/ Rhy. Fig. 3 (1st 7 meas.)
Gtr. 4 tacet
Asus2 Bsus4 D6sus2 Asus2 Bsus4
damn cold night, I'm try-in' to fig - ure out this
Gtr. 3
Riff A
w/ dist.
Gtr. 5
let ring
D6sus2
Gtr. 3 tacet
Asus2 Bsus4 D6sus2
life. Won't you take me by the hand, take me some - where new? I don't
End Riff A
let ring
F♯m7add4 E Dsus2
Gtrs. 1 & 2: w/ Rhy. Fig. 2 (1st 4 meas.)
F♯5
Gtrs. 1 & 2
know who you are but I, I'm with you.
Gtr. 5
let ring

D5
F#5
D5
I'm with you,
yeah, yeah,
oh.
let ring
Bridge
E5
Bsus4
Gtrs. 1 & 2
Why is ev - 'ry - thing so con - fus - ing?
Gtr. 3
w/ dist.
*Gtrs. 4 & 5
Rhy. Fig. 4
End Rhy. Fig. 4
*Gtr. 4: w/ dist.; Gtr. 5: w/ clean tone
Gtr. 4: w/ Rhy. Fig. 4
May - be I'm just out of my mind.
Yeah,
Gtr. 5

E5
D6sus2
Gtrs. 1 & 2
yeah, _ yeah,
yeah, _ yeah,
yeah, _ yeah,
yeah, _ yeah,
Gtrs. 3 & 4
Gtr. 5
C♯m7
E5
yeah.
It's a
let ring
let ring

Chorus
Gtrs. 1 & 2: w/ Rhy. Fig. 1 (2 times)
Gtrs. 3, 4 & 5 tacet
A5 B5 D5 A5 B5
damn cold night. Try-in' to fig - ure out this
D5 A5 B5 D5
life. Won't you take me by the hand, take me some - where new? I don't
Gtrs. 1 & 2
P.M.
(cont. in slashes)
F#m7add4 E D5open type2
Gtrs. 1 & 2
know who you are but I, I'm with
Gtr. 3
w/ clean tone
Gtr. 3
Gtr. 6 (elec.)
divisi
mf
w/ slight dist.
let ring
Gtr. 4
w/ increased gain
(cont. in slashes)
P.M.

Gtrs. 1 & 2: w/ Rhy. Fig. 3
Gtr. 3: w/ Riff A
Rhy. Fig. 5
End Rhy. Fig. 5
A5
B5
D5
Gtr. 4
you.
I'm with
*Gtrs. 5 & 7
let ring
*Gtr. 7 (acous.), played mf
Gtr. 6
Gtr. 4: w/ Rhy. Fig. 5 (2 times)
Asus2
Bsus4
D6sus2
Asus2
Bsus4
you.
Take me by the hand take me

1.
Gtrs. 5 & 7 tacet
D6sus2
F♯m7add4
E
Dsus2
some - where - new. I don't know who you are but I, I'm with
Gtr. 4
let ring
let ring
P.M.
let ring
2.
Gtrs. 5 & 7 tacet
F♯m7add4
E
Dsus2
know who you are but I, I'm with
Outro
Gtrs. 1 & 2: w/ Rhy. Fig. 2 (1st 4 meas.)
Gtr. 6 tacet
F♯5
you.
Gtr. 4
Gtr. 6
let ring
D5
F♯5
D5
Gtr. 4 tacet
A5
Oh, I'm with you. I'm with you.
Gtr. 4
mp
dist. off
1/2
Gtrs. 1 & 2

Island in the Sun

Words and Music by Rivers Cuomo

Chorus
Gtrs. 2 & 3: w/ Rhy. Figs. 2 & 3 (4 times)
3rd time, Gtr. 6: w/ Fill 1
Em Am D G Em Am D G
* Voc. Fig. 2
End Voc. Fig. 2
On an is - land in the sun, we'll be play - ing and hav - ing fun.
(Oo. Oo. Oo.
Gtr. 4 (elec.)
Riff A
End Riff A
w/ clean tone
let ring
* Refers to upstemmed notes.
** 3rd time, Lead voc. tacet for beats 1 & 2.
Gtr. 4: w/ Riff A (2 times)
Em Am D G Em Am D G
Voc. Fig. 3
End Voc. Fig. 3
1.
And it makes me feel so fine I can't con - trol my brain.
Oo. Oo.)
Interlude
Gtrs. 1 & 2: w/ Rhy. Figs. 1 & 2 (2 times)
Em Am D G Em Am D G
2.
D G
Hip, hip. Hip, hip. my brain.
Oo.)
Bridge
D G5 D G5
Gtr. 4
We'll run a - way to - geth - er. We'll spend some time, for - ev - er.
*** Gtr. 5 (elec.)
w/ dist.
*** Doubled throughout
Fill 1
Gtr. 6
fdbk.

To Coda
C
Am7
D
We'll nev - er feel bad an - y - more.
Hip, hip.
Interlude
Gtrs. 1 & 2: w/ Rhy. Figs. 1 & 2 (2 times)
Gtrs. 4 & 5 tacet
Em Am D G Em Am D G
Hip, hip. Hip, hip.
Guitar Solo
Gtrs. 1 & 2: w/ Rhy. Figs. 1 & 2 (4 times)
Em Am D G
Gtr. 6 (elec.)
f
Harm.
w/ heavy dist.
D.S. al Coda
(take 2nd ending)
Em Am D G Em Am D G Em Am D G
Coda
Outro
Bkgd. Voc.: w/ Voc. Fig. 1 (7 times)
Gtrs. 1 & 2: w/ Rhy. Figs. 1 & 2 (7 times)
Gtrs. 4 & 5 tacet
Em Am D G Em Am D G
We'll nev - er feel bad an - y - more.
Bkgd. Voc.: w/ Voc. Fig. 2
Gtr. 4: w/ Riff A (5 times)
Em Am D G Em Am D G
No, no.
Bkgd. Voc.: w/ Voc. Fig. 3 (3 times)
Em Am
We'll nev - er feel bad an -
Begin fade
Fade out
D G Em Am D G Em Am D G
- y - more. No, no. No, no.

The Kids Aren't Alright

Words and Music by Dexter Holland

Ab5
Gtr. 1: w/ Rhy. Fig. 3
Bb5
Gb5
End Rhy. Fig. 3
Db5
Ab5
Verse
Bb5
Gtr. 3 tacet
Gb5
1. When we were young the fu-ture was so bright, the old neigh-bor-hood was so a - live.
(Whoa. Whoa.
2. See Additional Lyrics
Gtr. 3
Gtr. 1
Rhy. Fig. 4
P.M.
Db5
Ab5
And ev-'ry kid on the whole damn street was gon-na make it big and not be beat.
Whoa.
End Rhy. Fig. 4

Gtr. 1: w/ Rhy. Fig. 4
Bb5
Gb5
Now the neigh-bor-hood's cracked and torn, _
Whoa. _
the kids are grown up but their lives are worn. _
Whoa. _
Db5
Ab5
How can one lit - tle street _ swal - low so man - y lives? _ Chanc - es
_)
Chorus
Gtr. 1: w/ Rhy. Fig. 3, 2 times
Bb5
Gb5
thrown, _ noth - ing's free, _ long - ing
* Harmony voc. tacet 1st time
Db5
Ab5
Bb5
for _ what used to be. _ Still it's hard, _
Gb5
Db5
_ hard to see. _ Frag - ile lives, _ shat - tered
Guitar Solo
Gtr. 1: w/ Rhy. Fig. 2, 2 times
Ab5
Bb5
Gb5
dreams. _ Go!
Gtr. 3

Db5
Ab5
full
Bb5
Gb5
Db5
Ab5
Chances
Chorus
Gtr. 1: w/ Rhy. Fig. 3, 2 times
Gtr. 3 tacet
Bb5
Gb5
thrown, nothing's free,
Riff A
Gtr. 4 (dist.)
mf

Additional Lyrics

2. Jamie had a chance, well, she really did;
Instead she dropped out and had a couple of kids.
Mark still lives at home 'cause he's got no job;
He just plays guitar and smokes a lot of pot.
Jay committed suicide,
Brandon O.D.'d and died.
What the hell is going on?
The cruellest dream, reality.

Kings and Queens

Words and Music by Jared Leto

Tune down 1/2 step:
(low to high) Eb-Ab-Db-Gb-Bb-Eb

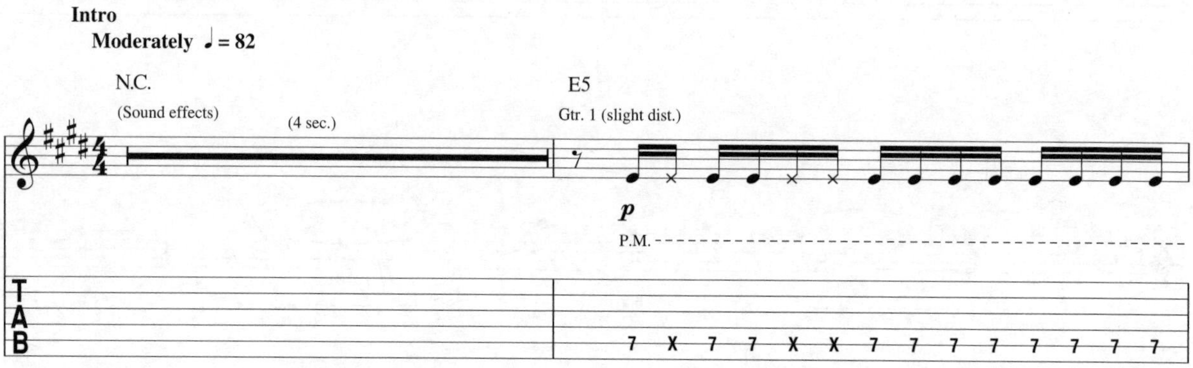

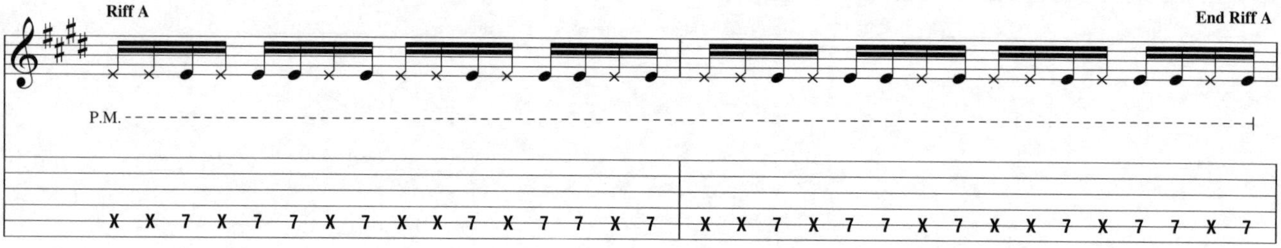

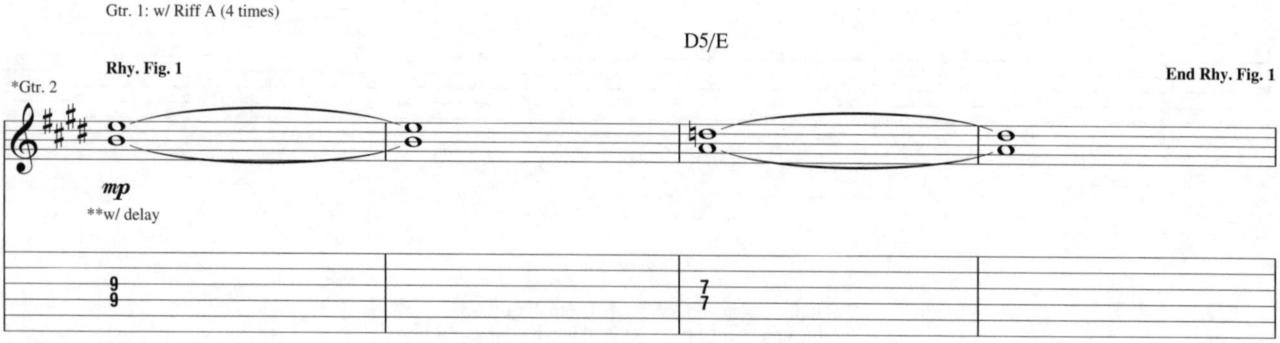

*Elec. piano arr. for gtr.

**Set for dotted eighth-note regeneration w/ 8 repeats.

Gtr. 2: w/ Rhy. Fig. 1
E5
D5/E
Gtr. 4 (dist.)
***
9
***Vol. swell
*Gtr. 3
**
7
*Doubled throughout
**Vol. swell
E5
F#5
A5
E5
F#5
Voc. Fig. 1
(Oh.
Oh.
Riff C
Gtr. 4
mf
let ring
let ring
let ring
9 9 9 12 9 12 9 9 9 12 9 12
9 9 9 9 9 9 9 9 9 10 9 10
9 9 9 12 9 12 9 9 9 12 9 12
Riff C1
Gtr. 5 (dist.)
mf
let ring
let ring
let ring
9 9 9 12 9 12 9 9 9 12 9 12
9 9 9 9 9 9 9 9 9 9 9 9
9 9 9 12 9 12 9 9 9 12 9 12
Riff B
Gtr. 3
f
0 0 0 0 0 0 0 0 2 2 2 2 2 2 2 2
5 5 5 5 5 5 5 5 5 5 5 5 5 5 5 5
0 0 0 0 0 0 0 0 2 2 2 2 2 2 2 2

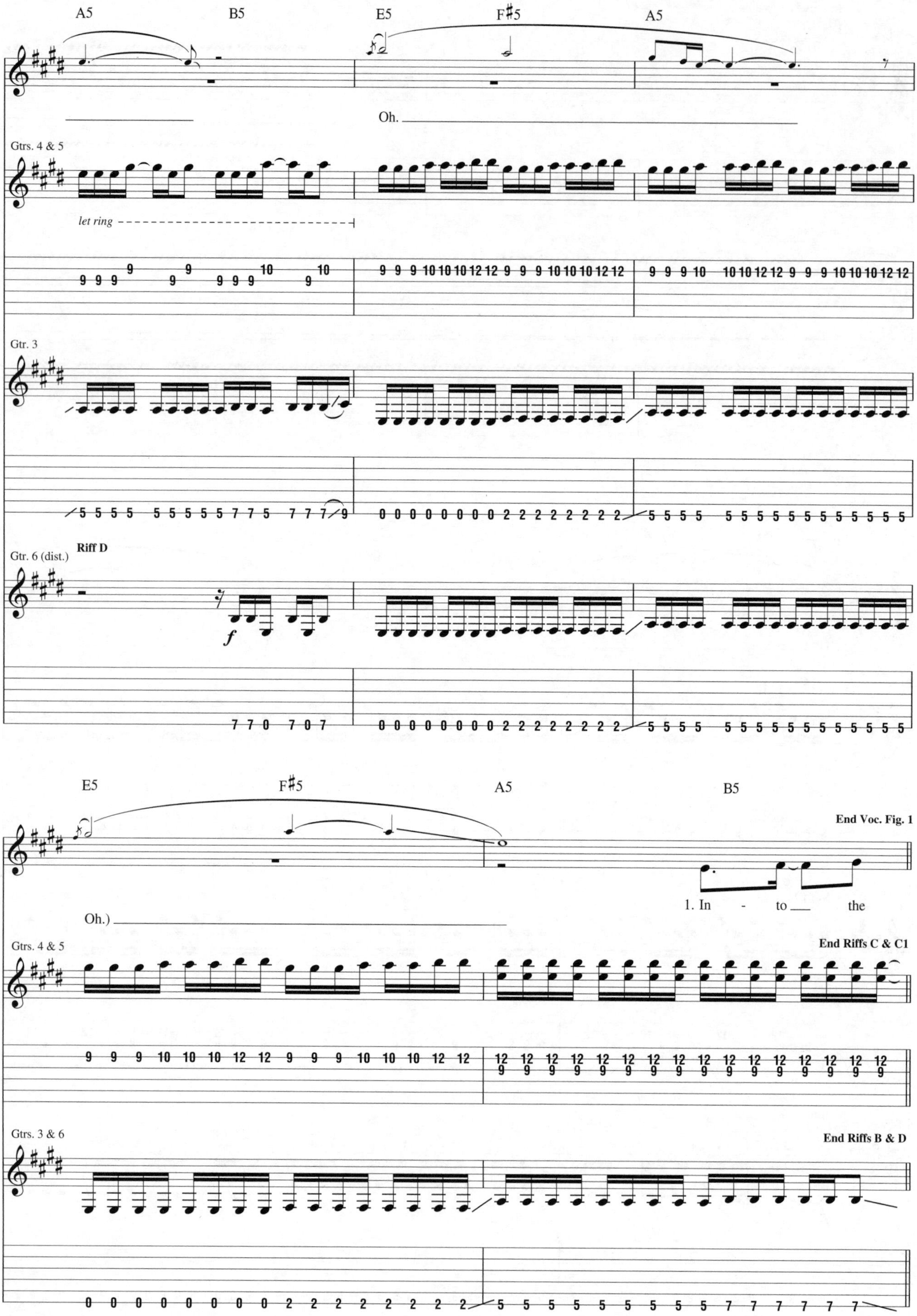
A5
B5
E5
F♯5
A5
Oh.
Gtrs. 4 & 5
let ring
Gtr. 3
Gtr. 6 (dist.)
Riff D
f
E5
F♯5
A5
B5
End Voc. Fig. 1
Oh.)
1. In - to the
Gtrs. 4 & 5
End Riffs C & C1
Gtrs. 3 & 6
End Riffs B & D

Verse
Gtr. 2: w/ Rhy. Fig. 1 (1st 3 meas.)
Gtrs. 3 & 6 tacet
Gtrs. 4 & 5 tacet
E5
D5
night
des - p'rate and bro - ken.
Gtrs. 4 & 5
Riff E
End Riff E
Gtr. 7 (clean)
mf
let ring
Gtr. 7: w/ Riff E
E5
D5
A5
The sound of a fight,
fa - ther has spo - ken.
(Ah.)
Gtr. 2
Rhy. Fig. 2
End Rhy. Fig. 2
Interlude
Bkgd. Voc.: w/ Voc. Fig. 1 (1st 4 meas.)
Gtr. 2 tacet
Esus4/2
Riff F
End Riff F
Gtr. 8 (slight dist.)
mp
Riff F1
End Riff F1
Gtr. 9 (slight dist.)
mp

**Set for eighth-note regeneration w/ 4 repeats.

A5
E5
We stole our new lives through blood and pain.
(12) 10
9 10 12 12 12
Gtr. 10: w/ Riff G (4 times)
D5
A5
E5
In de - fense
10 12 10 9
Gtr. 11 tacet
D5
A5
E5
of our dreams.
In de - fense
D5
A5
of our dreams.
We were the
Gtr. 4
let ring
9 12 9 9 9 12 9 9 9 12 9 9 9 12 9 9
*Lead Voc.: w/ echo set for half-note regeneration w/ 2 repeats.
Chorus
Gtr. 3: w/ Riff B (1st 6 meas.)
Gtr. 4: w/ Riff C (1st 6 meas.)
Gtr. 5: w/ Riff C1 (1st 6 meas.)
E5
F♯5
A5
E5
F♯5
kings and queens of prom - ise.
We were the vic - tims of our -

Gtr. 6: w/ Riff D (1st 3 meas.)
A5 B5 E5 F#5 A5
selves. May-be the chil - dren of a les - ser god be-tween
Bridge
E5 B5 A
heav - en and hell, heav - en and hell.
Gtr. 4
Gtr. 5
Gtrs. 3 & 6
*w/ echo set for dotted half-note regeneration w/ 1 repeat.
Gtrs. 3 - 6 tacet
F#m E Emaj7 A
The age of man
**w/ echo set for half-note regeneration w/ 1 repeat (next 17 meas.).
Gtr. 10: w/ Riff G (7 times)
F#m E Emaj7 A
is o - ver. The dark - ness comes
F#m E A
and all. These les - sons that

F♯m
E
Emaj7
we've learned here have on -
Gtr. 12 (dist.)
w/ heavy reverb
mp
*Fade in
A
F♯m
E
- ly just be - gun.
We were the
Chorus
Bkgd. Voc.: w/ Voc. Fig. 1 (2 times)
Gtr. 3: w/ Riff B (1st 4 meas.)
Gtrs. 4 & 5: w/ Riffs C & C1 (1st 6 meas.)
Gtr. 10: w/ Riff G (8 times)
Gtr. 12 tacet
E5
F♯5
A5
kings and queens of prom - ise.
We were the vic - tims of our -
A5
B5
selves.
May-be the chil - dren of a les - ser god be-tween
Gtr. 6
Gtrs. 3 & 6
Riffs H & H1

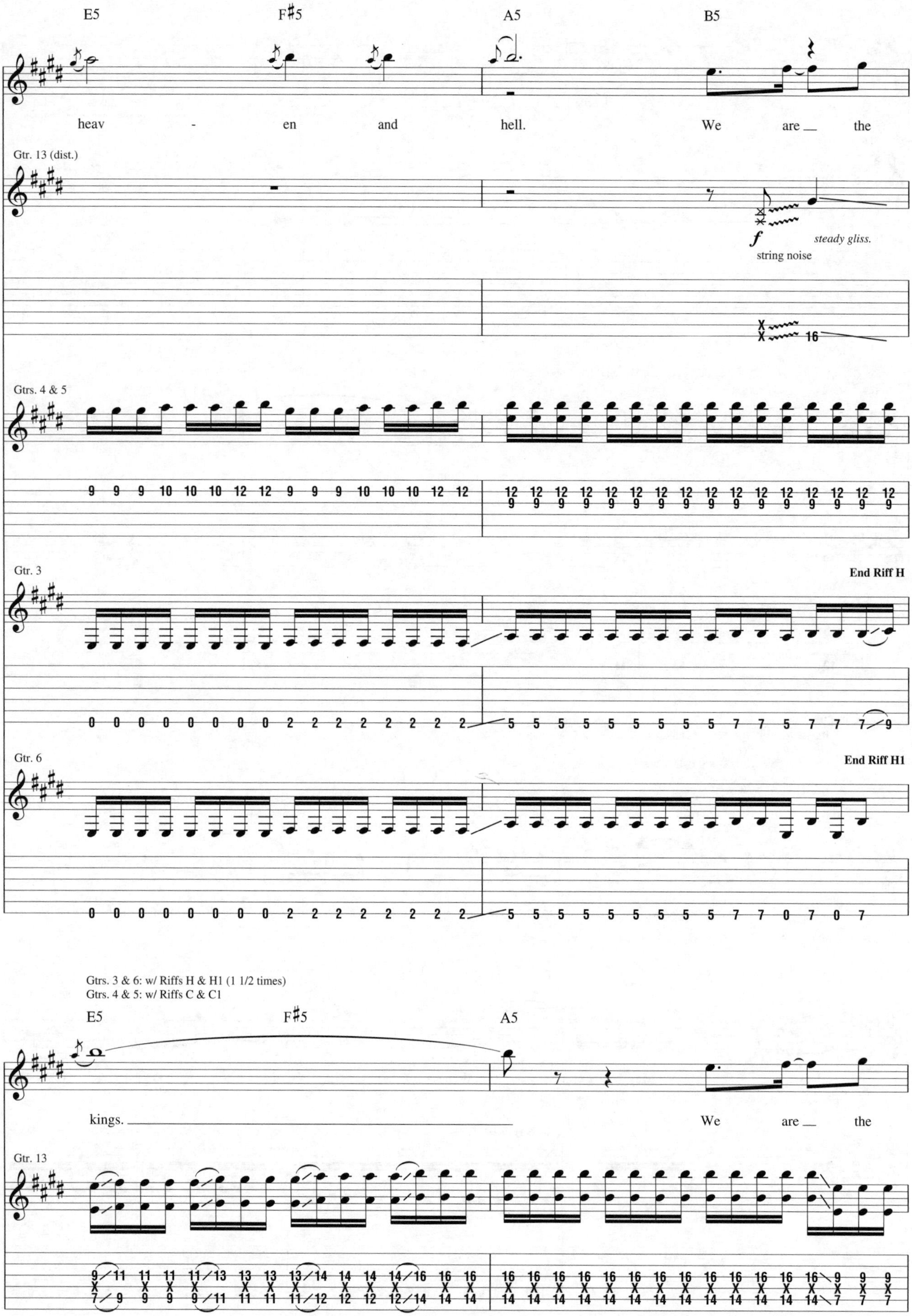
E5
F♯5
A5
B5
heav - en and hell. We are the
Gtr. 13 (dist.)
string noise
steady gliss.
Gtrs. 4 & 5
Gtr. 3
End Riff H
Gtr. 6
End Riff H1
Gtrs. 3 & 6: w/ Riffs H & H1 (1 1/2 times)
Gtrs. 4 & 5: w/ Riffs C & C1
E5
F♯5
A5
kings. We are the
Gtr. 13

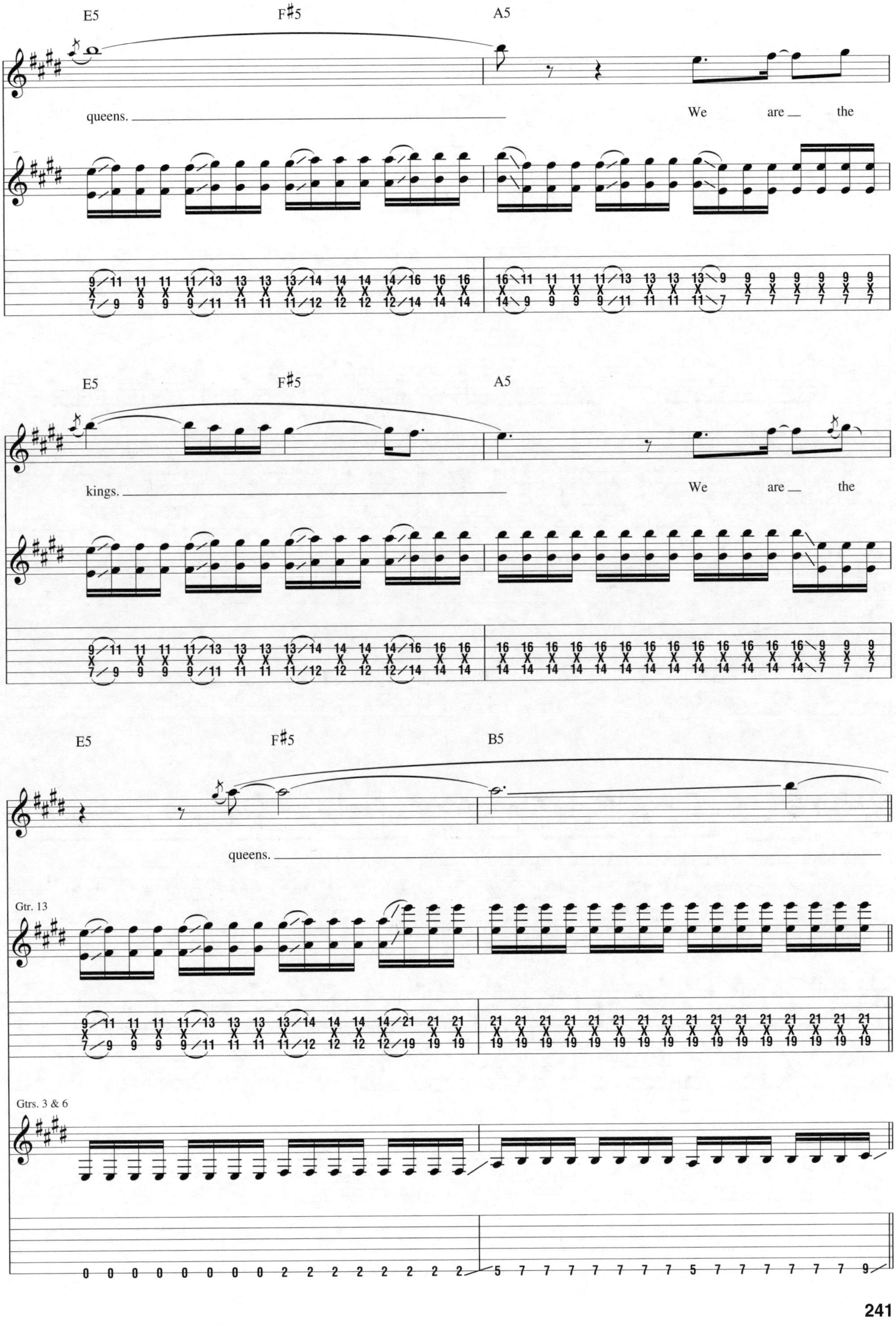
E5
F♯5
A5
queens.
We are the
E5
F♯5
A5
kings.
We are the
E5
F♯5
B5
queens.
Gtr. 13
Gtrs. 3 & 6

Outro
*Bkgd. Voc.: w/ Voc. Fig. 1
Gtrs. 3, 6 & 13 tacet
E5
Gtr. 13
Gtr. 14 (slight dist.)
mp
w/ reverb & delay
let ring throughout
Gtrs. 3 & 6
steady gliss.
*Sung by children's choir.
A5
E5
Gtr. 14
A5
F♯5
A5
E5

Let Me Be Myself

Words by Brad Arnold
Music by Brad Arnold, Robert Harrell, Christopher Henderson and Matthew Roberts

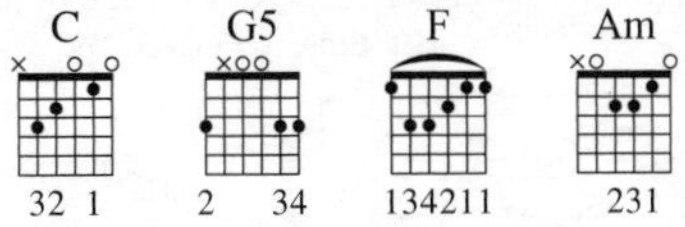

Fsus2
Gsus4
G5
C
but noth-ing ev - er helped. I left my-self be-hind some-where a-long the way,
of day liv-ing in this cell. It's time to make my way in-to the world I knew
End Riff B
Gtr. 3: w/ Riff B
Am
Fsus2
Gsus4
G5
hop-ing to come back a-round to find my-self some-day.
and then take back all of these times that I gave in to you.
Pre-Chorus
Fadd9 Fmaj7
C
G5
Late - ly I'm so tired of wait - ing for you
*Gtrs. 4 & 5
mf
let ring throughout
*Gtr. 4 (acous.); Gtr. 5 (elec.) w/ clean tone.
Composite arrangement
**T = Thumb on 6th string
Fadd9 Fmaj7
Am
G5
to say that it's o - kay. But tell me,
***Gtr. 6 (elec.)
†pp
w/ dist.
fdbk.
***Doubled throughout
Pitch: C
†Vol. swell
Gtrs. 4 & 5
(cont. in slashes)

Chorus
3rd time, Gtr. 1 tacet
C
G5
Rhy. Fig. 1
Gtrs. 4 & 5
please, would you one time just let me be my - self so I can shine
Riff C
Gtr. 7 (elec.)
mf
w/ dist.
let ring throughout
Rhy. Fig. 1A
Gtr. 6
mf
1.
F
Am
G5
End Rhy. Fig. 1
with my own light? Let me be my - self.
End Riff C
End Rhy. Fig. 1A

Interlude

Gtrs. 1 & 2: w/ Riff A
C
Gtrs. 4 & 5 tacet
Am
Would you let me be my -
Gtr. 7
pp
Gtr. 8 (elec.)
mp
w/ clean tone
let ring throughout
Gtr. 6
Gtr. 9 (elec.)
mp
w/ clean tone
Gtrs. 6 & 7 tacet
Fsus2
Gsus4
G5
self?
2. I'll nev - er find my heart
Gtr. 8
Gtr. 9

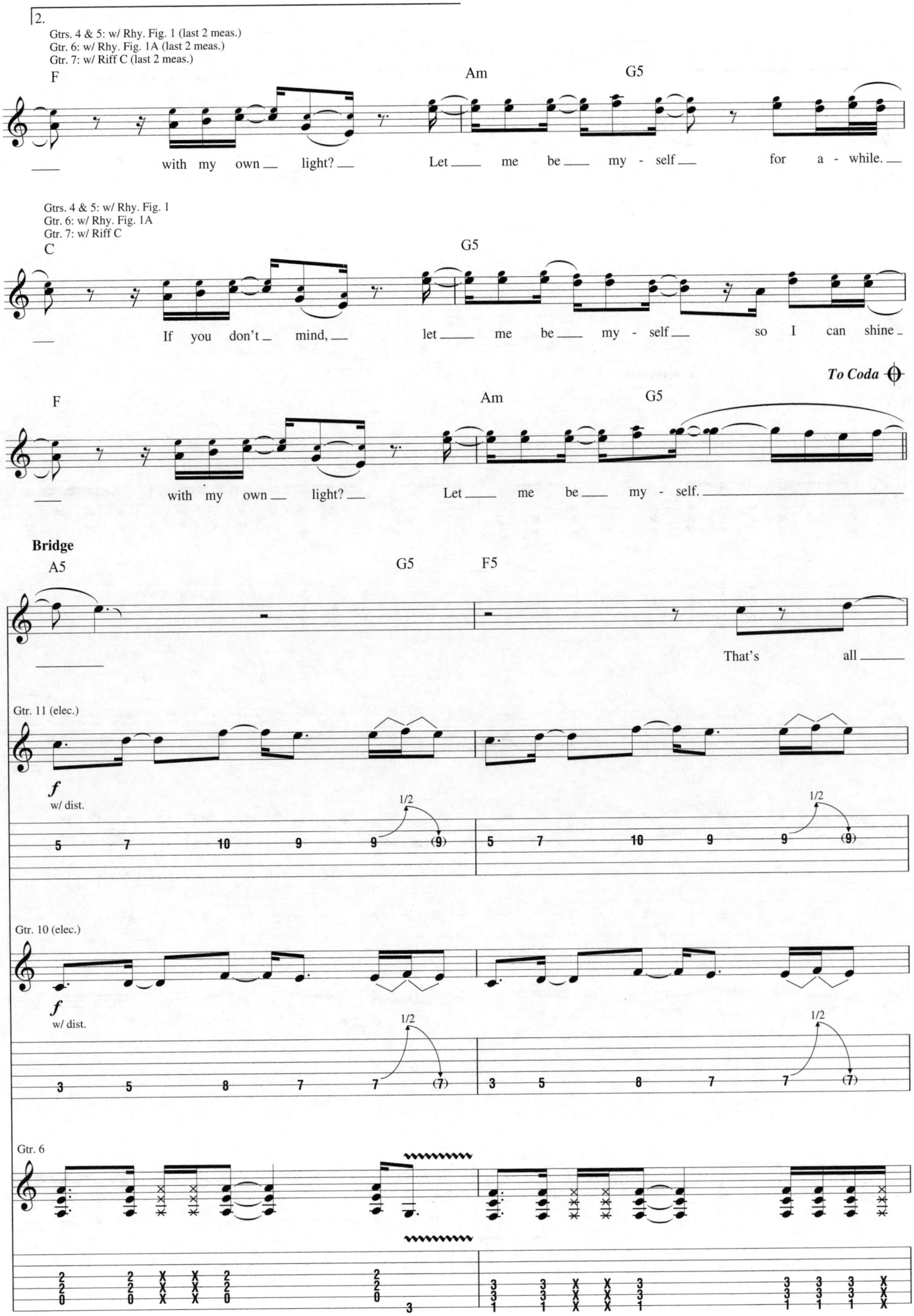
2.
Gtrs. 4 & 5: w/ Rhy. Fig. 1 (last 2 meas.)
Gtr. 6: w/ Rhy. Fig. 1A (last 2 meas.)
Gtr. 7: w/ Riff C (last 2 meas.)
F
Am
G5
with my own light? Let me be my - self for a - while.
Gtrs. 4 & 5: w/ Rhy. Fig. 1
Gtr. 6: w/ Rhy. Fig. 1A
Gtr. 7: w/ Riff C
C
G5
If you don't mind, let me be my - self so I can shine
To Coda
F
Am
G5
with my own light? Let me be my - self.
Bridge
A5
G5
F5
That's all
Gtr. 11 (elec.)
f
w/ dist.
1/2
Gtr. 10 (elec.)
f
w/ dist.
1/2
Gtr. 6

G5
C5
G/B
I've ever want-ed from this world,
A5
G5
F5
is to let me be me.
1/2

G5
P.M.
Chorus
Gtrs. 6, 10 & 11 tacet
C
G
Please, would you one time let me be my-self so I can shine
Gtrs. 1 & 4
D.S. al Coda
(take 2nd ending)
F
C
G
with my own light? Let me be my-self,
(Gtr. 4, cont. in slashes)

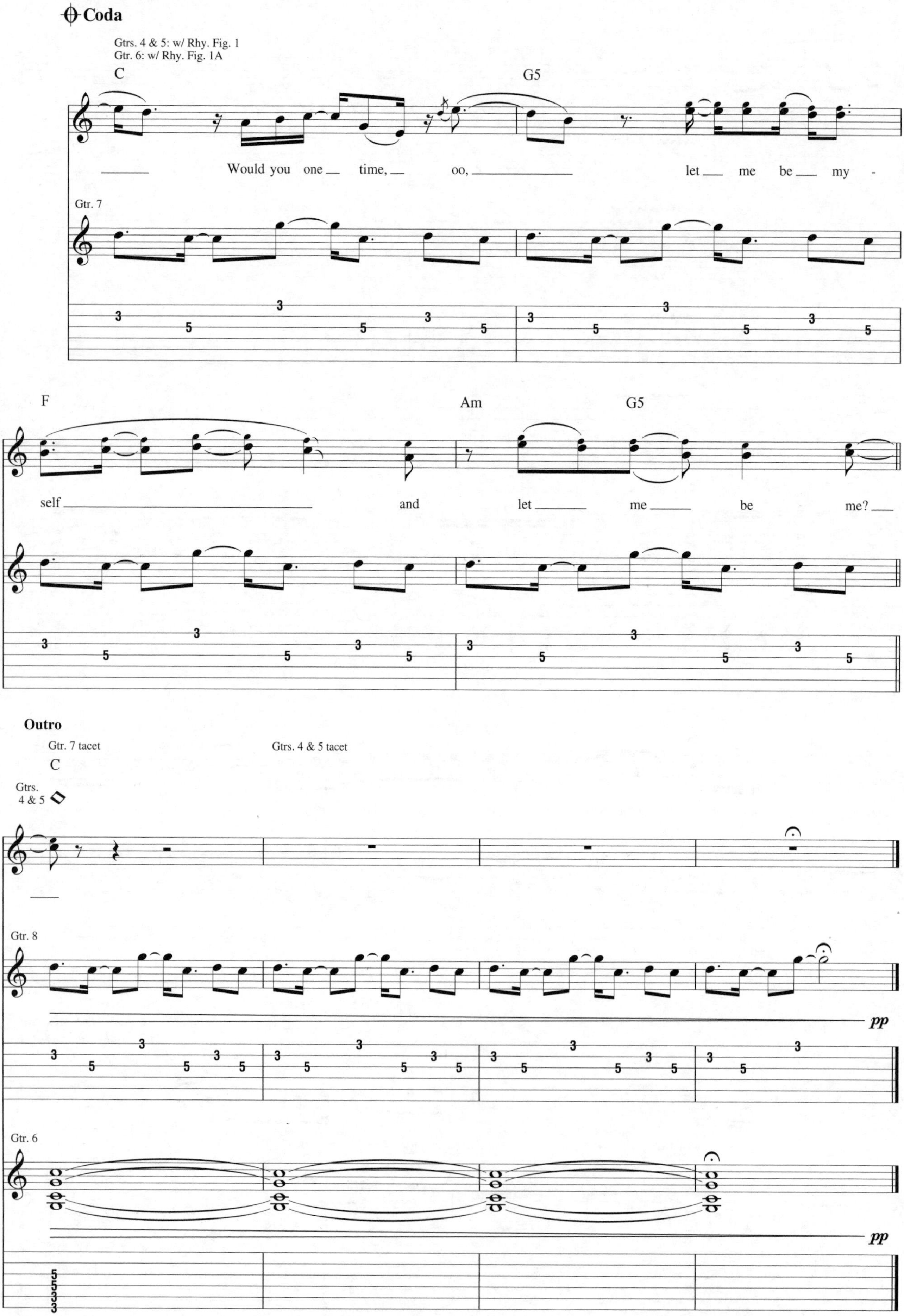
Coda
Gtrs. 4 & 5: w/ Rhy. Fig. 1
Gtr. 6: w/ Rhy. Fig. 1A
C
G5
Would you one time, oo, let me be my-
Gtr. 7
F
Am
G5
self and let me be me?
Outro
Gtr. 7 tacet
Gtrs. 4 & 5 tacet
Gtrs. 4 & 5
Gtr. 8
pp
Gtr. 6
pp

Lips of an Angel

Words and Music by Austin Winkler, Ross Hanson, Lloyd Garvey, Mark King, Michael Rodden and Brian Howes

Pre-Chorus
Gtr. 2 tacet
E
Bsus4
C#m7
Asus2
Rhy. Fig. 2
Gtr. 1
my girl's in the next room. Some - times I wish she was you.
Rhy. Fig. 2A
Gtr. 3 (elec.)
mf
w/ slight dist.
End Rhy. Fig. 2
I guess we never really moved on. It's real - ly good to
End Rhy. Fig. 2A
(cont. in slashes)
Chorus
2nd time, Gtr. 5 w/ Fill 1
Dsus2
*Gtrs. 1 & 3
hear your voice say - in' my name. It sounds so sweet com - in' from the
Gtr. 4 (elec.)
f
w/ dist.
*Composite arrangement
Fill 1
Gtr. 5
let ring

E Bsus4 Dsus2 Asus2
Rhy. Fig. 3
End Rhy. Fig. 3
(Gtr. 3, cont. in notation)
lips of an an - gel. Hear - in' those words, it makes me weak. And
Rhy. Fig. 3A
End Rhy. Fig. 3A
P.M.
To Coda
C#m7 Bsus4
Rhy. Fig. 4
End Rhy. Fig. 4
Gtr. 1
I nev - er wan - na say good - bye. But, girl, you make it
Rhy. Fig. 4A
End Rhy. Fig. 4A
**Gtrs. 3 & 4
**Composite arrangement
F#5 E/G# Asus2
Rhy. Fig. 5
End Rhy. Fig. 5
(cont. in notation)
hard to be faith - ful with the lips of an
Rhy. Fig. 5A
End Rhy. Fig. 5A

Interlude
Gtr. 4 tacet
C♯m7
Bsus4
Asus2
an - gel.
Gtr. 5 (elec.)
mf
w/ dist.
let ring
Gtr. 1
Gtr. 3
P.M.
Verse
Bsus4
C♯m7
Asus2
E
2. It's fun - ny that you're call - in' me to - night,

Bsus4
C♯m7
Asus2
E
and, yes, I've dreamt of you too.
let ring
Bsus4
C♯m7
Asus2
E
And does he know you're talk - in' to me, will it start a fight?
let ring

Pre-Chorus
Gtrs. 1 & 3: w/ Rhy. Figs. 2 & 2A
Bsus4
C♯m7
Asus2
E
Bsus4
No, I don't think she has a clue.
Well, my girl's in the next room.
let ring
D.S. al Coda
C♯m7
Asus2
E
Bsus4
C♯m7
Asus2
Some-times I wish she was you.
I guess we nev-er real-ly moved on.
It's real-ly good to
Gtr. 5
Coda
F♯5
E/G♯
Asus2
Rhy. Fig. 6
End Rhy. Fig. 6
hard to be faith - ful with the lips of an
Rhy. Fig. 6A
End Rhy. Fig. 6A
(Gtr. 3, cont. in slashes)

Guitar Solo

*Composite arrangement

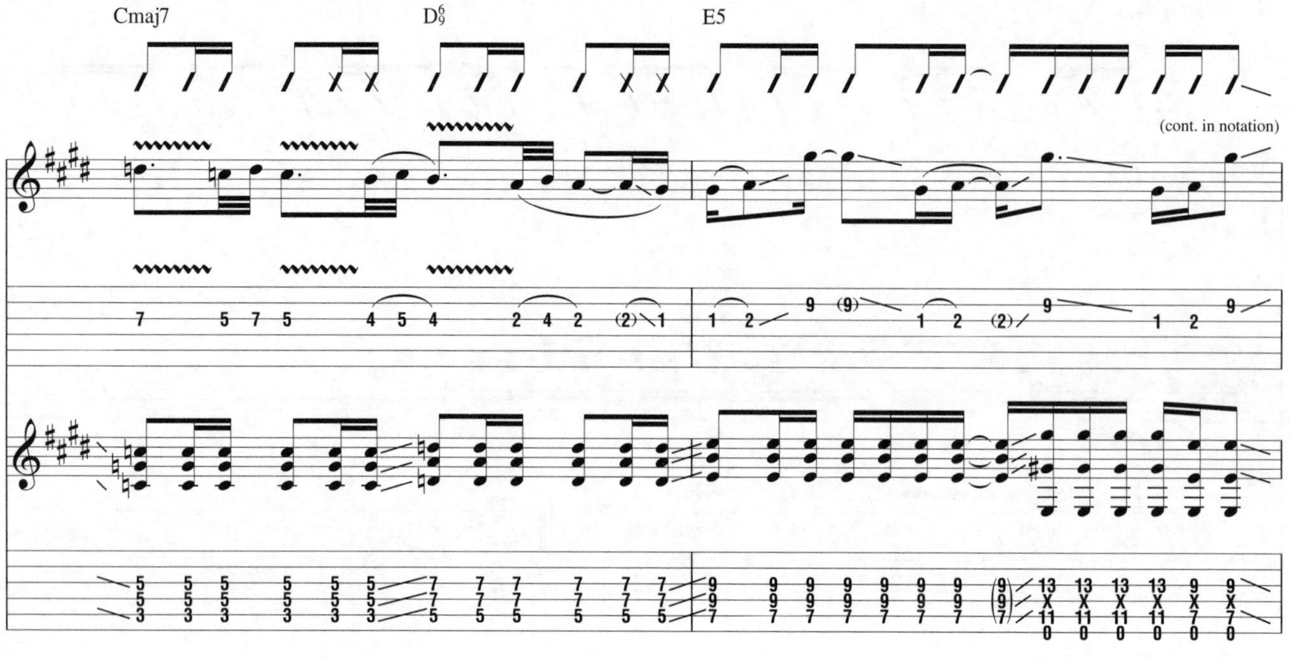
Cmaj7
D6/9
E5
(cont. in notation)

Cmaj7
D6/9
B5
Bsus4
It's real - ly good to
Gtr. 6
8va
loco
grad. bend
Gtrs. 1 & 3
*P.M.
(Gtr. 1, cont. in slashes)
*Gradually lift P.M.
Gtr. 4
**P.M.
**Gradually lift P.M.

Chorus

Gtr. 6 tacet
E5
Bsus4
Dsus2
Asus2
Gtr. 1
hear your voice say - in' my name. It sounds so sweet com - in' from the
Gtr. 6
Gtr. 4
fdbk.
Pitch: C♯
Gtr. 3
*mp
let ring
**mf
*1/2 vol.
**Full vol.
Gtrs. 1 & 3: w/ Rhy. Fig. 3
Gtr. 4: w/ Rhy. Fig 3A
E
Bsus4
Dsus2
Asus2
lips of an an - gel. Hear - in' those words, it makes me weak. And
Gtr 1: w/ Rhy. Fig. 4
Gtrs. 3 & 4: w/ Rhy. Fig. 4A
C♯m7
Bsus4
I nev - er wan - na say good - bye. But, girl, you make it

Gtr. 1: w/ Rhy. Fig. 6
Gtrs. 3 & 4: w/ Rhy. Fig. 6A
F♯5
E/G♯
Asus2
hard to be faith - ful with the lips of an an -
Gtr. 5
Gtr. 1: w/ Rhy. Fig. 4
Gtrs. 3 & 4: w/ Rhy. Fig. 4A
C♯m7
Bsus4
gel.
I never wan - na say good - bye. But, girl, you make it
Gtr. 1: w/ Rhy. Fig. 5
Gtrs. 3 & 4: w/ Rhy. Fig. 5A
F♯5
E/G♯
Asus2
hard to be faith - ful with the lips of an
let ring

Outro
Gtr. 5 tacet
C#m7
Bsus4
Asus2
an - gel.
Gtr. 1
Gtr. 3
mp
w/ clean tone
w/ fingers
let ring
Harm.
Bsus4
C#m7
Asus2
E
rit.
Hon-ey, why you call - in' me so late?

Lit Up

Words and Music by Joshua Todd Gruber, Keith Edward Nelson, Jonathan Brightman and Devon Glenn

Gtrs. 1 & 2: w/ Rhy. Figs. 1 & 1A
C G C G C F/C C F/C C F/C C G
Come on, yeah!
1. I'm on a
Gtr. 3 (dist.)
fdbk.
*vol. swell
Verse
Gtrs. 1 & 2: w/ Rhy. Figs. 1 & 1A, 2 times
Gtr. 3 tacet
C G C G C F/C C F/C C F/C C G
plane with co-caine and, yes, I'm all lit up a-gain. Cup of
train and right on, you know the train is stay-in' off the track. I'm in touch,
C G C G C F/C C F/C C F/C C G
love and touch-in'. Your ma-ma said pack-in' lines a sin.
love, from this crutch. When you're in tempt of mon-ey I'm on e-lev-en.
And, yes, I'm
Chorus
Gtr. 2: w/ Rhy. Fill 1, 3rd time
E♭ B♭ F C
Gtr. 2
all lit up a-gain, on the couch, in my bed.
Gtr. 1
w/ slide
Rhy. Fill 1
Gtr. 2

Csus4 C Eb Bb G5
(cont. in notation)
And, yes, I'm all lit up a - gain, fly - in'.
steady gliss.
To Coda
C G C G C G F C G Bb G Bb G
I love the co-caine, I love the co-caine. Ma - ma, can you wait? Ma - ma, can you wait? Go 'head!
Gtr. 1
Rhy. Fig. 2
End Rhy. Fig. 2
w/o slide
w/o slide
Gtr. 2
Rhy. Fig. 2A
End Rhy. Fig. 2A
1.
Interlude
Gtrs. 1 & 2: w/ Rhy. Figs. 1 & 1A
C G C G C F/C C F/C C F/C C G
2. I'm on a
Gtr. 3 (dist.)
f
full
full
full
1/4

2.
Gtrs. 1 & 2: w/ Rhy. Figs. 2 & 2A
C G C G C G F C G B♭ G B♭ G
I love the co-caine, I love the co-caine. Ma - ma, can you wait? Oh, can you wait long?
Guitar Solo
G5 F5 C Csus4 C B♭ B♭sus4 B♭ G5
Gtr. 2
Gtr. 3
hold bend
1/2
full
Gtr. 1
w/o slide
F5 C Csus4 C B♭ B♭sus4 B♭ G5
full
full
full

Bridge
Gtrs. 1, 2 & 3 tacet
N.C.(F)
(C)
(B♭)
You cracked the door for the cu - ri - ous girl 'cause she's wait - in', she's been wait - in'.
(G)
(F)
(C)
(B♭)
I chop a line for the fiend-in' man 'cause he wants one.
You know, you know you got to.
Can you feel it? Can you feel it to - night? Are you a - lone? Tell me, are you fuck-in' high?
Gtr. 1
D.S. al Coda
G5
F5
C5
B♭5
Gtr. 2
In a mo-ment you just so right. You're right, love. Are you right, love? are And, yes, I'm
w/ slide

Coda
Gtrs. 1 & 2: w/ Rhy. Figs. 2 & 2A
C G C G
C G
F
C
G B♭ G B♭ G
I love the co-caine, I love the co-caine. Ma - ma, can you wait? Oh, can you wait long?
Gtr. 3
Outro - Guitar Solo
Gtrs. 1 & 2: w/ Rhy. Figs. 1 & 1A, 3 times
C G C G C F/C C F/C C F/C C G
Oh, yeah!
1/2
full
C G C G C F/C C F/C C F/C C G
Don't wan-na fight you.
full
full
C G C G C F/C C F/C C F/C C G
Al-right, yeah!
Uh.

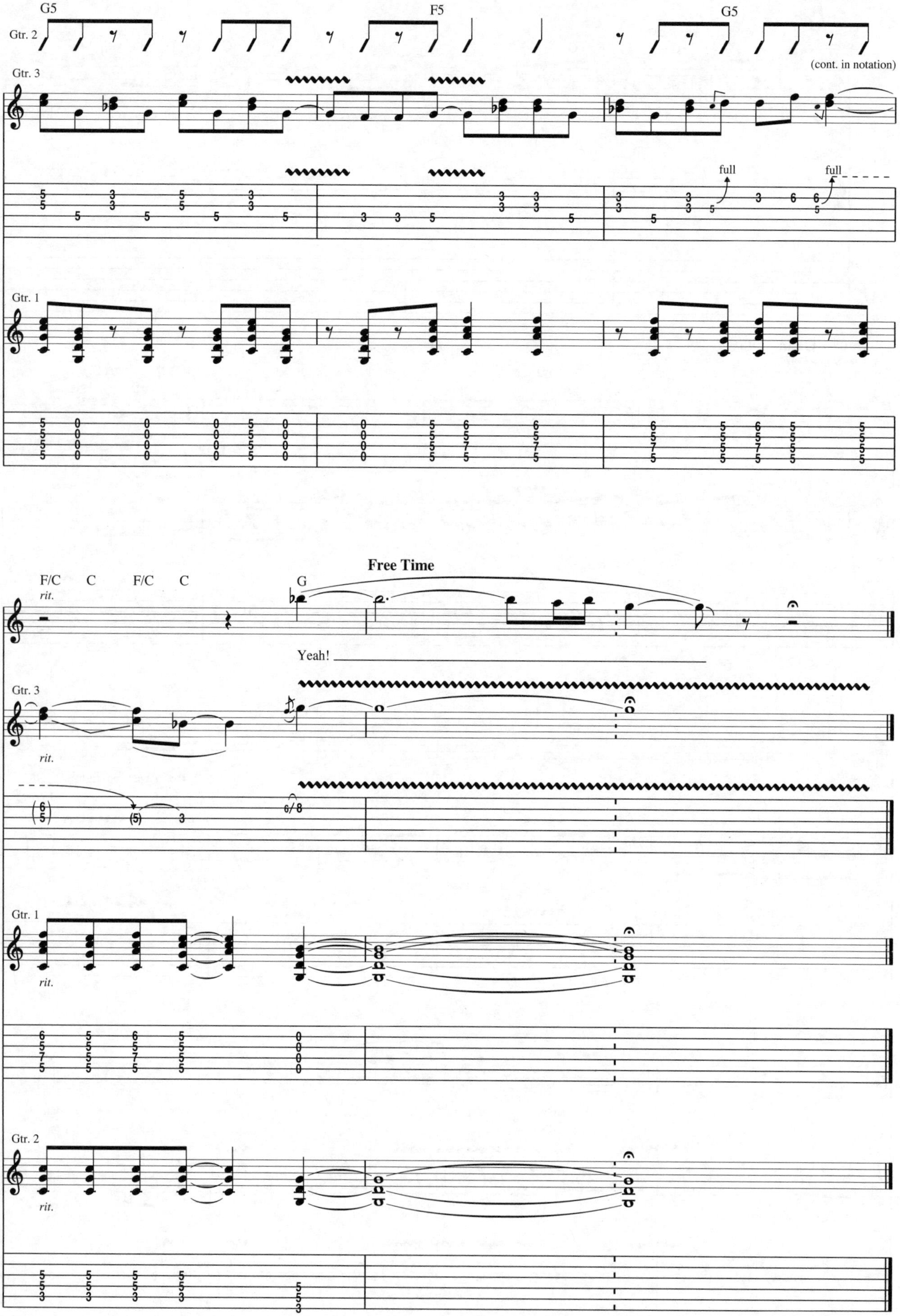
G5
F5
G5
Gtr. 2
(cont. in notation)
Gtr. 3
full
full
Gtr. 1
Free Time
F/C
C
F/C
C
G
rit.
Yeah!
Gtr. 3
rit.
Gtr. 1
rit.
Gtr. 2
rit.

Live Forever

Words and Music by Noel Gallagher

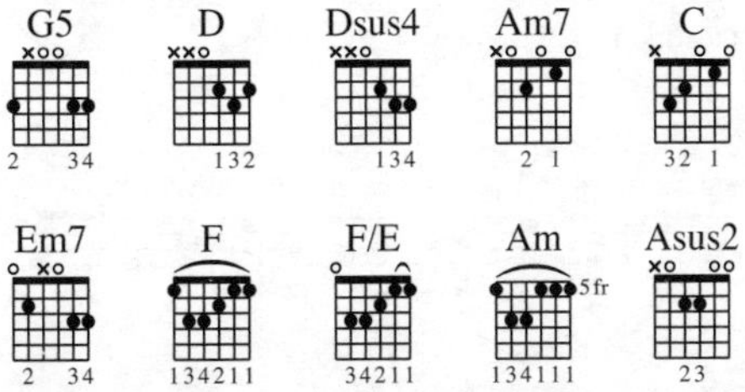

D Dsus4 D Am7 C D G5
End Rhy. Fig. 1
ev-er feel the pain in the morn - ing rain as it soaks _ you to the bone? _
(cont. in slash)
Chorus
Em7 D Dsus4 D Am7
Rhy. Fig. 2
Gtrs. 1 & 2
May-be I ___ just wan-na fly. Wan-na live, _ I don't wan-na die. May-be I ___ just wan-na
C D Em7 D Dsus4 D
breathe, may-be I ___ just don't be-lieve. _ May-be you're _ the same _ as me, ___ we see things they'll nev-er
Am7 F F/E F F/E F F/E F
End Rhy. Fig. 2
Rhy. Fill 1A
Gtr. 2
End Rhy. Fill 1A
(Gtr. 1 cont. in notation)
8va
loco
see. You and I ___ are gon-na live for-ev - er. 2. I said,
Rhy. Fill 1
Gtr. 1
End Rhy. Fill 1

Verse
Gtrs. 1 & 2: w/ Rhy. Fig. 1
G5 D Dsus4 D Am7
may - be I don't real-ly wan-na know how your gar - den grows 'cause I
Gtr. 3 (elec.)
Rhy. Fig. 3
w/ dist.
let ring
C D G5 D Dsus4 D
just wan - na fly. Late - ly, did you ev - er feel the pain in the morn -
Am7 C D G5
- ing rain as it soaks you to the bone?
End Rhy. Fig. 3
Chorus
Gtrs. 1 & 2: w/ Rhy. Fig. 2
Em7 D Dsus4 D Am7
May - be I will nev - er be all the things that I wan - na be. Now is not the time to
Rhy. Fig. 4

C D Em7 D Dsus4 D
cry, now's the time to find out why. I think you're the same as me. We see things they'll nev-er
let ring
let ring
let ring
Am7
8va
Gtr. 3 tacet
Gtrs. 1 & 2: w/ Rhy. Fills 1 & 1A
F F/E F F/E F F/E F
see. You and I are gon-na live for-ev - er.
End Rhy. Fig. 4
Gtr. 4 (elec.)
let ring
w/ dist.
Guitar Solo
Gtrs. 1 & 2: w/ Rhy. Fig. 1
G5 D Dsus4 D Am7 C D G5
full
full
D Dsus4 D Am7 C D G5
full
Gtrs. 1 & 2: w/ Rhy. Fig. 2
Gtr. 3: w/ Rhy. Fig. 4
Em7 D Dsus4 D Am7
full

C D Em7 D Dsus4 D
full full
Gtrs. 1 & 2: w/ Rhy. Fills 1 & 1A
Gtr. 3: w/ Rhy. Fill 1
Am7 F F/E F F/E F F/E F
full
full full
Verse
Gtrs. 1 & 2: w/ Rhy. Fig. 1
Gtr. 3: w/ Rhy. Fig. 3
G5 D Dsus4 D Am7 C D G5
loco
3. May - be I don't real-ly wan-na know how your gar - den grows 'cause I just wan - na fly.
pp f
Gtr. 4 tacet
D Dsus4 D Am7 C D G5
Late - ly, did you ev-er feel the pain in the morn - ing rain as it soaks you to the bone?
Chorus
Gtrs. 1 & 2: w/ Rhy. Fig. 2
Gtr. 3: w/ Rhy. Fig. 4
Em7 D Dsus4 D Am7
May - be I just wan - na fly. Wan - na live, I don't wan - na die. May - be I just wan - na
Gtr. 4

C D Em7 D Dsus4 D
breathe, may - be I just don't be - lieve. May - be you're the same as me, we see things they'll nev - er
Am7 F F/E F Am
Rhy. Fig. 5A
Gtr. 2
End Rhy. Fig. 5A
8va
see. You and I are gon - na live for - ev - er, gon - na live for - ev -
Rhy. Fig. 5
Gtr. 1
Gtr. 4
divisi
End Rhy. Fig. 5
Rhy. Fig. 5B
Gtr. 3
End Rhy. Fig. 5B
let ring
Gtrs. 2 & 3: w/ Rhy. Figs. 5A & 5B
F F/E F Am
Gtrs. 2 & 3: w/ Rhy. Figs. 5A & 5B, 3 times
F F/E F
8va
loco
- er, gon - na live for - ev - er,

Gtrs. 1, 2 & 3: w/ Rhy. Figs. 5, 5A & 5B
Am
play 3 times
F
F/E
F
Am
gon-na live for-ev - er.
Gtr. 4
full
Outro-Guitar Solo
Gtr. 1 tacet
Gtrs. 2 & 3: w/ Rhy. Figs. 5A & 5B, 7 1/2 times
Free Time
Begin Fade
Fade Out
Asus2
Gtr. 2
Gtr. 3
* 8va
w/ clean tone
*fdbk.
let ring
pitch: B

Lucky

Words and Music by Jason Mraz, Colbie Caillat and Timothy Fagan

Am
Dm7
G
*G/F
dreams. I feel your whis - per a - cross the sea. I keep you
P.M.
*Bass plays F.
E7
Am
Dm7
with me in my heart. You make it eas - i - er when
P.M.
Chorus
Half-time feel
G
G#°
Am
Dm7
life gets hard. Luck - y I'm in love with my best friend,
Rhy. Fig. 2
strum w/ fingers
let ring
let ring
G
C
Gadd4/B
Am
luck - y to have been where I have been. Luck - y to be
let ring
sim.

Dm7
Gsus4
G
coming home again.
End Rhy. Fig. 2
C
Am
Em
G
Oo,
oo.
Bridge
Dm7
Am7
G
Dm7
They don't know how long it takes, waiting for a love like this.
They don't know how long it takes, waiting for a love like this.
Am7
G
Dm7
Ev'ry time we say goodbye, I wish we had
Ev'ry time we say goodbye, I wish we had
one more kiss. I'll

Am7
G
Am7
G7/B
wait for you, I prom - ise you I will.
I'm
Gtr. 1
*Gtr. 2
mf
w/ fingers
*Kybds. arr. for gtr.
Chorus
Gtr. 1: w/ Rhy. Fig. 2 (1st 4 meas.)
Am7
Dm7
G7
C
C/B
luck - y I'm in love with my best friend,
luck - y to have been where I have been.
Rhy. Fig. 3
Gtr. 2
let ring
let ring
sim.
*2nd time, Voc. tacet on beats 1 and 2.
Am7
Dm7
Gsus4
G
N.C.
Luck - y to be com - ing home a - gain.
Gtr. 1
Gtr. 2
End Rhy. Fig. 3

1st time, Gtr. 1: w/ Rhy. Fig. 2
2nd time, Gtr. 1: w/ Rhy. Fig. 2 (1st 7 meas.)
Gtr. 2: w/ Rhy. Fig. 3
Am7 Dm7 G7 C C/B
Luck - y we're in love in ev - 'ry way, luck - y to have stayed where we have stayed.
To Coda
End half-time feel
Am7 Dm7 Gsus4 G
Luck - y to be com - ing home some - day.
2. And so I'm
Verse
Gtr. 1: w/ Rhy. Fig. 1
C Am Dm7
sail - ing through the sea to an is - land where we'll
G E7 Am
meet. You'll hear the mu - sic fill the air; I'll put a
Dm7 G C
flow - er in your hair.
Though the breez - es through the
Gtr. 1
let ring
3 2 0 1 0 3
Am Dm7 G *G/F
trees move so pret - ty, you're all I see. As the
let ring
sim.
0 2 2 3 2 0
5 7 5 6 5 5
3 5 5 4 5 3
*Bass plays F.

D.S. al Coda
E7 Am Dm7 G G#°
world keeps spin - ning 'round, you hold me right here, right now.
strum w/ fingers
Coda
Outro
G C Am
Oo,
Gtr. 1
Em G C
oo.
Oo,
Am Em G C
oo.
Oo.
w/ thumb

Megalomaniac

Words and Music by Brandon Boyd, Michael Einziger, Jose Pasillas II, Chris Kilmore and Ben Kenney

G
Gm
E♭
C7
G
Gm
Oh,
let ring
E♭
C7
G
Gm
E♭
C7
G
Gm
oo,
let ring
E♭
C7
G5
B♭5
E♭5
C7
ah,
ah.
Gtr. 2 (dist.)
Rhy. Fig. 1
*Gtrs. 1 & 2
f
*Composite arrangement
Gtr. 1
(cont. on higher staff)

G5 B♭5 E♭5 C7 G5 B♭5
Gtrs. 1 & 2
E♭5 C7 G5 B♭5 E♭5 C7
End Rhy. Fig. 1
Verse
Gtr. 2 tacet
Gm7
Csus2/4
1. I hear you on the ra - di - o.
Gtr. 1
let ring
E♭add2
* G7/F
You per - me - ate my screen.
Riff A
*Bass plays F.

E♭add2
Csus
G7
It's un - kind but, if I
End Riff A
Riff B
*
let ring
*w/ pick & finger
Csus
E♭add2
met you in a scis - sor fight
End Riff B
G7/F
G7sus4
G7
E♭add2
I'd cut off both your wings on
1/2
Csus
G5
Gm
E♭
C7/E
prin - ci - ple a - lone. On prin - ci - ple a - lone.
(Prin - ci - ple a - lone.)
Riff C

Chorus
Gtrs. 1 & 2: w/ Rhy. Fig. 1
G5 Gm E♭ B♭ G5 B♭5
⑥ 11fr ⑥ 6fr
Gtr. 2
Yeah, meg - a - lo - ma -
Gtr. 1
End Riff C
let ring
E♭5 C7 G5 B♭5 E♭5 C7
- ni - ac, you're no Je - sus, yeah, you're no fuck - ing El - vis.
G5 B♭5 E♭5 C7 G5 B♭5 E♭5 C7
Wash your hands clean of your - self, ba - by, and step down, step down, step down.
Interlude
Gm7 E♭add2 Csus2/4
Oo.
Gtr. 1
let ring
let ring
let ring
*w/ pick & finger
Gtr. 3 (slight dist.)
mf
let ring

Verse
Gtr. 1: w/ Riff B
Gtr. 3 tacet
G7
Csus2/4
E♭add2
2. If I were your ap - pend - ag - es
Gtr. 1: w/ Riff A
G7/F
E♭add2
Csus2/4
I'd hold o - pen your eyes so you would see
G7
Csus2/4
E♭add2
that all of us are Heav - en sent,
(And there was nev - er meant to be on - ly one.)
Gtr. 1
let ring
*w/ pick & finger
Gtr. 3
let ring
Gtr. 3 tacet
G7/F
G7sus4
G7
E♭add2
Csus2/4
and there was nev - er meant to be on - ly one,
(Be on - ly one.)
Gtr. 1
let ring
1/2

Gtr. 1: w/ Riff C
G5 Gm E♭ C7/E G5 Gm E♭5 C7
to be the on - ly one. Hey,
Gtr. 2
6
Chorus
Gtrs. 1 & 2: w/ Rhy. Fig. 1 (2 times)
2nd time, Gtrs. 1 & 2: w/ Rhy. Fig. 1 (1 7/8 times)
G5 B♭5 E♭5 C7 G5 B♭5 E♭5 C7
meg - a - lo - ma - ni - ac, you're no Je - sus, yeah, you're no fuck - ing El - vis.
G5 B♭5 E♭5 C7 G5 B♭5 E♭5 C7
Wash your hands clean of your - self, ba - by, and step down, step down, step down.
Gtr. 4 (dist.)
f
w/ step flanger
15 0
Gtr. 4: w/ Rhy. Fig. 1
2nd time, Gtr. 4: w/ Rhy. Fig. 1 (1st 7 meas.)
G5 B♭5 E♭5 C7 G5 B♭5 E♭5 C7
Step down! Step down!
To Coda
Interlude
G5 B♭5 E♭5 C7 G5 B♭5 E♭5 C7 D5 F5
Whoa, step down! Oo,
Gtr. 2
17 8 5

Gtr. 2 tacet
D5 F5 A5
oo, do, do, do, do, do.
D5 F5 D5 F5 C
Yeah.
Dm7 F6 Dm11 F6/9 Am11
You're,
Gtr. 1
w/ clean tone
let ring
Dm7 F6 Dm11 F6/9
you're, you're,
let ring
Bridge
Dm11 Fsus2 Dm11 Fsus2 Am7
you're no Je - sus, you're no
Rhy. Fig. 2
End Rhy. Fig. 2
w/ dist.

Dm11 Fsus2 Dm11 Fsus2 Am7
El - vis, you're no Je - sus. You're no
Gtrs. 1 & 4: w/ Rhy. Fig. 2 (2 times)
Dm11 *C/E Fsus2 Dm11 C/E Fsus2
Je - sus, you're no El - vis, you're no
*Bass plays E
Dm11 C/E Fsus2 Dm11 C/E Fsus2
an - swer, oo.
D.S. al Coda
G5 Gm E♭ C5 G5 Gm E♭ C5
Whispered: Step down, step down, step down, step down, hey, hey, hey.
Gtr. 1
** mf
P.M.
f
1/4 1/4
**1/4 dist.
†Increase to full dist.
Coda
Outro
Free time
Gtr. 4 tacet
E♭5
C7/G
Gtr. 4
Step down.
Gtrs. 1 & 2
let ring
1/2 1/2 1/2

No Surprise

Words and Music by Chris Daughtry, Rune Westberg, Chad Kroeger and Eric Dill

**See top of page for chord diagrams pertaining to rhythm slashes.

***Doubled throughout

C♯m
Asus2
And as I say it loud - er, I love how it sounds. 'Cause I'm not tak - in' the eas - y way out.
End Riff A
let ring
F♯
Asus2
End Rhy. Fig. 2
Not wrap - ping this in rib - bons. Should - n't have to give a rea - son why. It's no sur-
Gtr. 4 (dist.)
Riff B
End Riff B
mf
let ring
w/ amp tremolo
Gtr. 2
Rhy. Fig. 3
End Rhy. Fig. 3

Chorus
Gtr. 3 tacet
E5
B5
prise I won't be here to-mor - row. I can't be - lieve that I stayed till to - day. Yeah, you and
Gtr. 4
Riff C
End Riff C
tremolo off
Gtr. 2
Rhy. Fig. 4
C#5
A5
B5
I will be a tough act to fol - low, but I know in time we'll find this was no sur - prise.
(Heh, na,
1/2
End Rhy. Fig. 4

E5
Gtr. 4 tacet
Gtr. 3
E
ho.)
Gtr. 4
Gtr. 5
mf
Gtr. 5 (elec.)
divisi
w/ slight dist.
let ring
Verse
Gtr. 2: w/ Riff A
Gtr. 3: w/ Rhy. Fig. 2
E
Badd4
2. It came out like a riv - er once I let it out, when I thought that I would-n't know how.
Gtr. 5
let ring
let ring
C♯m
Asus2
Held on to it for - ev - er, just push-ing it down. Felt so good to let go of it now.
let ring
let ring

Gtr. 2: w/ Rhy. Fig. 3
Gtr. 4: w/ Riff B
F#add2
Asus2
Not wrap-ping this in rib - bons. Should-n't have to give a rea - son why.
It's no sur-
Chorus
Gtr. 2: w/ Rhy. Fig. 4 (3 times)
Gtr. 4: w/ Riff C
Gtr. 5 tacet
E5
B5
prise I won't be here to-mor - row.
I can't be - lieve that I stayed till to - day.
There's noth-ing
C#5
A5
B5
here in this heart left to bor - row,
there's noth-ing here in this soul left to say.
Don't be sur-
Gtr. 4
1/2
E5
B5
prised when we hate this to-mor - row.
God knows we tried to find an ea - si - er way.
Yeah, you and
C#5
A5
B5
I will be a tough act to fol - low,
but I know in time we'll find this was no sur - prise.
Our fav -
1/2

Bridge
E
Bsus4
Rhy. Fig. 5
Gtr. 3
- 'rite place we used to go, the warm em-brace that no one knows. The lov-
Gtr. 4
1/2
Gtr. 6 (elec.)
mf
w/ dist.
C#m
Asus2
Bsus4
End Rhy. Fig. 5
(cont. in notation)
- ing look that's left your eyes. That's why this comes as no, as no sur-prise.

Verse
E
E5
3. If I could see the fu - ture and how this plays out,
(Heh, na, ho. Heh, na,
Gtr. 4
Gtr. 3
divisi
mf
*Gtr. 4 to left of slash in tab
Gtr. 6
dim.
Gtr. 2
dim.
Gtrs. 2, 4 & 6 tacet
Bsus4
C♯m
I bet it's bet - ter than where we are now. But af - ter go - ing
ho. Heh, na, ho.)
Gtr. 3
Asus2
through this, it's ea - si - er to see the rea - son why. It's no sur -

Chorus
Gtr. 2: w/ Rhy. Fig. 4 (3 times)
Gtr. 3 tacet
Gtr. 4: w/ Riff C
E5
B5
prise I won't be here to-mor - row. I can't be - lieve that I stayed till to - day. Yeah, you and
(Stayed till to - day.)
C♯5
A5
B5
I will be a tough act to fol - low, but I know in time we'll find this was no sur - prise.
The kiss
Gtr. 4
1/2
1/2
Gtr. 3: w/ Rhy. Fig. 5 (2 times)
E
Bsus4
good-night, it comes with me. Both wrong and right, our mem - o - ries. The whis -
(Our mem - o - ries.

C#m
Asus2
Bsus4
- per- ing ___ be - fore ___ we sleep, just one ___ more thing _ that you ___ can't keep. Our fav -
You _ can't keep.
1/2
E
Bsus4
- 'rite place ___ we used ___ to go, the warm ___ em - brace ___ that no ___ one knows. _ The lov -
In time this was no sur - prise.) _
C#m
Asus2
Bsus4
- ing look ___ that's left ___ your eyes, _ but I know in time _ we'll find this was no sur - prise. _
(Heh, na,
1/2

Outro
Gtr. 4 tacet
E5
(Heh, na, ho. Heh, na,
ho. Heh, na, ho.)
Gtr. 4
dim.
12
Gtr. 2
dim.
2
0
ho. Heh, na, ho.
Gtr. 2
fdbk.
(2)
(0)
(2)
(0)
N.C.
Heh, na, ho.
(2)
(0)

Real World

Written by Rob Thomas

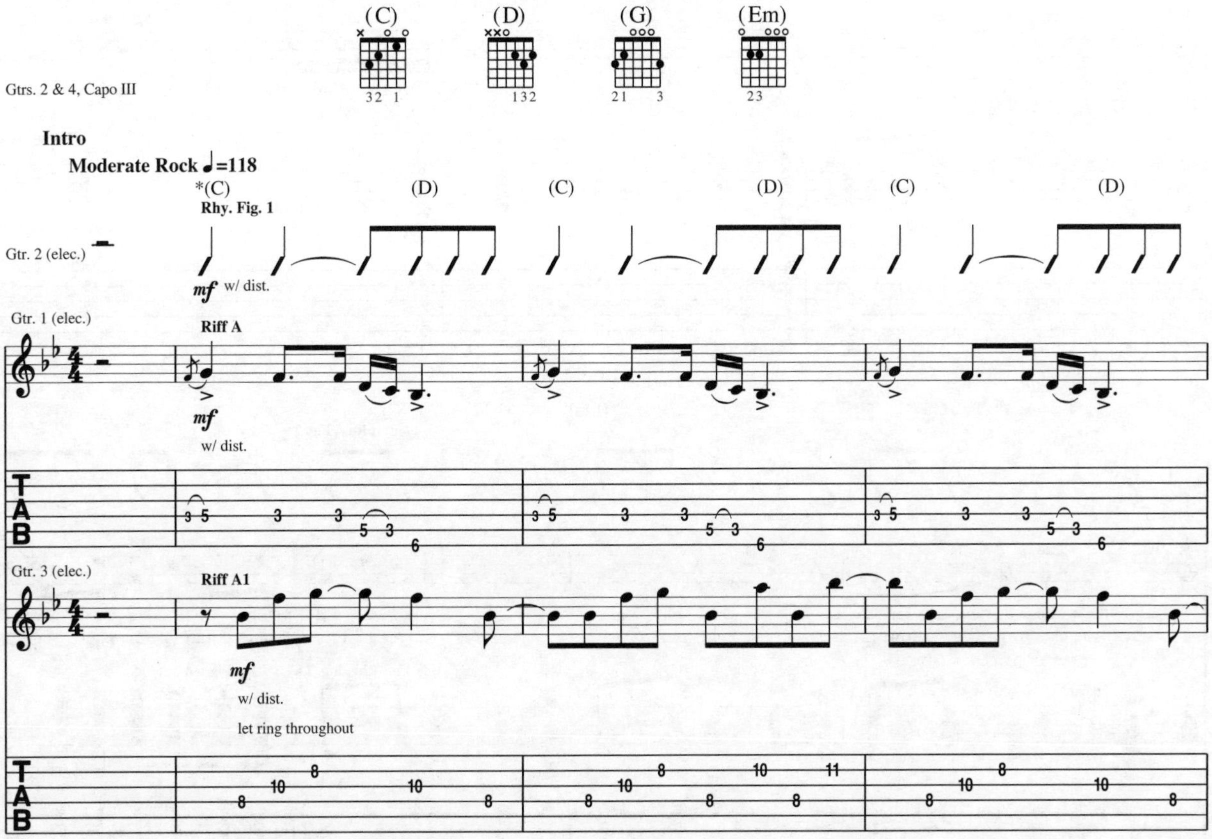

*Symbols in parentheses represent chord names respective to capoed guitar and do not reflect actual sounding chord.

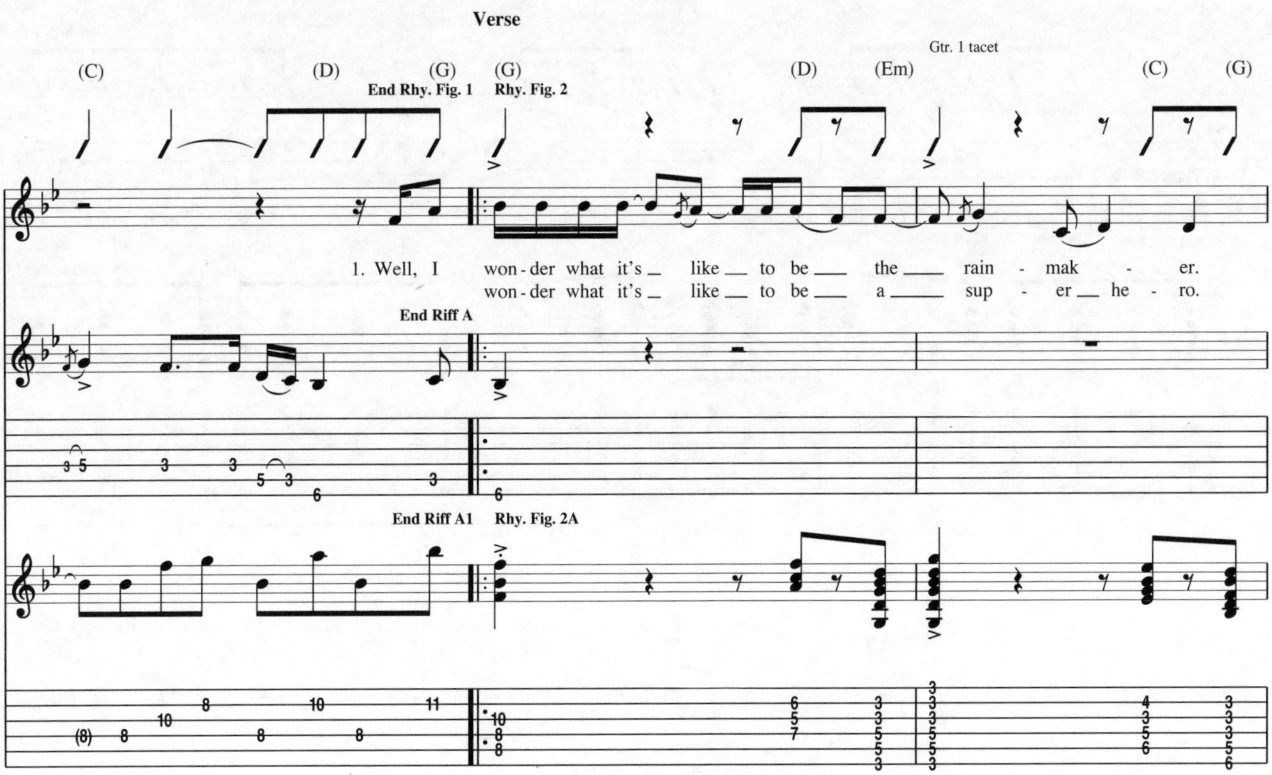

*Symbols in parentheses represent chord names respective to capoed guitar.
Symbols above reflect actual sounding chord.

2.
Chorus
Gtr. 1 tacet
(C) (D) (C) (G) (C) (D)
Rhy. Fill 1
End Rhy. Fill 1
Rhy. Fig. 4
Gtr. 2
yeah, yeah. Straight up, what did you
(Yeah.)
Gtr. 3
Gtr. 2: w/ Rhy. Fig. 4, 3 times, simile
(C) B♭ (G) E♭ (C) F (D) E♭ (C)
End Rhy. Fig. 4
hope to learn a-bout here? If I were some-one else would this all fall a-part?
Riff B
End Riff B
Gtr. 3: w/ Riff B, 2 times, simile
B♭ (G) E♭ (C) F (D) E♭ (C) B♭ (G) E♭ (C) F (D)
Strange, where were you when we start-ed this gig? I wish the real world
Gtrs. 1 & 3: w/ Riffs A & A1
Gtr. 2: w/ Rhy. Fig. 1
E♭ (C) F (D) E♭ (C) F (D) E♭ (C) F (D) E♭ (C) F (D) B♭ (G)
would just stop has-sl-in' me and you, to you, yeah, me.
Interlude
Gtrs. 2 & 3: w/ Rhy. Figs. 3 & 3A, simile
B♭ (G) F (D) Gm (Em) E♭ (C) B♭ (G) F (D) Gm (Em)
Gtr. 1
mp
f

Verse
Gtrs. 2 & 3: w/ Rhy. Figs. 2 & 2A, simile
*Gtr. 4: w/ Rhy.Fig. 3, 3 times, simile
Gtr. 1 tacet
Eb (C) Bb (G) F (D) Gm (Em) Eb (C) Bb (G) F (D) Gm (Em)
3. Well, I won-der what it's like to be the head hon-cho.
*Gtr. 4 is an acous. played mf.
I won-der what I'd do if they all did just what I said.
(Just what I said.)
Gtrs. 2 & 3: w/ Rhy. Figs. 3 & 3A, simile
Well, I'd shout out an ord-er, I think we're out of this, man, get me some.
Gtrs. 1 & 3: w/ Riffs A & A1
Gtrs. 2 & 4: w/ Rhy. Fig. 1, 1st. 3 meas., simile
Boy, don't make me wan-na change my tone, my tone, yeah,
(Yeah.
Chorus
Gtr. 2: w/ Rhy. Fig. 4, 4 times, simile
Gtr. 3: w/ Riff B, 4 times, simile
Gtrs. 1 & 4 tacet
Gtrs. 2 & 4: w/ Rhy. Fill 1, simile
yeah. Straight up, what did you hope to learn a-bout here?
)
If I were some-one else would this all fall a-part? Strange, where were you
when we start-ed this gig? I wish the real world would just stop has-sl-in' me.

Bridge
(Em)
(G)
(Em)
(G)
Gtr. 2
Please, don't change, please, don't break. Well, the on - ly thing
Gtr. 3
(Em)
(G)
that seems to work at all is you. Please, don't change at all from me,
Gtrs. 1 & 3: w/ Riffs A & A1
Gtr. 2: w/ Rhy. Fig. 1, 1st. 3 meas.
Gtr. 2: w/ Rhy. Fill 1, simile
E♭ (C)
F (D)
E♭ (C)
F (D)
E♭ (C)
F (D)
E♭ (C)
to you, and you to me, yeah, yeah.

Guitar Solo

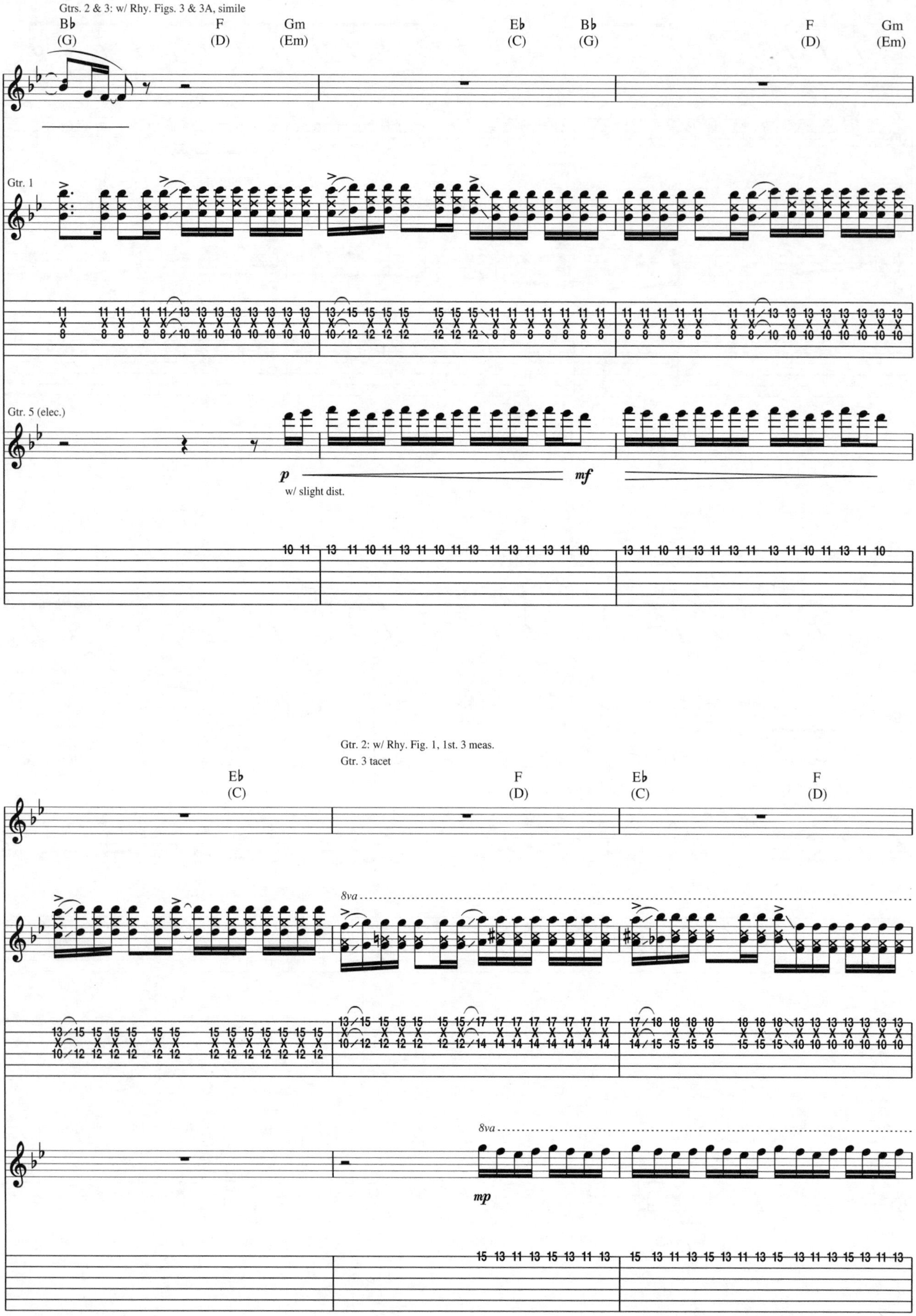
Gtrs. 2 & 3: w/ Rhy. Figs. 3 & 3A, simile
B♭ (G)
F (D)
Gm (Em)
E♭ (C)
B♭ (G)
F (D)
Gm (Em)
Gtr. 1
Gtr. 5 (elec.)
p
mf
w/ slight dist.
Gtr. 2: w/ Rhy. Fig. 1, 1st. 3 meas.
Gtr. 3 tacet
E♭ (C)
F (D)
E♭ (C)
F (D)
8va
8va
mp

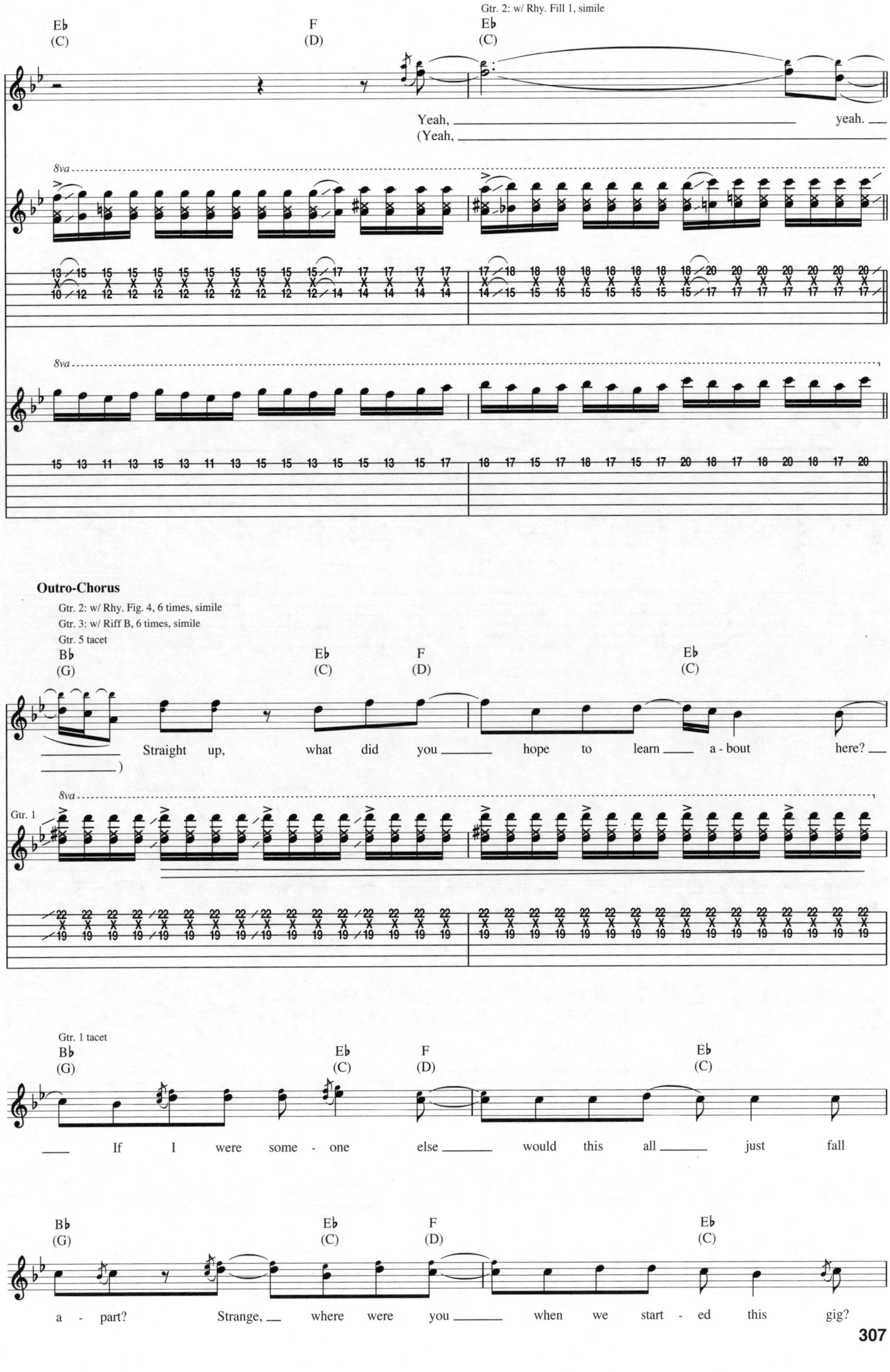
Gtr. 2: w/ Rhy. Fill 1, simile
E♭ (C)
F (D)
E♭ (C)
Yeah, ___ yeah. ___
(Yeah, ___
8va
Outro-Chorus
Gtr. 2: w/ Rhy. Fig. 4, 6 times, simile
Gtr. 3: w/ Riff B, 6 times, simile
Gtr. 5 tacet
B♭ (G)
E♭ (C)
F (D)
E♭ (C)
___ Straight up, what did you ___ hope to learn ___ a - bout here? ___
___)
Gtr. 1
Gtr. 1 tacet
B♭ (G)
E♭ (C)
F (D)
E♭ (C)
___ If I were some - one else ___ would this all ___ just fall
B♭ (G)
E♭ (C)
F (D)
E♭ (C)
a - part? Strange, ___ where were you ___ when we start - ed this gig?

B♭ (G) E♭ (C) F (D) E♭ (C) B♭ (G) E♭ (C) F (D)
I wish the real world would just stop has - sl - in' me. I wish the real world
Gtr. 1
E♭ (C) B♭ (G) E♭ (C) F (D) E♭ (C)
would just stop has - sl - in' me. I wish the real world would just stop has - sl - in'
(The real
Gtrs. 1 & 3: w/ Riffs A & A1, 1st 2 meas.
Gtr. 2: w/ Rhy. Fig. 1, 1st 2 meas.
F (D) E♭ (C) F (D) (C) (D) (C)
Gtr. 2
me, and you, and me.
world, the real world, the real world,)
Gtr. 1
Gtr. 3

Rollin'
(Air Raid Vehicle)

Words and Music by Fred Durst, Wesley Borland, Sam Rivers, John Otto, Leore Dimant and Kaseem Dean

Drop D tuning, down 1 1/2 steps:
(low to high) B-F♯-B-E-G♯-C♯

B5 A5 G5 F#5 E5 G5 E5
roll - in', roll - in', roll - in', roll - in'. Keep roll - in', roll - in', roll - in', roll - in'. Keep
(What? Come on.
To Coda
B5 A5 G5 F#5 E5 G5 E5
roll - in', roll - in', roll - in', roll - in'. Keep roll - in', roll - in', roll - in', roll - in'. 1. Now, I
Yeah.)
* Verse
2nd time, Gtr. 1 tacet (next 8 meas.)
3rd time, Gtr. 1: w/ Rhy. Fig. 2 (4 times)
N.C.
know y'all be lov - in' this right here. L. I. M. P. Biz - kit is right here.
2.,3. See additional lyrics
Gtr. 1
P.M.
*2nd & 3rd Verses w/ Bkgd. Voc. ad lib.
Peo - ple in the house put your hands in the air, cuz if you don't care, then we don't care.
Riff A
End Riff A
P.M.
1st time, Gtr. 1: w/ Riff A (2 times)
One, two, three times two to the six. Jolts in for your fix with the Limp Biz - kit mix. So
1.,2.
where the fuck you at? Punk, shut the fuck up. And back the fuck up be - fore we fuck this track up.
Rhy. Fig. 2
Gtr. 1
P.M.

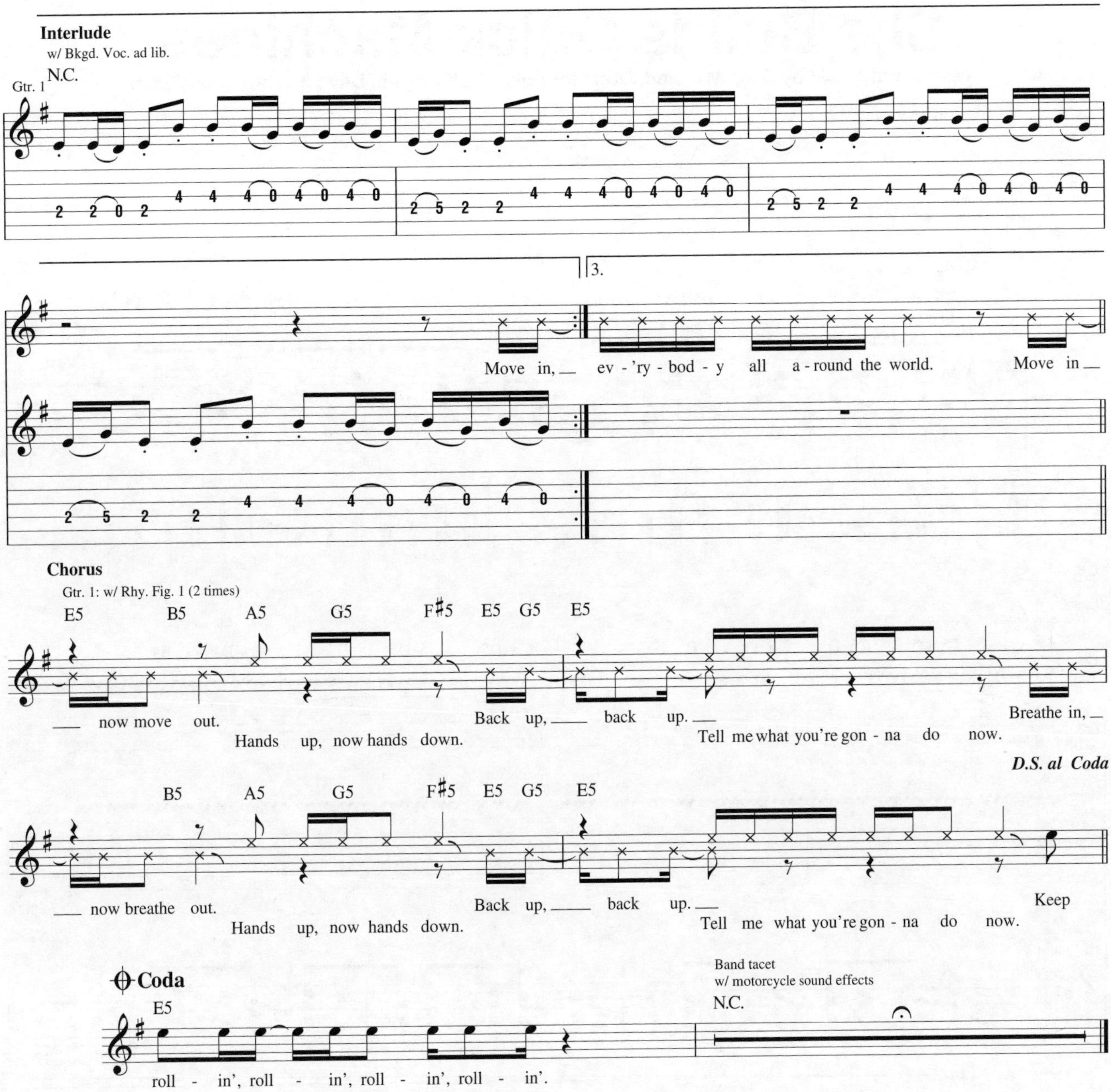

Additional Lyrics

2. You wanna mess with Limp Bizkit? You can't mess with Limp Bizkit
Because we it on every day and every night.
And this platinum thing right here, well we're doin' it all the time.
So you'd better get some better beats and, uh, get some better rhymes.
We got the gang set so don't complain yet.
Twenty-four seven, never begging for a rain check.
Old school soldiers passing out the hot shit.
That rock shit, putting bounce in the mosh pit. *(To Interlude)*

3. Hey ladies, hey fellas,
And the people that don't give a fuck.
All the lovers, all the haters,
And all the people that call themselves players.
Hot mommas, pimp daddies,
And the people rollin' up in Caddies.
Hey rockers, hip hoppers,
And everybody all around the world. *(To Chorus)*

She Builds Quick Machines

Words and Music by Scott Weiland, Duff McKagan, Matt Sorum, Dave Kushner and Slash

Verse
*C5 D5 C5 D5 C5 D5 B5 D5 B5 Dm C5 D5 C5 D5 C5 D5 B5 D5 B5 Dm
1. Hold fast, lit - tle off. Punch strong, let it roam.
Gtr. 2
Riff A
End Riff A
Gtr. 3
Riff A1
End Riff A1
P.M.
*Chord symbols reflect implied harmony.
Gtr. 3: w/ Riff A1 (3 times)
C5D5 C5D5 C5 D5 B5 D5 B5 Dm C5D5 C5D5 C5 D5 B5 D5 B5 Dm
Eyes cold as the snow. She built a quick dream.
Gtr. 2
Riff B
End Riff B
Gtr. 2: w/ Riff A
C5D5 C5D5 C5 D5 B5 D5 B5 Dm C5D5 C5D5 C5 D5 B5 D5 B5 Dm
Sis - ter keep her mo - tor clean. Sol - id vi - sions and a wet ma - chine.
C5D5 C5D5 C5 D5 B5 D5 B5 Dm C5D5 C5D5 C5 D5 B5 D5 B5 Dm
She's al - ways quick to fight. We'll break her through to - night.
Gtr. 2
Riff C

Pre-Chorus
Half-time feel
A5 G5 C5 A5 G5 C5
Gtr. 2 tacet
I can feel it when you push straight down.
Gtr. 2
End Riff C
pp
(14)
Riff D
Gtr. 4 (slight dist.)
End Riff D
mf
let ring throughout
Gtr. 3
Rhy. Fig. 3
*w/ echo set for quarter-note regeneration w/ 1 repeat, till Chorus.
Gtr. 4: w/ Riff D
A5 G5 C5 A5 G5 F5 G5
End half-time feel
I could feel it when they stood their ground.
Gtr. 3
End Rhy. Fig. 3
Chorus
Gtr. 2: w/ Rhy. Fig. 2 (2 times)
C5 D5 C5 D5 C5 D5 B5 D5 B5 F5 C5 D5 C5 D5 C5 D5 B5 D5 B5 F5
Roll o - ver right, keep it through to - night. Right, right, keep it through to - night.
Rhy. Fig. 4
End Rhy. Fig. 4
Gtr. 3: w/ Rhy. Fig. 4
C5 D5 C5 D5 C5 D5 B5 D5 B5 F5 C5 D5 C5 D5 C5 D5 B5 D5 B5 F5
Right in my sight, keep it through to - night. I'll smash right through your spot - light.

Verse
Gtrs. 2 & 3: w/ Riffs A & A1
C5 D5 C5 D5 C5 D5 B5 D5 B5 Dm C5 D5 C5 D5 C5 D5 B5 D5 B5 Dm
2. She ran a - way to Tex - as to keep a - way the ex - cess.
Gtr. 2: w/ Riff B
C5 D5 C5 D5 C5 D5 B5 D5 B5 Dm C5 D5 C5 D5 C5 D5 B5 D5 B5 Dm
Old ex in Veg - as don't back Tex - as.
Gtr. 3
Riff E
End Riff E
P.M.
Gtr. 2: w/ Riff A
Gtr. 3: w/ Riff E
C5 D5 C5 D5 C5 D5 B5 D5 B5 Dm C5 D5 C5 D5 C5 D5 B5 D5 B5 Dm
She burned through in - her - it - ance, dashed a - cross A - mer - i - ca.
Gtr. 2: w/ Riff C
C5 D5 C5 D5 C5 D5 B5 D5 B5 Dm C5 D5 C5 D5 C5 D5 B5 D5 B5 Dm
At the all night sex show, so far from home.
Gtr. 3
P.M.
Pre-Chorus
Half-time feel
Gtr. 3: w/ Rhy. Fig. 3
Gtr. 4: w/ Riff D (2 times)
2nd time, Gtr. 6: w/ Fill 1
A5 G5 C5 A5 G5 C5
I can feel it when you push straight down.
*w/ echo as before.
A5 G5 C5 A5 G5 F5 G5
End half-time feel
I could feel it when they stood their ground.
Chorus
Gtr. 2: w/ Rhy. Fig. 2
Gtr. 3: w/ Rhy. Fig. 4
C5 D5 C5 D5 C5 D5 B5 D5 B5 F5 C5 D5 C5 D5 C5 D5 B5 D5 B5 F5
Roll o - ver right, keep it through to - night. Right, right, keep it through to - night.
Voc. Fig. 1
End Voc. Fig. 1
(Ah, ah, ah, ah.)
Fill 1
Gtr. 6
8va

To Coda
Bkgd. Voc.: w/ Voc. Fig. 1
C5 D5 C5 D5 C5 D5 B5 D5 B5 F5 C5 D5 C5 D5 C5 D5 B5 D5 F5
Right in my sight, keep it through to-night. I'll smash right through your spot - light.
Gtr. 3
Gtr. 2
Interlude
D5
Ah.
Gtrs. 2 & 3
Bridge
D5
Gtrs. 2 & 3 tacet
What you give is what you take.
Gtr. 4
Riff F
End Riff F
mp
*w/ delay
*Set for quarter-note regeneration w/ 1 repeat.
Gtrs. 2 & 3
Gtr. 5 (slight dist.)
pp
mf
**w/ echo as before, next 32 meas.

Gtr. 4: w/ Riff F
Dsus4
D
What you bleed is what you break.
Gtr. 5
fdbk.
Harm.
Dsus4
D
I bleed for you.
Gtr. 4
Gtr. 5
fdbk.
fdbk.
Dsus4
D
I'd steal for you.

*Refers to down-stemmed voc. only.

***See top of first page of song for chord diagrams pertaining to rhythm slashes.

End half-time feel
Bkgd. Voc.: w/ Voc. Fig. 2
Gtrs. 2 & 3: w/ Rhy. Fig. 5
Gtr. 5: w/ Rhy. Fig. 5A
F
G
take,
I'd
take,
I'd
Gtr. 6 (dist.)
f
1/2
1
Guitar Solo
D5 C5 D5 C5 D5 C5 D5 C5 D5 C5 B5
take.
Gtr. 6
hold bend
Gtrs. 2 & 3
D5 C5 D5 C5 D5 C5 D5 C5 D5 C5 B5
hold bend
P.M.
Rhy. Fig. 6
End Rhy. Fig. 6

Gtrs. 2 & 3: w/ Rhy. Fig. 5
F5
G5
Gtr. 6
P.M.
Gtrs. 2 & 3: w/ Rhy. Fig. 6 (2 times)
D5 C5 D5 C5 D5 C5 D5 C5 D5 C5 B5
D5 C5 D5 C5 D5 C5 D5 C5 D5 C5 B5
Gtrs. 2 & 3: w/ Rhy. Fig. 5 (1st meas.)
F5
8va
D.S. al Coda
G5
F5
Gtr. 6
Gtrs. 2 & 3
*Played behind the beat.
Coda
Gtr. 2: w/ Rhy. Fig. 1 (last 2 meas.)
C5 D5 C5 D5 C5 D5 B5 D5 F5
I'll smash right through your spot - light.
Gtr. 3

This Ain't a Scene, It's an Arms Race

Words and Music by Patrick Stump, Peter Wentz, Andrew Hurley and Joseph Trohman

Gtr. 4: w/ Rhy. Fig. 1
Gtr. 5: w/ Riff A
Am
E7/G♯
(as) long as the room keeps sing-ing. That's just the busi-ness I'm in, yeah.
(Don't real-ly care which side wins...)
Pre-Chorus
Gtr. 4: w/ Rhy. Fig. 1 (1 1/2 times)
Gtr. 5: w/ Riff A (1 1/2 times)
Am
E7/G♯
This ain't a scene, it's a god - damned arms race.
(This ain't a scene, it's a
god - damned arms race.)
Am
This ain't a scene, it's a god - damned arms race.
E7/G♯
Gtr. 4 tacet
I'm not a shoul-der to cry on, but I di - gress.
Gtr. 4
Gtrs. 6 & 7 (dist.)
(cont. in lower staff)
Gtr. 5
P.M.
Chorus
Double-time feel
Gtr. 5 tacet
A5
F5
I'm a lead - ing man, and the lies I weave are oh, so in - tri - cate.
Riff B
Gtr. 8 (dist.)
Rhy. Fig. 2
Gtrs. 6 & 7

C5/G
E/G♯
*Voc. Fig. 1
End Voc. Fig. 1
Oh, so in - tri - cate, yeah.
(Doo, doo, doo, doo, doo. Doo, doo, doo, doo, doo.)
End Riff B
End Rhy. Fig. 2
*Applies to upstemmed voc. only.
To Coda
End double-time feel
Gtrs. 6 & 7: w/ Rhy. Fig. 2
Gtr. 8: w/ Riff B
Bkgd. Voc.: w/ Voc. Fig. 1
A5
F5
C5/G
E/G♯
I'm a lead - ing man, and the lies I weave are oh, so in - tri - cate. Oh, so in - tri - cate, yeah.
Verse
Gtr. 4: w/ Rhy. Fig. 1 (2 times)
Gtr. 5: w/ Riff A (2 times)
Am
Am
2. I wrote the gos - pel on giv - ing up, but the
(You look pret - ty sink - ing.
Gtr. 4
E7/G♯
Am
real bomb - shells have al - read - y sunk. At night we're paint - ing your trash gold
Pri - ma Don - nas of the gut - ter.
E7/G♯
while you sleep. Crash - ing not like hips or cars, no, more like p - p - p - par - ties.
Crash - ing not like hips or cars, no... par - ties.)

Pre-Chorus
Gtr. 4: w/ Rhy. Fig. 1 (1 1/2 times)
Am
E7/G♯
This ain't a scene, it's a god - damned arms race.
(This ain't a scene, it's a god - damned arms race.)
Gtr. 5
P.M.
Am
This ain't a scene, it's a god - damned arms race. This
D.S. al Coda
E7/G♯
E5
band - wag - on's full, please catch an - oth - er.
Gtr. 4
Gtr. 5
Gtrs. 6 & 7

Coda
Interlude
E/G♯
D5/A
A5
Whoa,
Gtr. 6
Rhy. Fig. 3
End Rhy. Fig. 3
Gtr. 7
E5
A5
G/B
G5
G/B
whoa,
oh.
Woo!
(Doo, doo, doo, doo, doo.)
Gtr. 7: w/ Rhy. Fig. 3
D5/A
Gtr. 6
A5

End double-time feel
*E5
Gtr. 7
Gtr. 6
*See top of first page of song for chord diagrams pertaining to rhythm slashes.
Bridge
Gtr. 4: w/ Rhy. Fig. 1 (3 times)
Gtr. 5: w/ Riff A (3 times)
Spoken: All the boys who the dance floor didn't love, and all the girls whose lips couldn't move fast enough, sing until your lungs give out.
A5
E7/G♯
Gtr. 6 tacet
Am
E7/G♯
Now, you...
(This ain't a scene, it's a god - damned arms race. This ain't a scene, it's a god - damned arms race.
Am
E7/G♯
Wear out the groove!
Uh, uh, uh, sing out
Voc. Fig. 2
End Voc. Fig. 2
This ain't a scene, it's a god - damned arms race. This ain't a scene, it's a god - damned arms race.)
Bkgd. Voc.: w/ Voc. Fig. 2
N.C.
loud!
Oh!
Oh!
Gtrs. 6 & 7
P.S.

Chorus
Double-time feel
Gtrs. 6 & 7: w/ Rhy. Fig. 2 (1 1/2 times)
Gtr. 8: w/ Riff B (1 1/2 times)
A5
F5
I'm a lead - ing man, and the lies I weave are oh, so in - tri - cate.
Riff C
Gtr. 10 (dist.)
mf
Bkgd. Voc.: w/ Voc. Fig. 1
C5/G
E/G#
Oh, so in - tri - cate, yeah.
End Riff C
Gtr. 10: w/ Riff C
A5
F5
I'm a lead - ing man, and the lies I weave are oh, so in - tri - cate.
Bkgd. Voc.: w/ Voc. Fig. 1
C5/G
E/G#
Oh, so in - tri - cate.
E5
A5
Gtrs. 6 & 7
Gtrs. 8 & 10

Times Like These

Words and Music by Foo Fighters

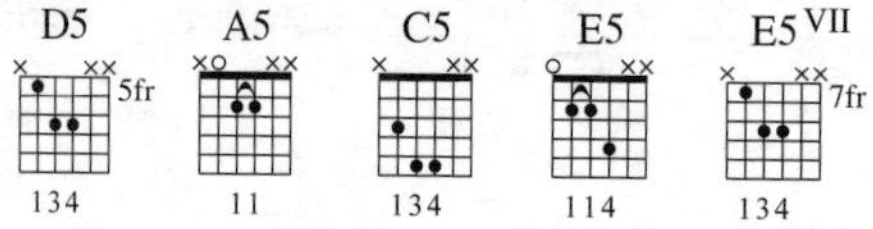

*Chord symbols reflect combined harmony.

Gtr. 3: w/ Riff A (6 times)
Bm
A5
D
End Rhy. Fig. 2
Gtr. 1
Gtr. 2
End Rhy. Fig. 2A
Csus2
D5
Bm
A5
D
Csus2
D5

*Gtrs. 1, 2 & 3: w/ Rhy. Fig. 1 (2 times)

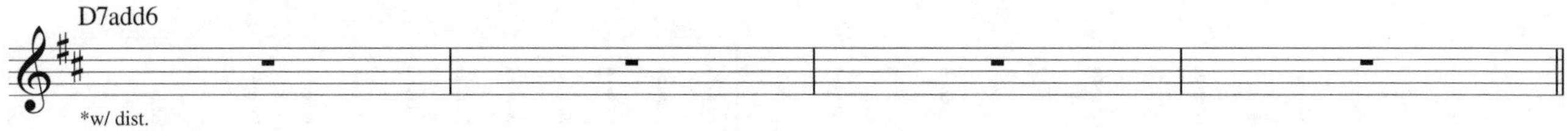

*Next 6 meas.

B
⑤
2fr
C5
E5
End Rhy. Fig. 4
I'm a road that drives a - way and fol - lows you back home.
I'm a brand new sky to hang the stars up - on to - night.
End Riff C
Gtrs. 1, 2 & 3: w/ Rhy. Fig. 1
D7add6
Gtr. 1: w/ Riff C
Gtr. 2: w/ Rhy. Fig. 4
*D
I,
But I,
*Chord symbols reflect overall harmony.
Am7
I'm a street - light shin - ing, I'm a white light blind -
I'm a lit - tle di - vid - ed. Do I stay or run
**Gtrs. 1, 2 & 3: w/ Rhy. Fig. 1 (2 times)
C
Em7
D7add6
- ing bright, burn - ing off and on.
a - way and leave it all be - hind?
**w/ dist.
Uh.
Uh.
It's times

Chorus
C5
E5 VII
D5
Rhy. Fig. 5A
End Rhy. Fig. 5A
Gtrs. 2 & 4 (dist.)
like these you learn to live a - gain. It's times
Gtr. 3
let ring throughout
Gtr. 1
Rhy. Fig. 5
End Rhy. Fig. 5
let ring
Gtr. 5 (dist.)
Riff D
End Riff D
Gtrs. 1, 2 & 4: w/ Rhy. Figs. 5 & 5A (2 times)
Gtr. 5: w/ Riff D (2 times)
C
Em7
Dadd4
like these you give and give a - gain. It's times
Riff E
End Riff E
Gtr. 3: w/ Riff E
To Coda
like these you learn to love a - gain. It's times

Gtrs. 1 & 2: w/ Rhy. Figs. 5 & 5A (1st 2 meas.)
Gtr. 3: w/ Riff E (1st 2 meas.)
Gtr. 5: w/ Riff D (1st 2 meas.)
1.
*Gtrs. 1, 2 & 3: w/ Rhy. Fig. 1 (2 times)
C
Em7
D7add6
like these time and time a - gain.
Gtr. 4
*w/ dist.
Gtr. 4 tacet
2.
Interlude
Gtrs. 1 & 2: w/ Rhy. Figs. 2 & 2A (3 2/3 times)
Gtr. 3: w/ Riff A (11 times)
Gtr. 4 tacet
Em7
D5
Csus2
D5
Bm
A5
and time a - gain.
Oh,
oh.
Gtr. 5
Gtr. 4

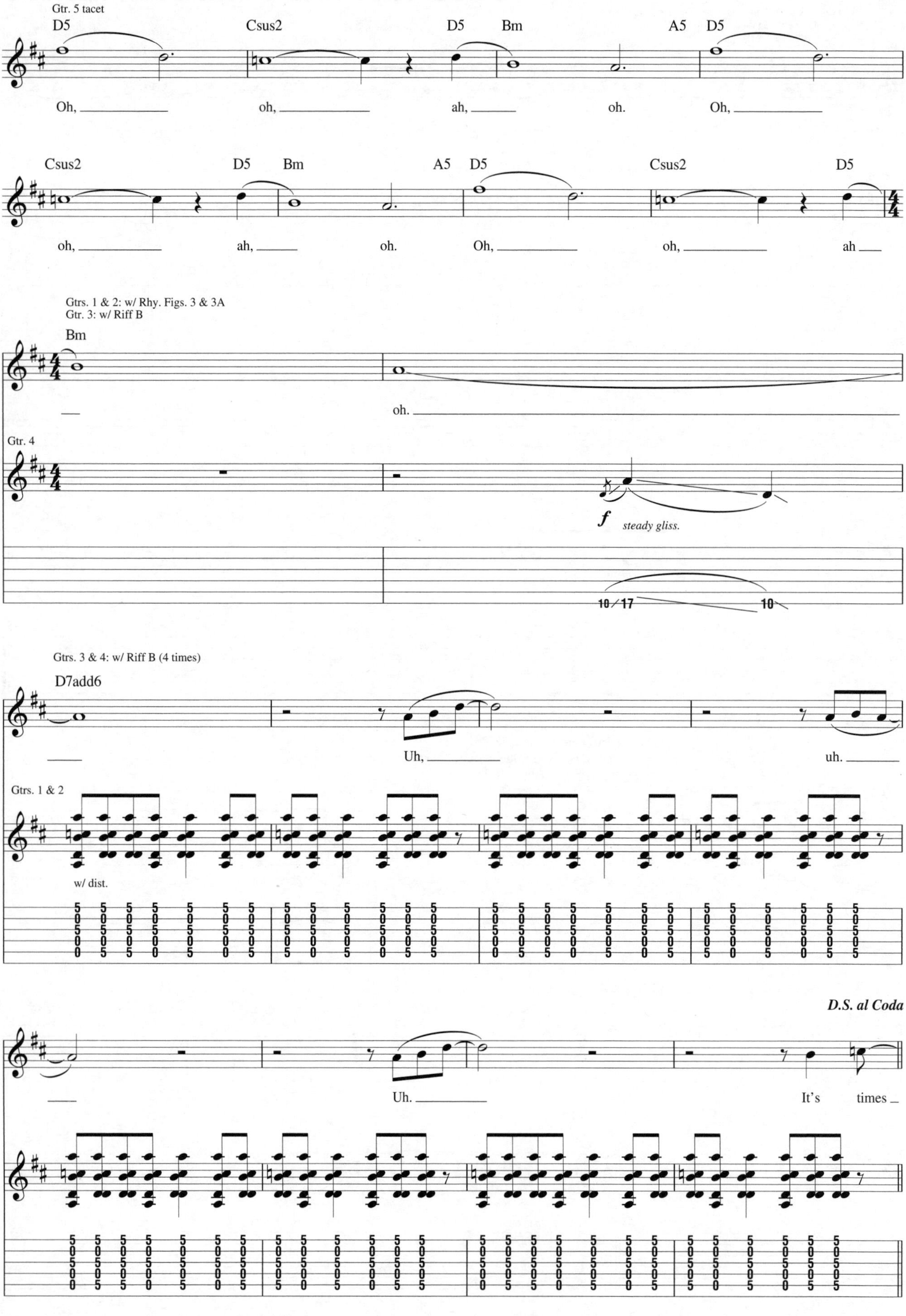

Gtr. 5 tacet
D5
Csus2
D5
Bm
A5
D5
Oh, oh, ah, oh. Oh,
Csus2
D5
Bm
A5
D5
Csus2
D5
oh, ah, oh. Oh, oh, ah
Gtrs. 1 & 2: w/ Rhy. Figs. 3 & 3A
Gtr. 3: w/ Riff B
Bm
oh.
Gtr. 4
f
steady gliss.
10 17 10
Gtrs. 3 & 4: w/ Riff B (4 times)
D7add6
Uh, uh.
Gtrs. 1 & 2
w/ dist.
D.S. al Coda
Uh. It's times

Coda
Gtrs. 1, 2 & 4: w/ Rhy. Figs. 5 & 5A (5 times)
Gtr. 3: w/ Riff E (5 times)
Gtr. 5: w/ Riff D (5 times)
C
Em7
Dadd4
like these time and time a - gain. It's times
Gtr. 2
C
Em7
Dadd4
like these you learn to live a - gain. It's times
Riff F
End Riff F
Gtr. 2: w/ Riff F (3 times)
C
Em7
Dadd4
like these you give and give a - gain. It's times
C
Em7
Dadd4
like these you learn to love a - gain. It's times
C
Em7
Dadd4
like these time and time a - gain. It's times

Outro
*Gtr. 1: w/ Rhy. Fig. 5 (3 times)
C
Em7
Dadd4
like these you learn to live a - gain. It's times
Gtr. 2
Gtr. 3
*w/ clean tone
Gtr. 3 tacet
Gtr. 2 tacet
C
Em7
Dadd4
like these you give and give a - gain. It's times
C
Em7
Dadd4
like these you learn to love a - gain. It's times
C
Em7
Dadd4
C
like these time and time a - gain.
Gtr. 1
let ring
let ring
let ring

Wherever You Will Go

Words and Music by Aaron Kamin and Alex Band

Gtr. 3 tacet
D Dsus2 Dsus2/C♯ Bm7 G6/9(no 3rd) Asus4
(C) (Csus2) (Csus2/B) (Am7) (F6/9(no 3rd)) (Gsus4)
If the great - er wave shall fall, and fall up - on us all.
Gtr. 2
mf
w/ slight dist.
let ring throughout
Gtr. 3
Gtr. 1: w/ Riff A (1st 3 meas.)
Gtr. 3: w/ Riff B
D Dsus2 Dsus2/C♯ Bm7
(C) (Csus2) (Csus2/B) (Am7) (F6/9(no 3rd))
Rhy. Fill 1
End Rhy. Fill 1
Gtr 1.
Then be - tween the sand and stone could you make it on your own?
Gtr. 2
Gtr. 4
(elec.)
mf
w/ dist.

Chorus
(C)
(Csus2/B)
(Am7)
(Fsus2(maj7))
Rhy. Fig. 1
End Rhy. Fig. 1
If I could, then I would, I'll go wher - ev - er you will go.
Gtr. 2
Gtr. 3
Rhy. Fig. 1A
End Rhy. Fig. 1A
let ring throughout
Gtr. 4
Rhy. Fig. 1B
Gtrs. 1 & 3: w/ Rhy. Figs. 1 & 1A
D
Dsus2
Dsus2/C♯
Bm7
Asus4
(C)
(Csus2)
(Csus2/B)
(Am7)
(Gsus4)
way up high, or down low, I'll go wher - ev - er you will go.
Gtr. 2
Gtr. 4
End Rhy. Fig. 1B

Verse
Gtr. 1: w/ Riff A (3 times)
Gtr. 4 tacet
D (C)
Dsus2 (Csus2)
Dsus2/C♯ (Csus2/B)
Bm7 (Am7)
G6/9(no 3rd) (F6/9(no 3rd))
Asus4 (Gsus4)
2. And may - be I'll find out a way to make it back some day.
Gtr. 2
Gtrs. 3 & 4
Gtr. 3
let ring throughout
To - wards you, to guide you through the dark-est of your days.
Gtr. 3 (elec.)
Riff B
mf

*Chord symbols in double parentheses represent chord names respective to Gtr. 5.

Gtr. 1: w/ Riff A (1st 3 meas.)
Gtr. 1: w/ Rhy. Fill 1
D (C) ((G))
Dsus2 (Csus2) ((Gsus2))
Dsus2/C♯ (Csus2/B) ((Gsus2/F♯))
Bm7 (Am7) ((Em7))
G6/9(no 3rd) (F6/9(no 3rd)) ((C6/9(no 3rd)))
Well then I hope there's some - one out there, who can bring me back too.
Gtrs. 3 & 4
Rhy. Fig. 2
End Rhy. Fig. 2
Chorus
Gtrs. 1 & 3 w/ Rhy. Figs. 1 & 1A (2 times)
Gtr. 4: w/ Rhy. Fig. 1B
Gtr. 5 tacet
D (C)
Dsus2/C♯ (Csus2/B)
Bm7 (Am7)
Gsus2(maj7) (Fsus2(maj7))
If I could, then I would, I'll go wher - ev - er you will go.
Gtr. 2
Rhy. Fig. 3
Way up high or down low, I'll go wher - ev - er you will
End Rhy. Fig. 3

Bridge
(Bm)
(F)
(G6)
(Em)
Gtr. 1
go.
Run a-way with my heart,
run a-way with my heart.
Gtr. 2
Gtr. 3
Gtr. 4
let ring throughout
(Bm)
(F)
(G6)
(Bm)
Run a-way with my love.
P.M.

Verse
Gtr. 1: w/ Riff A
D Dsus2 Dsus2/C♯ Bm7 G6/9(no 3rd) Asus4
(C) (Csus2) (Csus2/B) (Am7) (F6/9(no 3rd)) (Gsus4)
3. I know now just quite how my life and love might still go on.
Gtr. 1: w/ Riff A (1st 3 meas.)
Gtr. 3: w/ Riff B
Gtr. 5: w/ Rhy. Fig. 2
Gtr. 1: w/ Rhy. Fill 1
D Dsus2 Dsus2/C♯ Bm7 G6/9(no 3rd)
(C) (Csus2) (Csus2/B) (Am7) (F6/9(no 3rd))
((G)) ((Gsus2)) ((Gsus2/F♯)) ((Em7)) ((C6/9(no 3rd)))
In your heart, in your mind, I'll stay with you for all of time.
Gtr. 2
Gtr. 4
Chorus
Gtrs. 1 & 3: w/ Rhy. Figs. 1 & 1A (5 3/4 times)
Gtrs. 2 & 4: w/ Rhy. Figs. 3 & 1B (2 7/8 times)
D Dsus2/B Bm7 Gsus2(maj7)
(C) (Csus2/B) (Am7) (Fsus2(maj7))
If I could, then I would, I'll go wher - ev - er you will go.
D Dsus2/C♯ Bm7 Gsus2(maj7)
(C) (Csus2/B) (Am7) (Fsus2(maj7))
way up high or down low, I'll go wher - ev - er you will go.

D (C) Dsus2/C# (Csus2/B) Bm7 (Am7) Gsus2(maj7) (Fsus2(maj7))
If I could turn back time, I'll go wher - ev - er you will go.
D (C) Dsus2/C# (Csus2/B) Bm7 (Am7) Gsus2(maj7) (Fsus2(maj7))
If I could make you mine, I'll go wher - ev - er you will go.
(Go.
D (C) Dsus2/C# (Csus2/B) Bm7 (Am7)
I'll go wher -
Gtr. 6 (elec.)
Riff C
End Riff C
mf
w/dist.
Gtr. 6: w/ Riff C (4 times)
Gsus2(maj7) (Fsus2(maj7)) D (C) Dsus2/C# (Csus2/B) Bm7 (Am7) (Fsus2(maj7)) (Fadd9)
ev - er you will go.
Go.)
Gtr. 6
Gtrs. 2 & 3
Gtr. 4

Wrong Way

Words and Music by Brad Nowell, Eric Wilson and Floyd Gaugh

A5 G5 A5 G5
I'm gon-na make it hard to live. Sog-gy tears run-nin' down to her chin, and it
A5 C F# E
ru-ins up her make - up and nev-er want - ed… A cig-a-rette pressed be-tween her lips but I'm
End Rhy. Fig. 1
Rhy. Fig. 2
let ring
* Key signature denotes F# Mixolydian.
F# E F# E
star-in' at her tits, it's the wrong way. Strong if I can, but I am on-ly a man so I
Verse
F# E B5 A5
take her to the can. It's the wrong way.
3. The on-ly fam-i-ly that she's ev-er had is her
6. I gave her all that I had to give; she
End Rhy. Fig. 2
Rhy. Fig. 3
let ring
* Key signature denotes B Mixolydian.

B5 A5 B5
sev - en horn - y broth - ers and her drunk ass dad. He need - ed mon - ey so he
still would - n't take it. Whoa, no. Her two brown eyes are leak - in'
To Coda
A5 B5 D5
put her on the street. Ev - 'ry - thing was go - in' fine un - til the day she met me.
like a sieve and it
End Rhy. Fig. 3
E D E D
Hap - py are you sad? Wan - na shoot your dad? I'll do an - y - thing I can the wrong way.
Rhy. Fig. 4
E D E D
We talk all night, tried to make it right. Be - lieve me, shit was tight. It was the wrong way.
End Rhy. Fig. 4

Verse
Gtr. 1: w/ Rhy. Fig. 1, simile
A5 G5 A5 G5
4. Don't run a - way if you wan - na stay 'cause I ain't here to make you, oh no.
A5 G5 A5
It's up to you, what you real - ly wan - na do. Spend some time in A - mer - i - ca,
Trombone Solo
Gtr. 1: w/ Rhy. Fig. 2, simile
w/ Voc. ad lib.
Verse
Gtr. 1: w/ Rhy. Fig. 3, simile
C F♯ E B5 A5
play 4 times
ha, dub style! 5. She'll give you all that she got to give, but
B5 A5 B5 A5
I'm gon - na make it hard to live. Big salt - y tears rol - lin' down to her chin, and it
Gtr. 1: w/ Rhy. Fig. 4, simile
B5 D5 E
smears up her make - up and nev - er want - ed... So we ran a - way and I'm
D E D
sor - ry when I say that straight to this ver - y day, it was the wrong way.
E D E
She took a hike, it don't mat - ter if I like it or not be - cause she on - ly wants the
D.S. al Coda
D B5
wrong way.
Gtr. 1
Coda
B5 D
rit.
still ru - ins her make - up and nev - er want - ed...
Gtr. 1
rit.

Guitar Notation Legend

Guitar music can be notated three different ways: on a *musical staff*, in *tablature*, and in *rhythm slashes*.

RHYTHM SLASHES are written above the staff. Strum chords in the rhythm indicated. Use the chord diagrams found at the top of the first page of the transcription for the appropriate chord voicings. Round noteheads indicate single notes.

THE MUSICAL STAFF shows pitches and rhythms and is divided by bar lines into measures. Pitches are named after the first seven letters of the alphabet.

TABLATURE graphically represents the guitar fingerboard. Each horizontal line represents a string, and each number represents a fret.

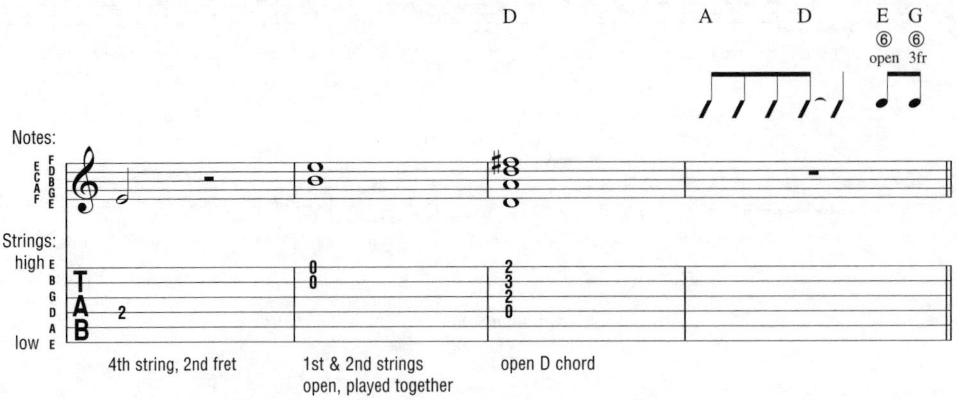

Definitions for Special Guitar Notation

HALF-STEP BEND: Strike the note and bend up 1/2 step.

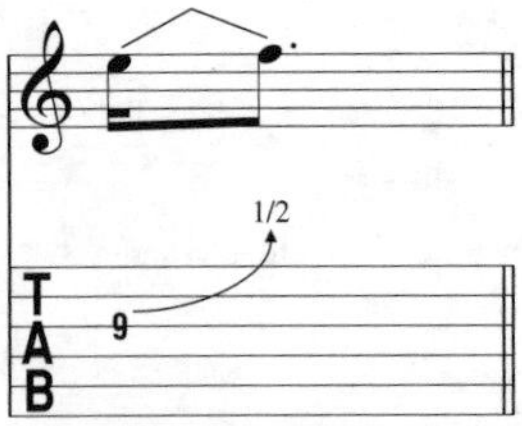

WHOLE-STEP BEND: Strike the note and bend up one step.

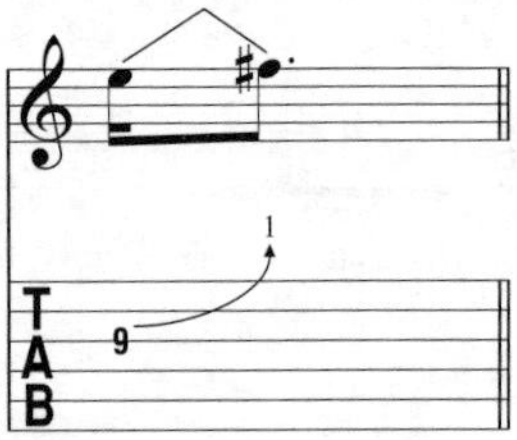

GRACE NOTE BEND: Strike the note and immediately bend up as indicated.

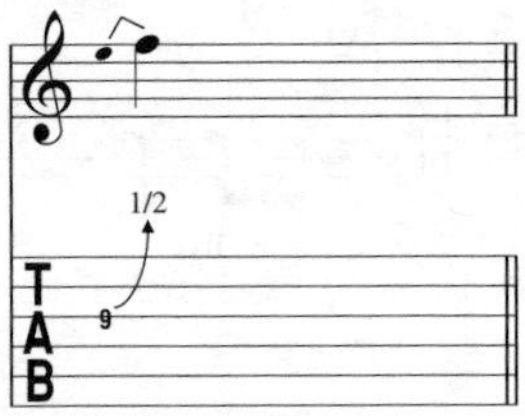

SLIGHT (MICROTONE) BEND: Strike the note and bend up 1/4 step.

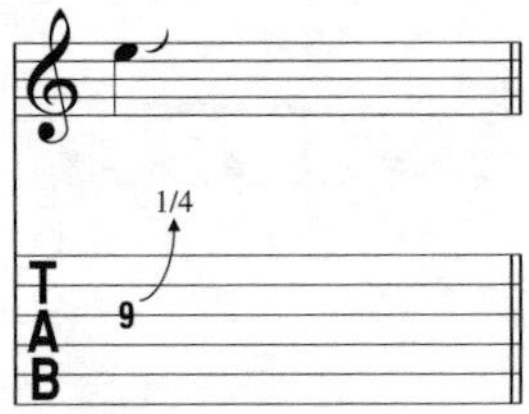

BEND AND RELEASE: Strike the note and bend up as indicated, then release back to the original note. Only the first note is struck.

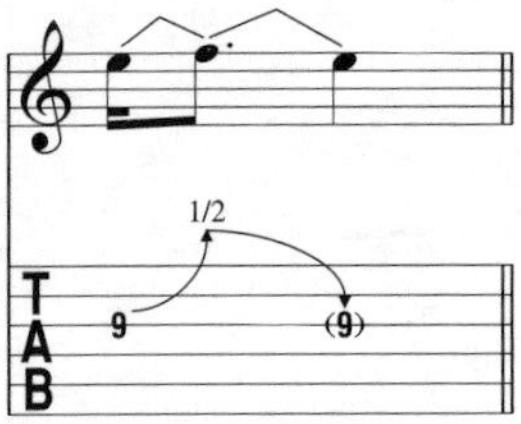

PRE-BEND: Bend the note as indicated, then strike it.

PRE-BEND AND RELEASE: Bend the note as indicated. Strike it and release the bend back to the original note.

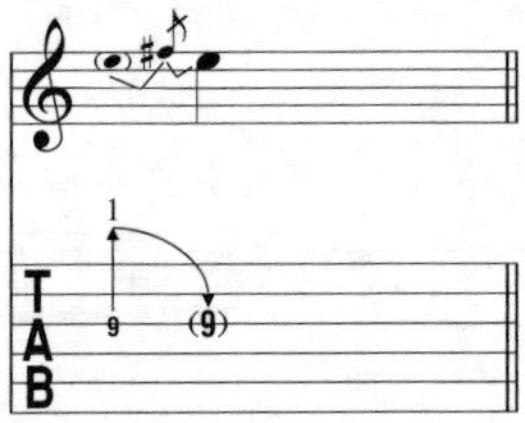

UNISON BEND: Strike the two notes simultaneously and bend the lower note up to the pitch of the higher.

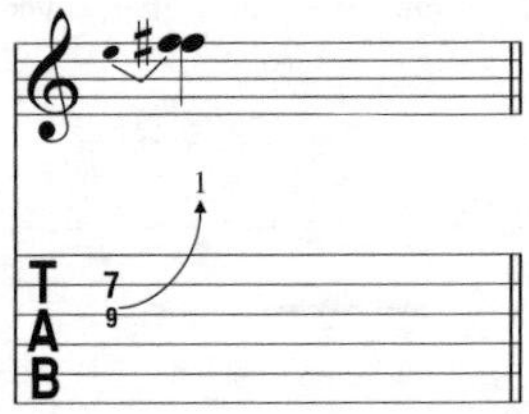

VIBRATO: The string is vibrated by rapidly bending and releasing the note with the fretting hand.

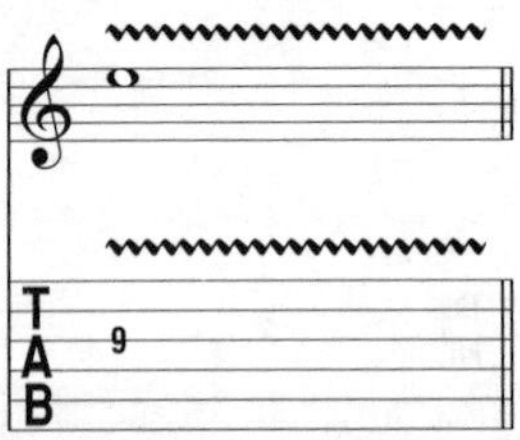

WIDE VIBRATO: The pitch is varied to a greater degree by vibrating with the fretting hand.

HAMMER-ON: Strike the first (lower) note with one finger, then sound the higher note (on the same string) with another finger by fretting it without picking.

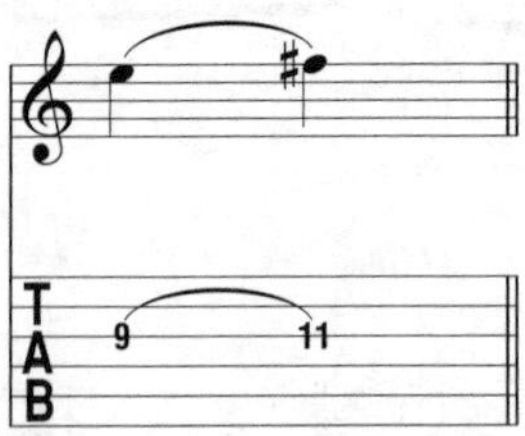

PULL-OFF: Place both fingers on the notes to be sounded. Strike the first note and without picking, pull the finger off to sound the second (lower) note.

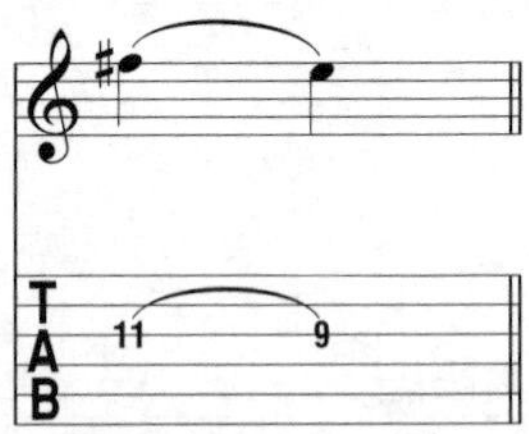

LEGATO SLIDE: Strike the first note and then slide the same fret-hand finger up or down to the second note. The second note is not struck.

SHIFT SLIDE: Same as legato slide, except the second note is struck.

TRILL: Very rapidly alternate between the notes indicated by continuously hammering on and pulling off.

TAPPING: Hammer ("tap") the fret indicated with the pick-hand index or middle finger and pull off to the note fretted by the fret hand.

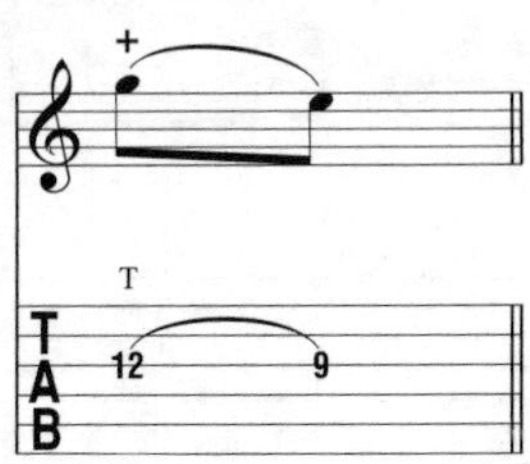

NATURAL HARMONIC: Strike the note while the fret-hand lightly touches the string directly over the fret indicated.

PINCH HARMONIC: The note is fretted normally and a harmonic is produced by adding the edge of the thumb or the tip of the index finger of the pick hand to the normal pick attack.

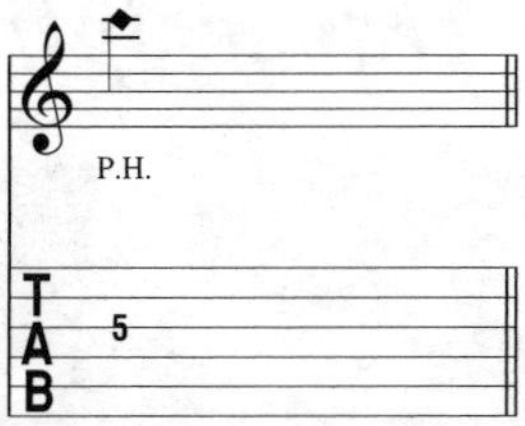

HARP HARMONIC: The note is fretted normally and a harmonic is produced by gently resting the pick hand's index finger directly above the indicated fret (in parentheses) while the pick hand's thumb or pick assists by plucking the appropriate string.

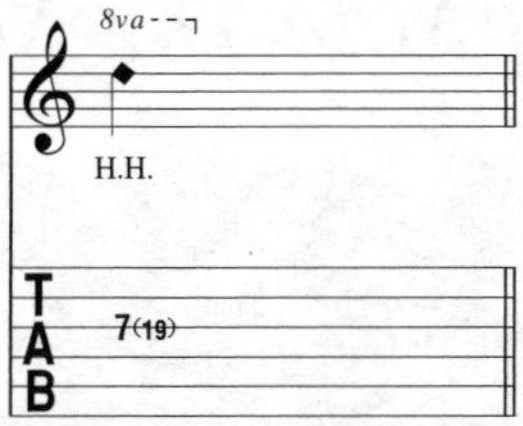

PICK SCRAPE: The edge of the pick is rubbed down (or up) the string, producing a scratchy sound.

MUFFLED STRINGS: A percussive sound is produced by laying the fret hand across the string(s) without depressing, and striking them with the pick hand.

PALM MUTING: The note is partially muted by the pick hand lightly touching the string(s) just before the bridge.

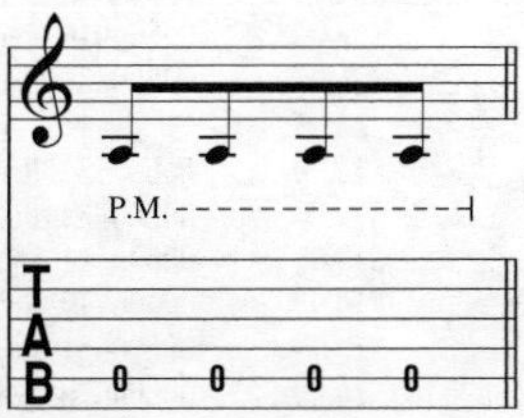

RAKE: Drag the pick across the strings indicated with a single motion.

TREMOLO PICKING: The note is picked as rapidly and continuously as possible.

ARPEGGIATE: Play the notes of the chord indicated by quickly rolling them from bottom to top.

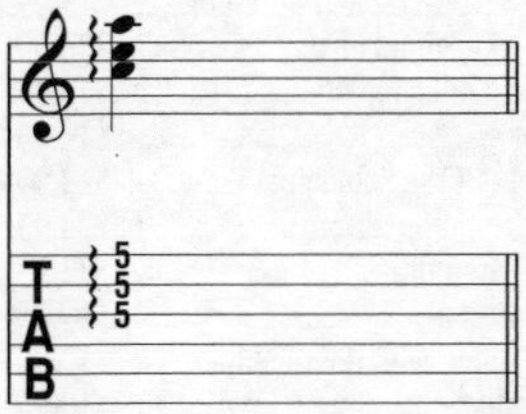

VIBRATO BAR DIVE AND RETURN: The pitch of the note or chord is dropped a specified number of steps (in rhythm), then returned to the original pitch.

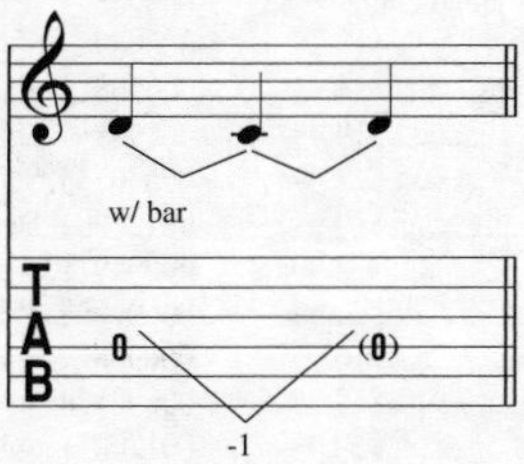

VIBRATO BAR SCOOP: Depress the bar just before striking the note, then quickly release the bar.

VIBRATO BAR DIP: Strike the note and then immediately drop a specified number of steps, then release back to the original pitch.

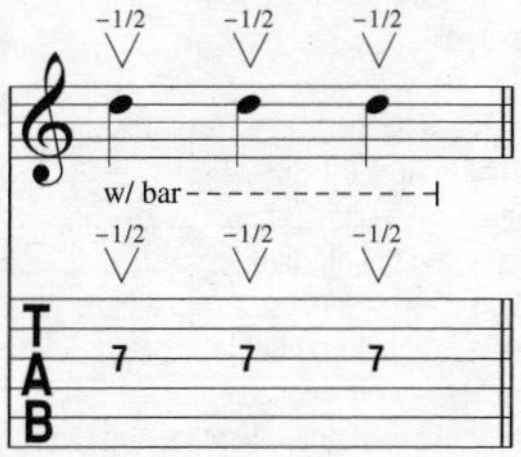

Additional Musical Definitions

 *(accent)*

- Accentuate note (play it louder).

 *(accent)*

- Accentuate note with great intensity.

 *(staccato)*

- Play the note short.

⊓

- Downstroke

V

- Upstroke

D.S. al Coda

- Go back to the sign (𝄋), then play until the measure marked "***To Coda,***" then skip to the section labelled "**Coda.**"

D.C. al Fine

- Go back to the beginning of the song and play until the measure marked "***Fine***" (end).

Rhy. Fig.

- Label used to recall a recurring accompaniment pattern (usually chordal).

Riff

- Label used to recall composed, melodic lines (usually single notes) which recur.

Fill

- Label used to identify a brief melodic figure which is to be inserted into the arrangement.

Rhy. Fill

- A chordal version of a Fill.

tacet

- Instrument is silent (drops out).

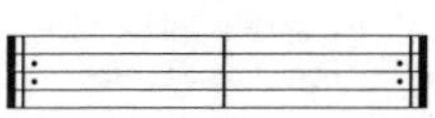

- Repeat measures between signs.

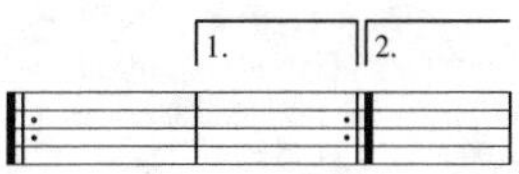

- When a repeated section has different endings, play the first ending only the first time and the second ending only the second time.

NOTE: Tablature numbers in parentheses mean:

1. The note is being sustained over a system (note in standard notation is tied), or
2. The note is sustained, but a new articulation (such as a hammer-on, pull-off, slide or vibrato) begins, or
3. The note is a barely audible "ghost" note (note in standard notation is also in parentheses).

RECORDED VERSIONS®

The Best Note-For-Note Transcriptions Available

RECORDED VERSIONS GUITAR®

ALL BOOKS INCLUDE TABLATURE

00692015 Aerosmith – Greatest Hits $22.95
00690178 Alice in Chains – Acoustic $19.95
00694865 Alice in Chains – Dirt $19.95
00690812 All American Rejects – Move Along $19.95
00690958 Duane Allman Guitar Anthology $24.99
00694932 Allman Brothers Band – Volume 1 $24.95
00694933 Allman Brothers Band – Volume 2 $24.95
00694934 Allman Brothers Band – Volume 3 $24.95
00690865 Atreyu – A Deathgrip on Yesterday $19.95
00690609 Audioslave $19.95
00690820 Avenged Sevenfold – City of Evil $24.95
00690366 Bad Company – Original Anthology $19.95
00690503 Beach Boys – Very Best of $19.95
00690489 Beatles – 1 $24.99
00694832 Beatles – For Acoustic Guitar $22.99
00691014 Beatles Rock Band $34.99
00690110 Beatles – White Album (Book 1) $19.95
00692385 Chuck Berry $19.95
00690835 Billy Talent $19.95
00690901 Best of Black Sabbath $19.95
00690831 blink-182 – Greatest Hits $19.95
00690913 Boston $19.95
00690932 Boston – Don't Look Back $19.99
00690491 David Bowie – Best of $19.95
00690873 Breaking Benjamin – Phobia $19.95
00690451 Jeff Buckley – Collection $24.95
00690957 Bullet for My Valentine – Scream Aim Fire $19.95
00691004 Chickenfoot $22.99
00690590 Eric Clapton – Anthology $29.95
00690415 Clapton Chronicles – Best of Eric Clapton $18.95
00690936 Eric Clapton – Complete Clapton $29.99
00690074 Eric Clapton – The Cream of Clapton $24.95
00694869 Eric Clapton – Unplugged $22.95
00690162 The Clash – Best of $19.95
00690828 Coheed & Cambria – Good Apollo I'm Burning Star, IV, Vol. 1: From Fear Through the Eyes of Madness $19.95
00690593 Coldplay – A Rush of Blood to the Head $19.95
00690962 Coldplay – Viva La Vida $19.95
00690819 Creedence Clearwater Revival – Best of $22.95
00690648 The Very Best of Jim Croce $19.95
00690613 Crosby, Stills & Nash – Best of $22.95
00690967 Death Cab for Cutie – Narrow Stairs $22.99
00690289 Deep Purple – Best of $17.95
00690784 Def Leppard – Best of $19.95
00692240 Bo Diddley $19.99
00690347 The Doors – Anthology $22.95
00690348 The Doors – Essential Guitar Collection $16.95
00690810 Fall Out Boy – From Under the Cork Tree $19.95
00690664 Fleetwood Mac – Best of $19.95
00690870 Flyleaf $19.95
00690931 Foo Fighters – Echoes, Silence, Patience & Grace $19.95
00690808 Foo Fighters – In Your Honor $19.95
00690805 Robben Ford – Best of $19.95
00694920 Free – Best of $19.95
00690848 Godsmack – IV $19.95
00690601 Good Charlotte – The Young and the Hopeless $19.95
00690943 The Goo Goo Dolls – Greatest Hits Volume 1: The Singles $22.95
00694854 Buddy Guy – Damn Right, I've Got the Blues $19.95
00690840 Ben Harper – Both Sides of the Gun $19.95
00694798 George Harrison – Anthology $19.95
00690841 Scott Henderson – Blues Guitar Collection $19.95
00692930 Jimi Hendrix – Are You Experienced? $24.95
00692931 Jimi Hendrix – Axis: Bold As Love $22.95
00692932 Jimi Hendrix – Electric Ladyland $24.95
00690017 Jimi Hendrix – Live at Woodstock $24.95
00690602 Jimi Hendrix – Smash Hits $24.99
00690793 John Lee Hooker Anthology $24.99
00690692 Billy Idol – Very Best of $19.95
00690688 Incubus – A Crow Left of the Murder $19.95
00690544 Incubus – Morningview $19.95
00690790 Iron Maiden Anthology $24.99
00690721 Jet – Get Born $19.95
00690684 Jethro Tull – Aqualung $19.95
00690959 John5 – Requiem $22.95
00690814 John5 – Songs for Sanity $19.95
00690751 John5 – Vertigo $19.95
00690845 Eric Johnson – Bloom $19.95
00690846 Jack Johnson and Friends – Sing-A-Longs and Lullabies for the Film Curious George $19.95
00690271 Robert Johnson – New Transcriptions $24.95
00699131 Janis Joplin – Best of $19.95
00690427 Judas Priest – Best of $22.99
00690742 The Killers – Hot Fuss $19.95
00690975 Kings of Leon – Only by the Night $22.99
00694903 Kiss – Best of $24.95
00690355 Kiss – Destroyer $16.95
00690930 Korn $19.95
00690834 Lamb of God – Ashes of the Wake $19.95
00690875 Lamb of God – Sacrament $19.95
00690823 Ray LaMontagne – Trouble $19.95
00690679 John Lennon – Guitar Collection $19.95
00690781 Linkin Park – Hybrid Theory $22.95
00690743 Los Lonely Boys $19.95
00690720 Lostprophets – Start Something $19.95
00690955 Lynyrd Skynyrd – All-Time Greatest Hits $19.99
00694954 Lynyrd Skynyrd – New Best of $19.95
00690754 Marilyn Manson – Lest We Forget $19.95
00694956 Bob Marley– Legend $19.95
00694945 Bob Marley– Songs of Freedom $24.95
00690657 Maroon5 – Songs About Jane $19.95
00120080 Don McLean – Songbook $19.95
00694951 Megadeth – Rust in Peace $22.95
00690951 Megadeth – United Abominations $22.99
00690505 John Mellencamp – Guitar Collection $19.95
00690646 Pat Metheny – One Quiet Night $19.95
00690558 Pat Metheny – Trio: 99>00 $19.95
00690040 Steve Miller Band – Young Hearts $19.95
00694883 Nirvana – Nevermind $19.95
00690026 Nirvana – Unplugged in New York $19.95
00690807 The Offspring – Greatest Hits $19.95
00694847 Ozzy Osbourne – Best of $22.95
00690399 Ozzy Osbourne – Ozzman Cometh $19.95
00690933 Best of Brad Paisley $22.95
00690995 Brad Paisley – Play: The Guitar Album $24.99
00690866 Panic! At the Disco – A Fever You Can't Sweat Out $19.95
00690938 Christopher Parkening – Duets & Concertos $24.99
00694855 Pearl Jam – Ten $19.95
00690439 A Perfect Circle – Mer De Noms $19.95
00690499 Tom Petty – Definitive Guitar Collection $19.95
00690428 Pink Floyd – Dark Side of the Moon $19.95
00690789 Poison – Best of $19.95
00693864 The Police – Best of $19.95
00694975 Queen – Greatest Hits $24.95
00690670 Queensryche – Very Best of $19.95
00690878 The Raconteurs – Broken Boy Soldiers $19.95
00694910 Rage Against the Machine $19.95
00690055 Red Hot Chili Peppers – Blood Sugar Sex Magik $19.95
00690584 Red Hot Chili Peppers – By the Way $19.95
00690852 Red Hot Chili Peppers –Stadium Arcadium $24.95
00690511 Django Reinhardt – Definitive Collection $19.95
00690779 Relient K – MMHMM $19.95
00690631 Rolling Stones – Guitar Anthology $27.95
00694976 Rolling Stones – Some Girls $22.95
00690264 The Rolling Stones – Tattoo You $19.95
00690685 David Lee Roth – Eat 'Em and Smile $19.95
00690942 David Lee Roth and the Songs of Van Halen $19.95
00690031 Santana's Greatest Hits $19.95
00690566 Scorpions – Best of $22.95
00690604 Bob Seger – Guitar Collection $19.95
00690803 Kenny Wayne Shepherd Band – Best of $19.95
00690968 Shinedown – The Sound of Madness $22.99
00690813 Slayer – Guitar Collection $19.95
00690530 Slipknot – Iowa $19.95
00690733 Slipknot – Vol. 3 (The Subliminal Verses) $22.99
00120004 Steely Dan – Best of $24.95
00694921 Steppenwolf – Best of $22.95
00690655 Mike Stern – Best of $19.95
00690877 Stone Sour – Come What(ever) May $19.95
00690520 Styx Guitar Collection $19.95
00120081 Sublime $19.95
00120122 Sublime – 40oz. to Freedom $19.95
00690929 Sum 41 – Underclass Hero $19.95
00690767 Switchfoot – The Beautiful Letdown $19.95
00690993 Taylor Swift – Fearless $22.99
00690830 System of a Down – Hypnotize $19.95
00690799 System of a Down – Mezmerize $19.95
00690531 System of a Down – Toxicity $19.95
00694824 James Taylor – Best of $16.95
00690871 Three Days Grace – One-X $19.95
00690737 3 Doors Down – The Better Life $22.95
00690683 Robin Trower – Bridge of Sighs $19.95
00699191 U2 – Best of: 1980-1990 $19.95
00690732 U2 – Best of: 1990-2000 $19.95
00660137 Steve Vai – Passion & Warfare $24.95
00690116 Stevie Ray Vaughan – Guitar Collection $24.95
00660058 Stevie Ray Vaughan – Lightnin' Blues 1983-1987 $24.95
00694835 Stevie Ray Vaughan – The Sky Is Crying $22.95
00690015 Stevie Ray Vaughan – Texas Flood $19.95
00690772 Velvet Revolver – Contraband $22.95
00690071 Weezer (The Blue Album) $19.95
00690966 Weezer – (Red Album) $19.99
00690447 The Who – Best of $24.95
00690916 The Best of Dwight Yoakam $19.95
00690905 Neil Young – Rust Never Sleeps $19.99
00690623 Frank Zappa – Over-Nite Sensation $19.95
00690589 ZZ Top Guitar Anthology $24.95

FOR A COMPLETE LIST OF GUITAR RECORDED VERSIONS TITLES, SEE YOUR LOCAL MUSIC DEALER, OR WRITE TO:

HAL•LEONARD® CORPORATION

7777 W. BLUEMOUND RD. P.O. BOX 13819 MILWAUKEE, WI 53213

Visit Hal Leonard online at
www.halleonard.com

Prices and availability subject to change without notice. Some products may not be available outside the U.S.A.

0310